# YOUNG PEOPLE, WELFARE AND CRIME

## Governing non-participation

Ross Fergusson

First published in Great Britain in 2016 by

Policy Press
University of Bristol
1-9 Old Park Hill
Bristol
BS2 8BB
UK
t: +44 (0)117 954 5940
pp-info@bristol.ac.uk
www.policypress.co.uk

North America office:
Policy Press
c/o The University of Chicago Press
1427 East 60th Street
Chicago, IL 60637, USA
t: +1 773 702 7700
f: +1 773-702-9756
sales@press.uchicago.edu
www.press.uchicago.edu

British Library Cataloguing in Publication Data
A catalogue record for this book is available from the British Library

Library of Congress Cataloging-in-Publication Data
A catalog record for this book has been requested

ISBN 978 1 44730 701 3 hardcover
ISBN 978-1-4473-2104-0 ePub
ISBN 978-1-4473-2105-7 Mobi

Cover design by Hayes Design

For Cally
and his generation of co-travellers

# Contents

# Detailed contents

# List of tables and figures

## Tables

## Figures

# List of tables and figures

# List of abbreviations

| | |
|---|---|
| ASBO | Anti-Social Behaviour Order |
| BME | Black and Minority Ethnic |
| CESI | Centre or Economic and Social Inclusion |
| CPAG | Child Poverty Action Group |
| Chav | Council-Housed and Violent or Council-House-Associated Vermin |
| CSEW | Crime Survey for England and Wales |
| DfES | Department for Education and Skills |
| DWP | Department for Work and Pensions |
| ECC | Economic Causes of Crime (thesis) |
| EMA | Education Maintenance Allowance |
| EU | European Union |
| GCSE | General Certificate of Secondary Education |
| GFC | Global Financial Crisis |
| IFS | Institute for Fiscal Studies |
| IGO | International Governmental Organisation |
| ILO | International Labour Organization |
| IMF | International Monetary Fund |
| JSA | Jobseeker's Allowance |
| LEP | Less Eligibility Principle |
| LEA | Local Education Authority |
| LPC | Low Pay Commission |
| NatCen | National Centre for Social Research |
| NCDS | National Child Development Study |
| NCB | National Children's Bureau |
| NDYP | New Deal for Young People |
| NTI | New Training Initiative |
| NGO | Non-governmental Organisation |
| NEET | Not in Employment, Education or Training |
| ONS | Office for National Statistics |
| OECD | Organisation for Economic Co-operation and Development |
| OED | Oxford English Dictionary |
| PSL | Pool of Surplus Labour |
| PSE | Poverty and Social Exclusion |
| PIP | Presumption of Innocence Principal |
| RWT | Reservation Wage Threshold |
| RFPP | Risk Factor Prevention Paradigm |
| SEU | Social Exclusion Unit |
| TUC | Trades Union Congress |

| | |
|---|---|
| TSPO | Two-step Prohibition Orders |
| UN | United Nations |
| UNDESA | United Nations Department for Economic and Social Affairs |
| UNESCO | United Nations Educational, Social and Cultural Organisation |
| UNICEF | United Nations International Children's Emergency Fund |
| US | United States (of America) |
| USA | United States of America |
| WEF | World Economic Forum |
| WHO | World Health Organization |
| YMCA | Young Men's Christian Association |
| YJB | Youth Justice Board |
| YLS | Youth Lifestyles Survey |
| YOT | Youth Offending Team |
| YTS | Youth Training Scheme |

# About the author

Ross Fergusson is Senior Lecturer in Social Policy in the Department of Social Policy and Criminology at The Open University, UK. His principal research interest is in policy development and the governance of young people at the interface between social policy and youth justice policies. The focus of this work is on young people who are defined as non-participants at the margins of compulsory participation in education, labour market entry, mandatory training and unemployment. His work explores these points of policy intersection theoretically and empirically and draws on a range of disciplines, including sociology and political economy as well as social policy and criminology. He publishes in policy, education, politics and criminology journals.

# Acknowledgements

Whatever its merits and limitations, this book is the outcome of a (very) long-standing project. As a result, I owe a debt of considerable gratitude to more people who variously provided motivation, inspiration and encouragement over the years than it is possible to mention here. There are many I do not know personally, but among those I know well, two good friends who were also one-time colleagues offered more by way of inspiration, guidance and support than they could possibly know. In many respects, my own intrinsic interest apart, the project began from my work alongside (and briefly with) Roger Dale, and was renewed and reoriented by working with John Muncie – both at The Open University at the time.

Much else was contributed by many others with whom I had the good fortune to write and research over the years: (chronologically) George Mardle, Geoff Esland, Lorna Unwin, Eugene McLaughlin, David Pye, Gordon Hughes, Deb Drake, Damon Briggs and Nicola Yeates. Alongside them, the support, guidance and kindness of John Clarke, Barry Goldson, Reece Walters and Steve Tombs have been considerable and instrumental.

During the immediate period of drafting this text I had the benefit of detailed and insightful comments from Deb Drake, Robin Simmons, Steve Tombs and Nicola Yeates – all of whom have provided much more generous support, guidance and encouragement than through their involvement in commenting (and re-commenting) on drafts alone. None of them or my other colleagues are in any way implicated in the outcome, and any shortcomings are of course mine alone.

At Policy Press, my greatest debt is to Emily Watt, for her confidence in, patience towards and encouragement of a project that had a longer gestation than anyone wanted. I have also variously enjoyed the benefits of encouragement, facilitation, patience and sheer hard work from Alison Shaw, Laura Vickers, Laura Greaves and Dave Worth. Joanne Osborn's editorial work at the first stage of production was a highly professional contribution. At The Open University I had the benefit of the hard work (reliably at short notice) of Donna Collins and Carol Fuller, and also of David Adamson, Sue Chaval, Adrian Gray and Kelly Staines.

My family and friends have been hapless but enthusiastic co-travellers, and also great supporters when it came to keeping up morale and reviving flagging energies. Foremost amongst them have been my daughter and son, Jo Maybin and Simon Maybin and their respective partners Duncan and Emma, my brother Malcolm, and my lifelong friends Adrian Briggs, Mic Dover, Graham Jarvis and Kate Laughton. My lovely grandson Cally took care to be born just around the time when writing began in earnest, and equal care to help keep my feet on the ground and my eyes on what really matters – and some of what will matter for his generation.

This book would not have been written without my partner Nicola. She made the project seem possible as well as worthwhile and has provided unstinting intellectual, emotional and practical encouragement, support, friendship and guidance – as well as forbearance and patience – in addition to her professional contributions mentioned above.

My heartfelt thanks to my family, my friends, my colleagues and my collaborators and co-workers, in ample due measure to all.

# Part One
# The crisis of non-participation

# ONE

# Crises of non-participation

## Introduction

The effects of the global financial crisis (GFC) on young people in and beyond the world's richer countries would be a compelling and deserving subject for a comprehensive analytical project in the social sciences. This is especially so for those young people whose prospects for becoming socially and financially independent adults have been severely delayed, significantly impaired or placed beyond reach as a result. An authoritative description of and explanation for mass unemployment, how it has become endemic amongst 16 to 24-year-olds, and why it shows serious signs of becoming a ubiquitous global phenomenon would be equally worthwhile. To differing degrees, these recent developments and the deep underlying concerns to which they give rise are one of the foci of this book. Not only do they set the context for what follows, they also direct the analytical gaze to the origins of the recent crises of young people's participation and non-participation in education, training and paid work.[1]

In the UK at least, these crises are not without precedents, recognisable precursors, and familiar responses in policy and in public discourse. What is new is the urgent need to understand how these developments − recurrent, endemic and ubiquitous as they are becoming − should be interpreted and theorised, by connecting the multiple elements of the study of young people across a range of disciplines and fields of study of the social sciences. While it is no longer the case that such studies proceed only or predominantly within the analytical and empirical confines of their own specialisms, attempts at genuinely integrative studies that traverse policy fields and disciplinary foci and methodologies remain a small minority. Even rarer are studies that are explicitly theoretical in origin and orientation. Rarest of all are those that endeavour to understand the plights of the most adversely and severely affected groups of young people in ways that cross policy fields, social science disciplines and theories, and the groupings and paradigms within which they are embedded.

The critical need for such an approach is in one sense simply explained. Although there are specific and powerful examples of the ways in which social science research and analysis has exerted direct, transparent and even tangible effects on policies addressed to some groups of young people that are most negatively affected by major social, political and economic changes, they too are rare. Conversely, little has been achieved by the hundreds of studies, analyses and extended narratives of potential relevance to understanding the conditions, causes and effects of mass non-participation in education, training or work, insofar as can be judged by its endemic nature. To make this claim is not to place undue responsibility at the door of academic research and policy analysis, and the extraordinarily modest resources available to them. However, the underlying consistency of policy responses and of the regular reapplication of variations on their dominant themes and methods, despite limited effectiveness, invokes three equally unpalatable interpretations: that most academic analyses and their putative policy implications are ineffective, mistaken or ignored.

Alternative explanations are that studies, interpretations and analyses have been too narrow in scope and too little aware of contextual complexity to offer convincing readings of persistent mass non-participation and the harms that flow from it; that they have lacked theoretical coherence; or that their theoretical premises and analyses have been too entrenched in particular paradigms or interpretations to have regard to the insights offered by their alternatives.

## Section 1: The crisis of non-participation

Evidence of policy failure is now palpable and transnational. Many years after the onset of the GFC, labour market conditions for young people continued to deteriorate throughout the world. The largest increases in youth unemployment occurred in the world's richest countries. By 2014, the International Labour Organization (ILO) reported that:

> unemployment among young people rose [further] to 18.3 per cent of the youth labour force. In total, 74.5 million young people aged 15–24 were unemployed in 2013, an increase of more than 700,000 over the previous year. There were 37.1 million fewer young people in employment in 2013 than in 2007, while the global youth population declined by only 8.1 million over the same period. The global youth labour force participation rate, at 47.4 per cent in 2013, remains more than 2 percentage points below the pre-crisis level, as more young people, frustrated with their

employment prospects, continue to drop out of the labour
market. (ILO, 2014, pp 21–2)

The ILO also reported that 'employment in Greece, Ireland and
Portugal as a whole declined by 1.6 million between 2007 and 2012,
but 75 per cent of this reduction, i.e. 1.2 million jobs, was concentrated
among younger people (aged 15–24 years)' (ILO, 2014, p 36).

Prior to the GFC, the rate of young people's participation in the
labour market in OECD and EU countries had been in a marked
and steady decline for many years (ILO, 2015, Box 2, p 13).One
international governmental organisation had already calculated that
'Youth make up 25 per cent of the global working-age population
but account for 43.7 per cent of the unemployed, which means that
almost every other jobless person in the world is between the ages of
15 and 24' (UNDESA, 2007, p 238). Modelled projections of actual
rather than declared unemployment massively raise this proportion.
For Ireland, for example, it increases from 28% to 47%, and for Spain
from 41% to 52%. In 2008, in Moldova, Bosnia and Herzegovina,
Lithuania and Macedonia, quite remarkably, fewer than one in five
15 to 24-year-olds were employed (ILO, 2010). In addition, the ILO
finds that far more young people are in working poverty: 'overall,
two in five (42.6 per cent) economically active youth are still either
unemployed or working yet living in poverty... In 2013, more than
one-third (37.8 per cent) of employed youth in the developing world
were living on less than US$2 per day. Working poverty, therefore,
affects as many as 169 million youth in the world. The number increases
to 286 million if the near poor are included (living below US$4 per
day)' (ILO, 2015, pp 1–2).

In the UK, according to ILO data, unemployment among young
people aged 15 to 24 reached 960,000 in 2011 and 2012, but has
fallen back since.[2] Almost half of the million who were recorded as
not in employment, education or training (NEET) by mid-2014 were
registered as unemployed, while the other half million are classified
as 'not working, not seeking work and/or not available to start work'
(that is, economically inactive).[3] This implies that up to half a million
young people have declared themselves to be living and surviving out
of sight of systems which record all recognised forms of economic and
educational participation. Analyses that look beyond such records find
rates of economic inactivity and underemployment amongst 16 to
24-year-olds totalling over 2 million (Figure 1.1). On this reckoning,
the total of un/underemployed young people increased by about three-

quarters of a million between 2005 and 2013, most of which occurred following the GFC (Figure 1.2).

**Figure 1.1** Summary of the total hidden talent of young people (16 to 24-year-olds), England and Wales, Oct 2012–Sept 2013

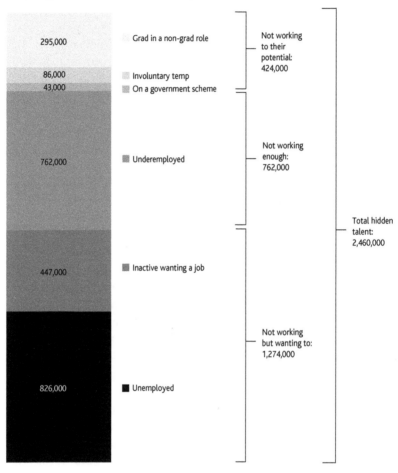

Source: Gardiner (2014)

But even these are not exceptional outcomes that can be attributed to the GFC alone. Clark (2014, pp 58-9) demonstrates that each recession since the 1970s has had a cumulatively harsher effect on young people in the UK. His data shows that, when young people classified as NEET (or underemployed) are excluded, recorded unemployment among 16 to 24-year-olds significantly exceeded 20% for at least a year either side of the 1980-81 and 1990-91 recessions, as well as after the GFC. However, the rate of recovery in youth unemployment during the four

**Figure 1.2** Total hidden talent, young people (16 to 24-year-olds), England and Wales

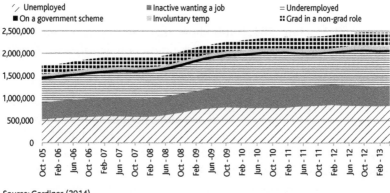

Source: Gardiner (2014)

years following the GFC-led recessions was negligible by comparison with the very rapid recovery after the 1990–91 recession, and periods of unemployment of more than two years more than trebled (Gardiner, 2014, Figures 1.1 and 4.2). Gardiner concludes that 'two in five young people in England and Wales can be considered not employed to their potential' (p 30).

The impact of the UK's post-GFC recessions fell especially heavily upon young people who were NEET. As Taylor-Gooby (2013, pp 7–8) points out, cuts have been targeted away from popular widely-used fields of the welfare state, and towards less popular benefits for lower income people, including the unemployed. The harshest cuts have concentrated on those with low skills, poor work opportunities and no dependent children (p 10), and the net effect is that 'the full impact is heaviest for poorer people of working age' (p 11). Consistent with this, the House of Commons Work and Pensions Committee (2013, p 167) received evidence that the Work Programme was giving least help to the worst off and largely ignoring the homeless and those with disabilities.[4] Similarly, the Social Mobility and Child Poverty Commission (2014, p 113) reported:

> The recession hit young adults harder and for longer than others in the labour market and the recovery has benefited them least. ... Despite large reductions in unemployment many young people remain out of work ... some groups of young people, notably those from non–white backgrounds, are still much worse off than others ... young people's

hourly pay ... has dropped in real terms to levels last seen 15 years ago.

Gregg and Machin (2012) also show that the depressive effect of unemployment on mean UK pay rates almost doubled after the GFC, while other data shows that the effect on young people has been considerably harsher.[5] Surveying conditions across Europe, Ellison (2014) draws attention to disadvantaged young people's entrapment in insecure work, zero hours contracts, extended periods of unemployment and a deeply discouraging absence of future possibilities. This also raises questions of intergenerational justice that have been widely aired in popular debate.[6] Jordan and Drakeford (2012) ask whether the current situation constitutes a relationship of injustice between older generations who enjoyed the heights of state welfare and pensions provision, and those who now struggle to find work, housing and an independent living, as growing proportions of young people prolong dependency on parents into their mid-twenties (see also Dorling, 2013; Social Mobility and Child Poverty Commission, 2014). Ainley and Allen (2009, p 104) argue that declining employment opportunities, student debt and adverse housing conditions mean that 'it is possible that many young people may no longer be able to "grow up" at all. They are not just "lost in transition" the notion of "transition" itself may be lost.'[7] Certainly, the Intergenerational Fairness Index (Leach and Hanton, 2015) demonstrates a major increase in unfairness between generations over the last 25 years, with a notional 10% decline in fairness in the years since the GFC, taking into account an ever-widening gap between 16 to 24-year-olds and the remainder of the population in employment rates, median annual income and housing affordability in particular. In 2015, the first Conservative Budget for almost two decades intensified intergenerational inequality considerably, with an anticipated allowance set at about half the minimum wage rate for 18 to 21-year-olds, the exclusion of 16 to 24-year-olds from the misleadingly named 'national living wage', and the removal of automatic housing benefit entitlement for 18 to 21-year-olds.[8]

Ellison (2014) also highlights the ill-effects of the GFC on young people's health, family life and life expectancy. She reports on the trajectory of suicide rates among young men aged 15 to 24 in the UK. Historically, the sharpest and longest sustained period of increase, from 10 to 16 per 100,000 of population during the 1980–81 recession, peaked around the 1990-91 recession, when parasuicide rates among young unemployed men were up to 25 times higher than among their employed counterparts (Bartley et al, 2004). The trend rapidly returned to pre-1980s levels between 2000 and 2006, during a period of low youth unemployment.[9] Most recently, Office for National Statistics (ONS) data for 2007-11 shows a 12% rise in suicides coinciding with the rise in unemployment (ONS, 2013),[10] while Barr et al (2012) show that this rise is regionally correlated with unemployment rates. One global health report has estimated that every percentage point increase in the general unemployment rate within the European Union is matched by a 0.8% increase in suicide rates (World Health Organization, 2011), and this finding is corroborated by alarming increases among young men without jobs in Greece and Spain (see Stuckler et al (2009); Katikireddi et al (2012); Chang et al (2013), summarised in Ellison (2014)). One extraordinary speech by the one-time Director-General of Schools at the UK Department for Children, Schools and Families during the GFC is said to have included an uncorroborated report that research in the North of England found that 15% of young people died within 10 years of being designated 'NEET'.[11]

Behind these disturbing reports sits the frustration of modest youthful ambitions to achieve economic and social independence, and the despair of the poor prospects for doing so. The potential psycho-social effects of 'never-worked' extended unemployment and hopeless prospects are amplified by the pressures of responsibilisation, of implied failure to achieve and progress, and by what Lea and Hallsworth (2013, p 22) refer to as '"self-warehousing" through encouraging passivity and self-blame', particularly among young people with criminal records. Others extend this line of analysis from the processes of despair to those of discontent. Jordan and Drakeford (2012, p 149) suggest that if young people's prospects of attaining economic independence are blocked, they have little to lose from rebellion. Internationally, there is also evidence that higher levels of social inequality are associated with an increased incidence of childhood conflict, particularly in the UK, and that this can also be a strong predictor of adolescent and adult violence.[12]

A number of these indicators are statistically associated with social unrest among young people. The incidence of mass public protests by young people burgeoned internationally in the wake of the GFC (Somavia/ILO, 2012a). One study has argued that 'globally, unemployment is the largest and most significant determinant of risk of unrest' (Institute for International Labour Studies, 2011), and this finding is consistent with long-term historical European trends which show that fiscal retrenchment is correlated with social instability and unrest (Ponticelli and Voth, 2011). Many interpretations and analyses of the August riots of 2011 in England focused on deep discontent among young people in impoverished localities (see for example Berman (2011); Lewis et al (2011); National Centre for Social Research (2011); Briggs (2012); General Synod (2012); Newburn (2012); Nwabuzo (2012)). An ILO (2011) report models indicators of social unrest derived from global survey data that includes respondents' confidence in their national governments and their perceptions of deteriorating national economies and standards of living. One predictive factor in the model is the proportion of 15 to 24-year-olds registered as unemployed. The report cites previous research which found that countries with large populations of young, educated people with limited employment prospects tend to experience unrest in the form of protests (Jenkins, 1983; Jenkins and Wallace, 1996). It notes that 'the inability to address the jobs crisis has led to rising social discontent' (ILO, 2011, p 1). And it estimates that 40% of the 119 countries with available information face the prospect of increased social unrest. The estimated risk of increased social unrest 'is especially high in advanced economies, the Middle East and North Africa' (ILO, 2011, pp 1-2). The follow-up report (ILO, 2013b) indicated a substantially increased risk of unrest, particularly in the EU in the five years following the GFC.[13]

More tenuously, connections are repeatedly asserted between young people's despair at their prospects and political extremism. In France, in the wake of the Charlie Hebdo killings in 2015, links have been made between the 25% unemployment rates among young Muslims and their supposed 'radicalisation' (Thomson and Stothard, 2015). In Bosnia and Herzegovina, Azinović and Jusić (2015, p 8) claim that some of the 63% of unemployed 15 to 24-year-olds are 'seen as most susceptible to radicalisation into violent extremism' in Syria and Iraq, particularly those who are geographically, economically and socially marginalised (p 42).

The connections and distinctions between social unrest, organised demonstrations of social discontent, riots and 'radicalisation' are complex and contested. The insistence on interpreting the August 2011 riots as criminal was viewed by many as a purposive political position adopted to delegitimise claims that they originated in expressions of mass discontent among young people. Yet protests and riots are the least significant axis for connecting unemployment and non-participation with crime. The most concerted claim of a systematic connection is that of the notorious assertions of the 'underclass' thesis, that poverty, low educational attainment, unemployment, delinquency, welfare dependency and crime among young people are attributable to the alleged decline of family structures and to poor parenting and a variety of forms of social amorality.[14] Numerous more measured empirically based academic studies have explored – and in many cases endorsed – these claims.[15] They have promoted lines of association that have exerted a major influence by informing targeted methods of pre-emptive intervention in the youth justice system. The Edinburgh Study of Youth Transitions and Crime offers this summary:

> Holding constant young people's actual level of offending, the system tends to target certain groups: males, those from manual and single-parent households and from deprived neighbourhoods, and users of alcohol and drugs. Also, it targets young people who are visible because they are hanging about on the street, truanting from school, and less subject to parental supervision. Further, it targets those who have already come into conflict with the police. (Pople and Smith, 2010, p 98)

Underlying such accounts, clear implications of causality nevertheless remain. The same study finds that 'lack of work opportunities is a cause of offending: the same individuals offend less often during periods of employment than when they are out of work' (Smith, 2010, p 385).

In other interpretations, these claims of association and inferred causality have provided a rationale for managing unemployment, non-participation and 'being NEET' using preventative and supervisory civil orders within and beyond the youth justice system. This approach is said to be focused on:

> the apparent failure of young people to act to help themselves, as evidenced by their withdrawal from education without qualifications. And, in a context in which the welfare system is considered to provide only perverse incentives to behave badly, the choices will be between work or subjection to social surveillance. (Rodger, 2008, pp 50-51)

France (2007, pp 113-14) takes this further by asserting that:

> in late modernity criminal behaviour of the young has been increasingly presented as individualised and driven by 'rational choices'. State policy has taken these conceptions and ideas and constructed policies that see punishment,

surveillance and control as rational responses to the 'problem'.

Altogether, the data, research findings, mooted effects of mass youth non-participation and various claims about its purported links to crime set out above also establish the parameters for emergent counter-claims that young people's non-participation in education, training or work is itself becoming the object of processes of criminalisation. A primary purpose of this book is to explore, explain and assess these claims and counter-claims empirically, theoretically, and in terms of the nature and extent of their realisation in policy.

## Section 2: A crisis of the analysis of non-participation

Alongside the crisis of non-participation, a crisis of analysis of the connected fields of non-participation amongst young people, welfare and crime has found the disciplines of social science ill-prepared to address the sources of the crisis of non-participation, and unable to propose policies capable of stemming endemic, ubiquitous mass non-participation.

Certainly, critical analysis has identified some of the sources of this crisis of analysis. France (2007, pp 113-14) criticises poor social science understandings of youth crime, their overreliance on positivistic methods for theorising it, and the disproportionate influence of this approach on policy. His own contribution has been to adopt a critical approach both to the Beck/Giddens individualisation thesis (see for example Beck, 1992; Beck et al, 1994), and to the ways in which it is challenged by persistent structures of inequality of class, race and gender (France, 2007, pp 72-4); and to poststructuralist theorisation, in terms of its failure to give due weight to socioeconomic and locational contexts, and to political economies of consumption (pp 130-32). His critique reasserts the irreducible importance of the local, interpreted in wider political-economic contexts for understanding youth in 'late modernity', and cautions against overemphasising young people's powers of agency.

Several years on from France's book, early in the GFC, an analysis of an intensive ethnographic study of 22 young non-participants in the North of England reinforces the argument that the processes of individualisation and reflexive modernisation 'have only obscured the ways in which social and economic structures shape young people's lives, not obliterated them ... the conditions of late modernity have diversified young people's biographies, but their trajectories remain profoundly influenced by their location in a matrix of class, gender and race positions' (Simmons et al, 2014, p 10).

Both these critiques are well founded and well substantiated. Nevertheless, both leave open the door to structuralist *and* poststructuralist theorisations without providing a convincing attempt to accommodate their contradictions, still less reconcile them. The difficulties of resolving tensions and dilemmas of this sort epitomise the ways in which theorisation typically remains trapped in competing paradigms, unable to suspend assumptions and switch interpretations or to contemplate alternatives to questions like those France (2007, p 114) raises about 'how the state might be criminalising the young'.

Analyses like these are important examples of research that theorises young people's experiences. However, they also illustrate the ways in which debate is locked into unresolved social science disputes about agency and structure, individualisation, structuration and poststructuralism. These parameters of theorisation may do at least as much to occlude debate and limit its advance as to enlighten it.

Whether or not academic research and its interpretation in this policy field are ineffective, mistaken or ignored, as was suggested earlier, the evidence of the ill-effects of the GFC on millions of young people is no indication of success. A brief scan of the field of contributions to better understanding suggests three possible related explanations for poor progress. The first concerns the range of academic fields and disciplines that any thoroughgoing analysis needs to consider. The second concerns some fundamental epistemological and methodological differences within the social sciences. The third concerns divisions at the levels of theory and of (meta-)paradigm. All three present major challenges. The divisions they describe cross-cut one another on multidimensional grids that delineate sharp boundaries at one extreme, while allowing fluid amalgams of focus and method at the other. Certainly, the best traditions of interdisciplinary social science strive to refuse such limitations of separation and (sometimes) the claimed paradigmatic monopolies of academic competence they reinforce. For some social scientists only hybrid and heterodox approaches can interpret complex social issues like non-participation and its relationship to crime *because* they encompass differences and traverse divisions. For others, they juxtapose and retrofit one approach to another in ways that compromise intellectual coherence.

In what follows in this book, the dangers identified by those who dispute the validity of genuinely interdisciplinary analysis will be visible. Sceptics will need to suspend disbelief to assess the benefits while recognising its risks. For less sceptical others, the claim of this book to address the 'crisis of analysis' stands or falls on its endeavour to encompass epistemological and methodological differences and traverse theoretical divisions. By way of illustration, France's (2007) claim about the limitations of social science applies more widely than to youth crime alone. Furlong et al (2011, p 356), for instance, have argued that 'There has been a long-standing separation (and on occasion a tension) between "cultural" and "transition" perspectives in youth studies which has had a negative impact on our understanding of experiences of youth.' Both views are modest understatements of the difficulties that have limited the capacity of the field of youth studies to shape policy and outcomes concerning young people's non-participation and its relationship to crime.

In recent decades, the conditions for mass unemployment and non-participation among young people began in the recession of 1980-81 as a by-product of the efforts of the incoming New Right monetarist-inspired Conservative government to control inflation, suppress the power of trades unions and radically restructure the economy and the labour market in the UK. They recurred in the recession of 1990-91. The outcomes of both recessions were politically traumatic as well as economically dramatic. As Jordan (1982, pp 162-3) argued, the government was troubled far more by youth than by adult unemployment, because of the growing impression that it created for parents that 'there will never be enough jobs for the new generation of children who will leave school in the 1980s', and by 'the threat to law and order posed by millions of young people out of work, particularly in inner-city areas'. He continued:

> The riots in Brixton, Toxteth, Moss Side and other inner city areas in June and July 1981 shook the Conservative government more than anything the Labour opposition or the trade union movement had done in the previous two years. They provided a dramatic demonstration of the scale of alienation, anger and despair in such areas. (Jordan, 1982, pp 164-5)

The recession of the early 1990s was similarly accompanied by riots, arson and looting. Almost three decades later, mass unemployment recurred, accompanied by more destructive and widespread rioting than during the earlier recessions. Unsurprisingly, the August 2011 riots prompted major anxiety in the political establishment. Yet mass non-participation, widely identified as contributory, has been met not with anxious urgency or major new employment measures, but with gestural make-work schemes, the inadequate effects of which barely registered on post-crisis concerns about major cuts in public spending.[16]

That academic analysis has had little to contribute to interpreting an unprecedented surge in non-participation, or to providing a theorised explanation for the ways in which mass non-participation is associated with crime and with increased reliance on welfare benefits, is in part attributable to divisions between analytical approaches. Furlong et al (2011, p 366) identified some rapprochement between the divided traditions of youth studies, but concluded that 'while there are clear signs of convergence between the "transitions" and "cultural" perspectives in the sociology of youth, as yet we do not have a conceptual framework that is accepted by those aligned to either tradition'. Instead of the 'false binary' between two traditions, Furlong et al adopt a paradigm-spanning 'social generation approach' based on changing socioeconomic structures *and* changes in young people's subjectivities, life contexts and meanings.

This book adopts a different approach to avoiding the same false divisions and traversing paradigms in pursuit of other interpretations. One explanation for the limited impact of the analyses developed since the 1980-81 recession can be traced to a different reading from that of Furlong and his colleagues of the prevailing state of convergence and division. It proposes that the divisions remain alive and deep, disguised much more than they have been resolved by the marked decline of the youth cultural studies tradition, which has been overwhelmed by the rise to prominence of one very particular branch of the 'youth transitions tradition'. The effects of these developments have been further exacerbated by separations between policy fields that miss the important relationship between unemployment, welfare and crime for understanding both the plight of many young people, and the responses with which it has been met.

One of the consequences of the historical division between the 'youth transitions' and 'youth cultural studies' traditions is that it has fostered an almost hermetic separation between the study of young people within a range of self-evidently interconnected policy fields, and the study of young people within criminology. To the extent that there has been traffic across the lines of separation, youth studies have engaged with criminology mainly within the youth cultural studies tradition. The core interests of that tradition in youth identities, cultural styles and meanings and group behaviours have built important bridges to criminologies of youth concerned with deviance and transgressive behaviours. Dominant interpretations of both approaches that highlight the socially constructed and normative nature of the precepts of youth criminal justice have made youth culture a productive focus for research, analysis and theorisation among criminologists.

Cultural criminology and youth cultural studies are symbiotic bedfellows (see most notably the work of Clarke and Jefferson (1973); Muncie (1999, 2015); Presdee (2000); Hayward (2002); and Ferrell et al (2004)). The affinity between them has nevertheless had a limiting effect on work within the youth transitions tradition, regarding analysis of the relationship between young people, non-participation and crime. The youth transitions tradition has constituted the dominant axis for the analysis of young people's post-school trajectories for more than three decades (among the first were Ashton and Field (1976); Brown (1987); Banks et al (1992); and Jones and Wallace (1992)). This dominance, in combination with the gulf between it and the youth cultural studies tradition, has meant that insights into the relationship between youth crime and young people's experiences as they are shaped by education, labour market and social and welfare policies have become obscured in analysis. This tendency has been further exacerbated by the propensity of studies concerned with young people's supposed 'exclusion', 'disconnection' or 'disengagement' to work in silos shaped by disciplinary boundaries, methodological divisions and political-ideological orientations.

The exception to this tendency is the branch of the youth transitions tradition that has been favoured by policy-driven research funding. It operates within a strongly positivist paradigm that relies on quantitative modelling and analysis using large-scale longitudinal datasets and regression techniques, to identify 'determinants' of 'failed transitions'. This approach is founded in the epistemological and methodological traditions of econometrics, epidemiology and aetiological criminology that are variously focused on economic-rationalist, behavioural, genetic, psychological and psychopathological factors for understanding the propensity to commit crimes.

Despite their common focus on crime, the youth cultural studies and quantitative modelling traditions follow almost entirely unconnected parallel paths, epistemologically, methodologically, paradigmatically and politically. Their respective approaches are emblematic of equivalent divisions in the social sciences. One historical outcome is that the affinities that connect youth cultural studies to cultural criminology result in limited attention to the ways in which youthful transgression may relate to material as well as cultural experiences, in terms of the political-economic conditions that prevent young people's secure transitions to economic and social adult independence. And, in turn, the quantitative methodologies that strive to identify defining personal, psychological, economic or other causes of crime remain largely oblivious to the entirely different meanings of transgressive and deviant behaviour assigned by the youth cultural studies tradition.

Between these polar positions sits an approach that has little alignment with or affinity to either. It is as yet an indistinct, un-defined, variegated approach. It lacks a label or a leading exponent. But it is one which leaves space for the relationship between young people, welfare and crime to be analysed and interpreted without recourse to the highly interpretive (and occasionally poorly grounded) perspectives of youth cultural studies, or to the relentlessly positivistic (and frequently narrowly dogmatic) approaches of quantitative modelling. What follows in this book has no pretensions to providing dazzling insights that define this messy middle ground, dissolving long-standing barriers, or bridging historic gulfs. Nor does it aspire to garner into a coherent frame of analysis the interpretations of the two ostensibly irreconcilable traditions. Still less does it aim to resolve profoundly conflicted epistemological histories that are rooted in the conflicted paradigms of the social sciences. It does, however, endeavour to draw attention to some of the analytical limitations of working within one tradition, and to circumnavigate some of the blind spots and separations they jointly create – *and* to highlight the intellectual costs of their separation. What follows is concerned with the adverse effects of the marginalisation of political-economic factors in some analyses within both traditions; the preoccupation with the sociocultural at the expense of political-economic, social and policy contexts in criminological analyses that focus on youth culture; and instrumental interpretations of motivation that are dominated by psychological or economic explanations for crime, without due regard to those contexts.

This book also has a second related aspiration. It is to extract and release investigation and analysis of the relationship between non-participation, welfare and crime from some of the confines of two (meta-)paradigmatic clusters into which so much study in this field has fallen. One can be characterised in terms of its focus on the individual, the personal, the emotional, the affective, the therapeutic and the psychosocial – and by association with a stress on endogenous influences on action, and idiographic levels of analysis that are primarily concerned with individual cases and instances. The focus of the other is on structures, material conditions, power, rationality, cognition and the political-economic – and by association a stress on exogenous influences on action, and nomothetic levels of analysis concerned with generalisable propositions that encompass entire categories of people, cases and recurrent instantiations.

These clusters are crude, over-differentiating heuristic devices for making sense of the lines that define and separate a huge diversity of approaches across a wide range of disciplines, epistemologies and methodologies. The fit of any theory into one or the other would need substantial qualification. However, their heuristic value is to draw attention to the propensity of theorisations of non-participation to incline towards one or the other, and towards the paradigm which it represents.

Few as they are, theories that work purposively across these clusters, and that refuse their separations (and their disregard for the complexities that separation conceals), have never been systematically applied to an understanding of young people's non-participation and its relationship to crime and welfare. In an endeavour to open up some trajectories for re-theorising this relationship, Part Three explores two exceedingly disparate theories that nevertheless have direct relevance to understanding both. This exploration offers two unfamiliar perspectives on non-participation, and a proposition that mass non-participation and its outcomes cannot be researched or interpreted effectively in isolation from an analysis of young people's entitlements to social protection and security, or from their involvement, however mediated, with systems of youth criminal justice.

## Section 3: Overview of key literature

The purposes of this book are more apparent if located in the limited literature of major original UK-based texts that are directly relevant.

A number of older texts dedicated to specialised areas of study within the broad field made critical contributions to establishing interest in youth studies that began from the political, social and economic transformations of the late 1970s.[17] Over the last two decades, a small number of original texts provided analyses across most of the policy fields included in this text: education, welfare, work, labour markets and crime. The most wide-ranging began to appear in the late 1990s. The earliest, most influential, widely used and cited is Andy Furlong and Fred Cartmel's (1997, 2007) *Young people and social change*. It is both a research-based text and a strongly theoretically framed textbook. It takes the form of a sociology of change in the late 20th century, realised through an analysis of the 'state of youth', largely framed as a critical assessment of the Beck/Giddens risk/individualisation and 'late modernity' thesis (noted earlier). Its equal attention to the theoretical frame and the substantive topic is exemplary, as are its breadth and scope in addressing education, labour markets, housing, youth culture, health, political participation and crime. Its analysis, though, is policy field by policy field, rather than integrative of the connections between these fields for understanding young people's non-participation and its consequences.

Phil Mizen's (2004) *The changing state of youth* is an introductory text that is politically engaged and infused with powerful critical analyses of the state in relation to a range of social spheres that shape the lives of young people. The emphasis is on change during the crisis of the state from 1979 through to the New Labour era, and it too undertakes its analysis by policy fields, covering education, work, social security, family, and law and order. It juxtaposes the growth of mass unemployment and the rising rates of youth crime, but consideration of how these two fields might be connected is not directly addressed or theorised.

Rob MacDonald and Jane Marsh's (2005) *Disconnected youth?* is closer to the concerns of this book. Its focus is on broadly the same 'disconnected' cadre as this book's non-participants, and its central fields of study are education and training, work and unemployment, welfare and crime, alongside families and housing. It touches on the interface between materialist-structuralist and postmodernist theorisation, including through strong references to youth culture. The principal axis of analysis is built around a sophisticated refutation of underclass theories of poverty, and its principal contribution among many is to report the findings of an impressively rich study of Teesside between 1998 and 2000, in which the dominant linkage between non-participation and offending is the misuse of drugs. This also sets crucial historical-contextual background for a follow-up study, reported in Shildrick et al's (2012) *Poverty and insecurity: Life in 'low-pay no-pay' Britain*. Both books offer important material upon which later chapters of this text draw, although neither claims any broader theorised focus on the relationship of crime to work, non-participation and welfare.

Alan France's (2007) *Understanding youth in late modernity* is an engaging, wide-ranging and valuable review that addresses most of the policy fields of relevance in this text. Its approach is committedly theoretical and it promises important debate about the nature of social science and its conflicted paradigms and epistemologies, as they impact on the study of young people, deploying key concepts of governance and criminalisation that are also central to the present text. France largely rejects poststructuralist analyses as a route to better understanding young people in late modernity, although the full complexity of the relationship between work, welfare, non-participation and crime is not assessed theoretically.

John Pitts' (2003) *The new politics of youth crime: Discipline or solidarity?* is predominantly criminological in orientation, but its explicitly political reading of shifting youth justice policies draws it into valuable analyses of social and labour market policies, social and economic restructuring, unemployment, marketisation, managerialisation, and policy alignment and coordination across these policy sites. It goes further than the texts described above in its recognition of the entwined nature of criminal activity in these wider contexts, without giving primary attention to non-participation.

Finally, John Muncie's *Youth and crime* (1999, 2015) also has an unequivocally criminological focus but it is uncompromising in giving equal attention to the wider social, economic and political contexts of crime, and to securing their integration into the analysis of youth crime. This, its encyclopaedic scope, and its renewed tracing of the trajectory of youth criminal justice policy over four editions, position it as a definitive work in this field, notable as much for its depth and breadth of theorisation and analysis as its extensive historical and contemporary coverage. Extensive chapters on youth culture and on control, regulation and governance in relation to policy afford particular attention to political-economic policy contexts, labour markets, unemployment, training, workfare, welfare, housing and social exclusion. They draw on key theorisations of the governance of young people in a range of spheres in which the control of crime is integrated and implicated. Moreover, they map some of the early linkages through which these lines of connection between policy spheres opened the doors to the importance of the concept of criminalisation, albeit without a primary parallel focus on non-participation.

## Section 4: Aims and structure of the book

*Young people, welfare and crime: Governing non-participation* aims to address some of the spaces defined *in absentia* by these texts, to rethink some of them theoretically, and *to make a concerted attempt to place the connections between non-participation and the governance of crime at the centre of a field of study*. All seven  texts described above have influenced this book because they have shown recognition of the importance of doing so, without making it their principal approach to analysis. Muncie's work comes closest to doing so, and the approach of this book is in some respects a deliberate obverse of Muncie's framing, in that it begins from the nature and drivers of mass non-participation and considers their points of intersection with youth crime as corollaries. It does so, in part, by developing an extended critical assessment of economic and aetiological analyses of those aspects of youth crime that relate to non-participation; in part by bringing to bear a different frame of theoretical reference for interrogating the relationship between non-participation and crime; and by taking further the insights of theories of governance for an assessment of the proposition that mass non-participation by young people is becoming criminalised.

In doing so, this book pays particular attention to a number of important changes. It considers aspects of the history of the relationship between young people's contribution to labour markets and their participation in school and college. It traces the ways in which the emergence of endemic mass non-participation has been represented, analysed and responded to. It maps some of the complex ways in which the multiple relationships between participation, non-participation, social and welfare policies, labour markets and youth wages have shifted in recent history. And ultimately it is concerned with the ways in which the social and economic position and status of identifiable groups of young people have been incrementally reconfigured, including through youth criminal justice policies.

These changes are fundamental to any analysis of young non-participants' involvement in crime, and of the ways in which the governance of identifiable groups of young people is undertaken. The analysis in Parts Three and Four is therefore centrally concerned with theorising the ways in which non-participation is interpreted, constructed and governed, and with a preliminary exploration of the ways in which the processes of 'governing non-participation' call upon tactics and policies whereby the choices and actions of problematised populations are criminalised.

This book focuses on the UK and the impact of the GFC, supported by some brief explorations of relevant histories, and of non-participation in other countries. These set an important perspective for the analysis of mass non-participation – and young people's responses to it – as an endemic, ubiquitous and increasingly transnational phenomenon.

In summary, then, the aims of the book are to take forward understanding of the relationship between non-participation, welfare and crime as it affects young people by:

- providing a wide-ranging critical assessment of existing evidence about the causes of non-participation, its interpretation and its impact on policy;
- locating the relationship between non-participation, welfare and crime in its historical, political-economic and policy contexts in the UK;

- considering the effects of the global financial crisis on the relationship, set in UK and international contexts;
- reviewing competing theorisations of key elements of the relationship;
- establishing the non-participation-welfare-crime relationship at the centre of critical policy analysis in the fields of social and criminal justice policies.

Of equal importance to these aims is the approach of the book to pursuing them. It endeavours to circumnavigate the analytical limitations of working within a single tradition of youth studies. It works deliberately across historical separations between policy fields, social science disciplines and theoretical approaches that have restricted the development of understanding of the non-participation-welfare-crime relationship. It strives to disrupt interpretations of the relationship founded on some dominant divided categories of analytical approach. It aims to place theories of governance and criminalisation at the centre of an analysis of the relationship. And it aspires to contribute towards a dedicated theorisation of the non-participation-welfare-crime relationship as it applies to young people.

The book is organised as follows. Part Two is focused on data, research and policy in relation to work, welfare and crime. Chapter Two begins from a brief contextualising history of the complex and conflicted relationship between the fluctuating needs for young people's labour and the legal requirement that they participate in schooling. It then offers a critical review of three discursive renditions of the evolving nature of this relationship. It traces the defining shift from three post-war decades of reliable transitions from school to work, to the unprecedented levels of youth unemployment of the 1980s and 1990s, and considers the conflicting analyses which explain them. It then develops a critical assessment of the rise of the social exclusion discourse during the New Labour era, which marked a major change to an emphasis on the responsibilisation of young people, and on the increasing conditionalisation of post-school provision and welfare entitlement. The chapter concludes with a critical analysis of the provenance and priorities of the disengagement discourse which has taken centre stage in the UK, especially since the GFC.

Chapter Three considers the claim that mass non-participation among young people is becoming an endemic, transnational and ubiquitous phenomenon. It traces the profile of post-war youth unemployment, and marks the emergence of a now enduring gulf between youth and adult unemployment, indicating exceptionally high levels of non-participation among young people in the UK, by international standards. It reviews claims about poor skills and qualifications as causes of mass non-participation, then focuses on the possible effects of the incremental withdrawal of state welfare for young people without jobs, courses or training places that began in the 1980s. The closing section offers an interpretation of the dynamic process of the determination of young people's wages, and its effects on young people's choices in heavily oversubscribed labour markets.

Chapter Four presents a detailed analysis of the extent and nature of the mooted relationship between non-participation and crime among young people. It considers the research and methodological underpinnings of this perceived relationship, and some of the key policies and policy discourses through which the claimed association is interpreted as causal. Central to this discussion is an extended assessment of the insights and limitations of the 'economic causes of crime' thesis, through which claims of a causal connection have achieved currency in debates about the nature and effects of mass non-participation.

Chapter Five revisits this discussion in the specific context of economic recession, and offers a critical analysis of the counter-typical findings of official data that youth offending in the UK declined in the wake of the GFC. The analysis considers major changes in policy, practice and recording methods which, taken together, inhibit claims that the historical association between increased unemployment and increased crime among young people has been broken in recessionary conditions. However, other analyses of recessions offer indications that workfare-based amelioration of economic duress is associated with reduced frequency of offending. This tentative finding is considered alongside analyses of extensive transnational evidence of social unrest among young people during the same period. These findings lead to a critical review of the 'economic causes of crime' thesis, and to reflections on the need to make good the absence of dedicated theorisation of the non-participation–welfare–crime relationship.

The Interlude between Parts Two and Three marks a shift in the focus of the book from policy and evidence concerning the relationship between non-participation, welfare and crime to theorising it. It makes the case for recognising the limits of empirical inquiry and the conflicting explanations and contested analyses that it has generated, and establishes the case for exploring the work of two theorists that opens up disparate but also surprisingly complementary possibilities for reanalysing the relationship.

Part Three therefore considers new ways of theorising non-participation and its relationship with crime. Chapter Six begins by exploring selected aspects of the work of Jürgen Habermas and Imogen Tyler that demonstrate a capacity to move beyond some of the damagingly-divisive binaries typifying interpretations of the non-participation-welfare-crime relationship. In particular, it seeks out the complementarities and intersectionalities of the work of these two social scientists, whose respective approaches are grounded in very different traditions and paradigms, and brings their analyses to bear on some of the conflicts and tensions between dominant interpretations of the non-participation-welfare-crime relationship. This opens up questions about the governance of non-participation.

Chapter Seven is concerned with theorising the governance of non-participation and with the ways in which Habermas' and Tyler's theories both reinterpret and disrupt the dominant interpretations of it that the earlier chapters of the book will assess. Application of Habermas' and Tyler's theories to case-study material demonstrates how their respective understandings of the governance of problematised populations enhance analysis of non-participation and its relationship to crime, while also querying aspects of both at the points where they work beyond their principal paradigms.

Part Four builds on the theorisations explored in Part Three to consider a number of approaches to the concept of criminalisation and how they inform understanding of the relationship between non-participation, welfare and crime. Chapter Eight shifts the theoretical frame from the governance of non-participation to its criminalisation, and to links and distinctions between the concepts of juridification and criminalisation. Using theories of criminalisation based in law, the chapter draws attention to a potentially insidious and opaque net-widening tendency in complex contemporary societies, constituted by the increasing encroachment of civil and criminal law into the governance of everyday problems. This can be traced to the prioritisation of the demands of competitive economic performance over sources of social integration and cohesion. These encroachments, the chapter argues, have begun to manifest themselves in conditions that significantly alter (and potentially override) the relatively recent intensification of the governance of non-participation, in ways that are redolent of and conducive to its increasing criminalisation.

Chapter Nine summarises and reviews the conclusions of Chapters Two to Eight and offers concluding comments, including priorities for reorienting research in this field.

# Notes

[1] Throughout this text, the term non-participation refers to young people who are not in education, training or paid employment, whether full-time or otherwise. For the purposes of 'positive' statistical analysis it is identical to 'NEET' (not in employment, education or training). But as Chapter Three shows the NEET count is also a considerable underestimate of non-participation.

[2] www.ilo.org/ilostat/faces/help_home/youthstats?_adf.ctrl-state=jhzkvq3jq_14&_afrLoop=99917879327219

[3] Mizra-Davies (2014, paragraph 1.2 (House of Commons Library Parliamentary briefing paper)).

[4] Evidence submitted to the Committee (Webster, 2014), http://eprints.gla.ac.uk/90147/.

[5] Data produced from multiple sources including Office for National Statistics (ONS) and the National Commission for Low Pay shows the substantial wage deficits experienced by young people. See Chapter Three.

[6] Most infamously, Howker and Malik (2010); Brand (2013).

[7] It is telling that several academic books published in the wake of the GFC included the word 'lost' in the title: Ainley and Allen (2009), Brinton (2010), Dillabough and Kennelly (2010), Smith et al (2011). Chapter Two considers the diminished relevance of the concept of 'transition'.

[8] See 'Paying the price of youth', *Guardian*, 10 July 2015; 'UK "fails its young" as gulf between generations grows', *Observer*, 12 July 2015.

[9] Data compiled from multiple sources by Pople and Smith (2010, Figure 3.24).

[10] 'The UK suicide rate increased significantly between 2010 and 2011, from 11.1 to 11.8 deaths per 100,000 population' (ONS, 2013).

[11] Vaughan (2009) reported that this evidence was given by the Director-General to a meeting of the Westminster Forum. All record of this reportage was withdrawn from government and Westminster Forum websites shortly after Vaughan's report was published.

[12] Wilkinson and Pickett (2009) propose that the UK has by far the highest incidence of childhood conflict (defined as fighting, bullying and unkindness) of more than a dozen OECD countries, and that this correlates highly with the UK's high incidence of inequality, the latter exceeded only by that of Portugal and the USA in the dataset selected (Figure 10.4).

[13] The assessed risk rose from 34% in 2006/07 to 46% in 2011/12 (ILO, 2013b, p 42).

[14] For useful critical accounts of underclass theory applied to young people, see MacDonald (1997); Rodger (2008); Jones (2009); Muncie (2015). Also Jones (2012) and Tyler (2013) for the extension of the underclass thesis.

[15] The most prominent is the Cambridge Study in Delinquent Development that resulted in the Risk Factor Prevention Paradigm (RFPP), considered in Chapter Four.

[16] Three years after its inception the Youth Contract had attracted barely 3% of its target participants (*Guardian*, 26 July 2013, p 16).

[17] Most notably Willis (1977); Hebdidge (1979); Ashton et al (1982, 1990); Muncie (1984); Brown(1987); Cockburn (1987); Finn (1987); Wallace (1987); Furlong (1992); Griffin (1993); Coles (1995); Roberts (1995); and Brown (1998).

# Part Two
# Work, welfare and crime:
# research and policy

# TWO

# Young people and non-participation: discourses, histories, literatures

> A very considerable number of the boys whose cases have occupied the attention of the Committee, have attributed the course of life, in which they have been engaged, to an association with bad companions ... [but] in many instances [the] cause has been want of employment. The moral culture of the boys has been neglected, and often the poverty of their parents has induced them to endeavour to place their children at an occupation rather than send them to school. Until a situation could be procured for a lad under these circumstances, his hours have usually been at his own disposal. The vivacity of youth has impelled him to action: he has had no legitimate object for the attention of his mind. Thus exposed to temptation, the wonder would rationally be, if he did, rather than if he did not, abstain from the suggestions of folly and vice.

> *The Report of the Committee for Investigating the Causes of the Alarming Increase of Juvenile Delinquency in the Metropolis*, London, 1816, columns 16-17

## Introduction

Non-participation in education, training, the labour market or other forms of approved productive activity is named and narrated in remarkably diverse ways. In the UK at least, young people who are not participants in recognised activities are variously described as unemployed, truants, disengaged, disconnected, marginalised, socially excluded, or as welfare dependants, dropouts, resistant refusers, victims of failed transitions or members of a new precariat. These terminologies and narrations manifest themselves as social-scientific concepts, administrative categories, historical accounts, policy discourses and scholarly literatures. Charting and analysing the ways in which they are constructed, propagated and afforded status as authoritative descriptors would provide an informative focus for the study and analysis of problematised populations of young people. The more modest aim of this chapter is to examine three principal discourses that purport to explain non-participation − those of transitions, social exclusion and disengagement. The chapter also provides a historical account of some major changes that have radically and apparently irreversibly altered the circumstances in which young people are able – or unable – to achieve social and economic independence as young adults; and of the policy shifts which have initiated, responded to or cemented those changes. It also draws on a range of literatures which variously expound, analyse and critique the changes, discourses and policies with which they are associated.

Section 1 focuses on the concept of transition as a metaphor and a discourse for explaining young people's attainment of adult economic independence at the critical juncture between the end of compulsory schooling and the start of paid employment. It gives particular attention to the major historical changes which first established and then disrupted the transition between them, particularly in the three decades after the Second World War. It also sets out and critiques the 'transitions discourse'. Section 2 concerns the New Labour governments between 1997 and 2010, and the policies and discourse associated with the concept of social exclusion. Section 3 considers the period since 2010, and the ascendancy of the discourse of disengagement and its policy corollaries.

By arguing that all three discourses under-recognise the significance of political-economic forces, and embody largely undemonstrated assertions of young people's inadequacies in achieving a transition to adult independence, the chapter sets the terrain for querying the three discourses that have dominated interpretation and analysis of young people's non-participation for more than half a century.

## Section 1: 'Transition' and the transitions discourse

### Introduction

The concept of 'transitions' as a way of describing and defining young people's activities after the age of 15 or 16 emerged in the literature in the 1960s, particularly in the USA (Wolfbein, 1959; Hill, 1969), but it was not until the 1970s that it proliferated in the UK (Ashton, 1973; Ashton and Field, 1976). By the 1980s faltering 'transitions' were the objects of government policy reports (Clarke, 1980). This concept is also formulated in broader terms as the 'transition from childhood/adolescence to adulthood', or the 'transition from dependency to independence'. Much of the early school-to-work literature was influenced by these 'life-course' related conceptions of transition, much of it grounded in social psychology (Hamilton and

Crouter, 1980; Buchmann, 1989; Farmer, 1993; Fend, 1994). This approach dominated the field, along with an associated preoccupation with individual behaviours, choices, abilities, characteristics and achievements.

The most significant development of this approach occurred through a series of major UK cohort tracking studies funded by government and research councils.[1] A distinctive field of 'transitions studies' evolved that was strongly driven by these studies. Key publications include Raffe's (1984) work based on the Scottish School Leavers Study, and an extensive series of publications arising from the UK government-funded Youth Cohort Study, beginning with Courtenay and McAleese (1986) and Courtenay and Britain (1988). Flowing from this, the concept of transition became the centrepiece of a *transitions discourse* which was for at least two decades the dominant discourse for interpreting post-16 trajectories, and which remains influential.

Most of the research and academic literature concerning young people's post-16 trajectories up to the 1990s refers to them as transitions, often supported by other metaphors of temporal-spatial progression. Some of this literature is sufficiently nuanced to recognise that the school-to-work transitions described are not universal and that some are interrupted, or broken. But these exceptions do not dispute normative understandings of appropriate trajectories across an identifiable critical 'boundary' in the life-course.

## 19th- and 20th-century configurations of work and school

Understanding the provenance, the foundations and the significance of the transitions discourse requires a historical understanding of the relationships between school and work, and between work and unemployment, particularly in terms of education and employment policies. An historical approach makes clear that mass non-participation, represented as a persistent social and economic problem in the UK, is a distinctive phenomenon of the late 20th and early 21st Centuries – not because it is new but because it is has made a significant shift from being sporadic, localised and conjunctural to being a continuing ubiquitous condition.

Historically, young people's non-participation could be almost exclusively accounted for by the absence of educational provision or employment. The contradictory struggles to free children from the competing demands of child labour markets, from the deprivations of joblessness at times of economic decline, and from households' perpetual dependence on them to maintain family incomes are a dominant theme of the history of state-provided compulsory schooling (see for example Maclure, 1986, pp 174-5). Before and after the pivotal 1870 Education Act, the devices of part-time attendance, day-release and 'post-compulsory' continuation day schools managed the conflicting demands of work against the reformist drive for mass schooling. Objections to the loss of household wages by families and the loss of labour power to factories were countered by objections about cheap young labour and the increased levels of adult unemployment that often resulted. The extent and force of contention fluctuated according to national economic conditions, the character of local labour markets, and the effects of wartime conscription.[2] Trade unionists and politicised sections of the working class were profoundly divided by the simultaneous need for children's incomes in impoverished households, and for stemming the supply of cheap child labour at times of mass adult unemployment.[3] Nonetheless, the contested apportionment of the available time for children and young people between schooling and the workplace from the late 18th century onwards did not prevent the growth of policy interventions about idleness, vagrancy, petty street crime and delinquency in the interstices of these competing activities (Pearson, 1983; Muncie, 2015).

Contemporary anxiety about non-participation as a problem for social and criminal justice policies has ample historical precedent. A focused political-economic history of 19th- and early 20th-Century youth unemployment has yet to be written, but Cunningham's (1990) paper is a valuable contribution. It argues that employment, overemployment, underemployment and unemployment coexisted alongside levels of educational participation that varied between marginal and extensive among working-class children; that 'there was in no sense a national labour market for children ... the child labour market was highly localized, and the employment opportunities could differ widely' (Cunningham, 1990, p 146); and that 'the increasing supply of children may be an indicator of a growing problem of unemployment rather than of strong demand for child labour (p 148).[4]

Perhaps even more notable is that, 20 years before the advent of legislated compulsory school attendance up to the age of 10 in 1870, and almost 50 years before the school leaving age was established at 13, in many parts of England, more than half of early adolescent boys and almost as many girls were already classified as 'scholars' in the 1851 Census (Cunningham, 1990). In practice, many children worked *and* attended school. At the turn of the 19th century, Vincent (1991, pp 19-20) observes that despite the requirement to spend so much of their time cooped up in a classroom, children had the widest opportunities for making a few pence. ... Almost as soon as they could walk, every member of the poor household had a duty to explore the possibilities of squeezing a few pence or shillings out of the local economy ... supplementary earnings were of far greater significance to the poor than all forms of welfare provision combined.

These brief 19th-century histories sketch the condition of working-class children and young people as workers, pupils, housekeepers, contributors to the family income, but also as vagrants, street urchins and minor miscreants. All these representations hold – many of them simultaneously – but they vary widely according to place, time and gender. Nevertheless, despite these caveats, from the early 20th century onwards (with the important exceptions of the economic crises of the 1920s and 1930s), mass unemployment and non-participation among young people aged 13 and above became largely confined to the frictional mismatches of labour supply and demand. This shift from the highly diverse circumstances of the previous century is largely attributable to the provision of compulsory schooling up to the ages of 13 (from 1899) and 14 (from 1922), to the legislative limitation of the exploitation of child labour, and to successive multiple periods of economic growth. Young people were largely prevailed upon to attend school (at least part-time) or to work, usually for a wage. From the turn of the 19th century, the separation of schooling from working, and pupildom from employee-hood became established.

Remarkably, there has been no dedicated academic study of the historical relationship between increases in the school-leaving age and rates of unemployment among young people and adults. Even the most cursory analysis of the earliest available state records of unemployment, however, makes it clear that, since the 1870 Act, increases in the school-leaving age have tended to follow peaks of unemployment (albeit often after many years) and, more predictably, have commonly resulted in temporary reductions in the total rate of unemployment.[5] A 'potted' history reveals striking synchronicities that began to emerge from the early 20th century onwards. Repeatedly, high unemployment rates informed recommendations for increases in the age of compulsory schooling, and were followed by declining unemployment.[6] Of greatest relevance here is that the period between the end of the Second World War and the mid-1970s was marked by extraordinarily low rates of youth and adult unemployment, mostly at around 2-3%, which have never since been approximated. The 1973 Education Act had temporarily stemmed a slightly rising trend in youth unemployment rates by implementing the 1944 Education Act to raise the school-leaving age to 16 – a three-decade gap that is at least as much attributable to the buoyancy of labour markets as to the extraordinary demands of the Second World War. But by 1976, this effect had declined and, as the next chapter shows, the underlying upward trend was restored – never to be reversed for more than a few years, to date.

## A 'transition' from school to work?

To many analysts, the end of the post-Second World War economic boom, between the early 1950s and the mid-1970s, marks a radical transformation in the options open to those who left school at the earliest opportunity, and a remarkably well-demarcated moment of the appearance of a permanent, substantial cadre of non-participant young people. During that period, smooth passage directly into the labour market at the age of 15 was normalised. Brief interludes, sometimes shorter than a school summer vacation, were the greatest interruption experienced by an overwhelming majority of the 1958 birth cohort as they continued along the pathway that was partly inscribed in their future prospects by their selection for differentiated modes of secondary education at the age of 11.[7] During this period, smooth passage had no need of nomenclatures: in conditions of unprecedented economic growth built on Keynesianism, post-war reconstruction and social-democratic policies for ameliorating some inequalities, smooth articulation between the end of compulsory schooling and the beginning of adult life occurred reliably for the vast majority of boys, and most girls.

From the early 1980s, there were three shifts that helped to determine the trajectories of young people's post-compulsory school experiences, and that brought into question the notion of transition. The first was the near-collapse in many localities of youth labour markets. They had contracted sharply at the peak of two recessions in 1980-81 and 1991-92, and this was experienced most acutely by young people in areas dominated by manufacturing and some primary industries (see Chapter Three). The second shift concerns the end of the post-war welfare settlement, and the erosion during the 1980s of young people's status as citizens with entitlements to welfare benefits (see Chapter Five). The third shift concerns major changes in the formulae for funding post-16 school students, and in the status of and funding arrangements for further education colleges, which introduced incentives to increase post-16 registrations, the sum impact of which was to intensify recruitment (Gleeson, 1993; Chadwick, 1997; Foskett and Hesketh, 1997). Other factors included the growth in part-time, temporary and low-paid employment under deregulated conditions, and the reduced power of trades unions (Muncie, 2015).

Seen in this light, it was a departure of the greatest significance that, in the critical recessionary moment of 1980–81, the new Conservative government's response to mass youth unemployment refused the historical precedent of a further increase in the school-leaving age to 17. Rather, the government made a policy shift that was to redraw the landscape of post-16 provision for young people for three decades. The New Training Initiative established work-related part-time training in the form of the Youth Training Scheme (YTS) up to the age of 18 for all young people not in full-time education (Department of Employment, 1981, para 1 (ii)).[8]

The impact of these changes was dramatic. They redrew the terrain of post-16 possibilities for a substantial proportion of young people who, throughout most of the previous century, would have left school to begin a life in paid employment – an altered terrain that now appears permanent. By the mid-1980s, the research literature had begun to explore in depth a fundamentally shifting relationship between academic attainment, socioeconomic class, remaining in full-time education and entering the labour market. As early as 1985, Roberts and Parsell (1989) had noted the trend towards lower aggregate qualifications of those young people who stayed on in full-time education, as post-16 provision expanded. And although in the early to mid-1980s there remained strong evidence of large numbers of very poorly qualified school-leavers finding low skilled work (Roberts, 1984; Ashton and Maguire, 1986), even by this time there was also clear evidence that inflating qualification demands for low-skilled work were squeezing young people who would previously have left school for a job out of the labour market (Ashton and Maguire, 1986).

Later studies provided more detailed analyses of young people's marginal decisions to remain in full-time education (Bynner and Ashford, 1990; Bynner and Roberts, 1991). Of particular importance, Raffe and Willms (1989) postulated their 'discouraged worker effect', which directly connected increased post-16 participation in education and training in Scotland to limited labour market opportunities. Taylor (1992) also found that the decisions of a substantial minority of young people to continue as students were in effect decisions to defer labour market entry. Gray et al's (1993) study, however, made clear that the underlying causes of changes in post-16 participation were complex, and could not be reduced to simple 'discouraged worker' prognostications.[9]

Nevertheless, 'positive' effects on staying-on rates triggered by high levels of youth unemployment continued to be observed long after the recession of 1980-81 (Roberts and Parsell, 1988; Gray and Sime, 1990). Roberts and Parsell (1989) found that almost a third of 16-year-olds who secured employment and YTS places had qualifications above the median. Other studies also noted an increasing prevalence of interludes between the end of school attendance and labour market entry (Furlong, 1992), and the tendency of such interruptions to be more intensive among the lowest socio-economic classes and some Black and Minority Ethnic (BME) groups (e.g. Drew et al, 1992; Furlong, 1992). Fergusson and Unwin's (1996) study suggested that a significant proportion of young people who stayed on, irrespective of academic achievements and parents' economic status, did so 'by default': they were not so much taking their first step towards financial independence, as making tactical responses to unemployment or training schemes. But the study also demonstrated great variability in the propensity of different schools to inhibit, allow or actively encourage extended full-time studentship beyond the age of 16 according to students' academic attainment. A partially instrumental convergence of the short-term interests of students and schools in favour of maximising post-16 participation was emerging, driven by the forces of collapsing youth labour markets and the quasi-marketisation of post-16 funding of schools and colleges.

## The fragmentation of transitions, and the transitions discourse

In the light of this brief summary of an extensive literature alone, it is puzzling and apparently paradoxical that the currency of the concept of 'transition' in relation to young people's post-16 trajectories has grown exponentially since (and in inverse relation to) the dramatic decline in what might, until the late 1970s, legitimately have been described as mainly seamless post-school transitions. Many studies had begun to query fundamentally the ubiquity of recognisable linear transitions. And yet as the evidence of smooth passage from school to work for a substantial minority of young people demonstrated sharp decline, the urgency of normalising the notion of 'transition' apparently increased, as a means of highlighting the fast-growing ranks of those who were not in school, college or work. As the reliability of the material transitions themselves dwindled with alarming rapidity from the early 1980s, the analytical tendency to compare young people's fragmented experiences of unemployment, short-term casual work, temporary training schemes and non-participation with pre-existing transitions intensified.

In this way, the continued use of a concept of transition that was redundant for a substantial minority of school-leavers transmogrified into a transitions discourse. Like all discourses, it served to do much more than achieve some common basis for understanding the transformation of the landscape of post-school trajectories. It also shaped, constructed and ultimately determined the meaning and interpretation of those trajectories. And in doing so it established dominant and highly normative understandings and expectations of them. Post-16 trajectories thereby came to be portrayed as the product of relatively rational processes whereby young people were matched to a range of possible places according to their preferences and educational performance (Bates et al, 1984). The objectifiable rationality of the process was established principally through the judgements, assessments and interventions of a wide range of professional gatekeepers to extended education, training or jobs (Fergusson et al, 2000). In this discourse, successful careers are founded in transfers from one activity category to another that are progressive, objectively linked and subjectively coherent.

Consequently, the transitions discourse carries with it a set of meanings that becomes difficult to query or refute, to the extent that it normalises and monopolises the possibilities for the interpretation of young people's post-16 trajectories, thereby closing off alternative understandings. As a result, failure to progress towards states of adult social and financial independence is principally explained by reference to the moment of transfer between activity categories. Whether for want of opportunity, poor provision, ill-advised choices, weak motivation or unrealistic expectations, this moment is taken to constitute a critical conjuncture at which transitions are broken. In effect, the transitions discourse defines the parameters of desirable trajectories, identifies the sources of failure to pursue them, and attributes responsibility accordingly.

## Culture and economy: conflicted paradigms?

By the late 1990s, the metaphor and discourse of transition had begun to attract significant criticism. In his review of the literature, Raffe (2003) notes three main criticisms: that they ignore complexities and overlaps, social (as distinct from economic) transitions, and social structures and inequalities (Evans and Furlong, 1997; Dwyer and Wyn, 1998; Cohen and Ainley, 2000). These oversights are respectively characterised as linearity, economism and individualism (Raffe, 2003, p 4).

MacDonald et al (2001, para 2.11) provide a comprehensive overview of the debate, drawing on four studies which argue that 'the over-riding failing of youth sociology over the past twenty years has been its preoccupation with the concept of transition'. The first, Cohen and Ainley's (2000), critiqued the narrow and restrictive economism of transitions studies. Jeffs and Smith (1998, p 59) attack the narrowness of transitions studies which 'has produced little of substance and certainly nothing fresh or original for nearly two decades'. Miles (2000, p 10) claimed that '[T]he most damaging problem with the "transitions debate" is that it has tended to treat young people as troubled victims of economic and social restructuring without enough recourse to the active ways in which young people negotiate difficulties in their every day lives'. Fergusson et al (2000, paras 2.11–12) argued that the language of transitions is not capable of interpreting the trajectories of at least a third of young people. In response, MacDonald et al (2001, para 2.14) reasserted the value of the transitions perspective, arguing that 'These critics tend to present a narrow and largely out-dated picture of the nature of transition studies and underplay the theoretical potential of contemporary studies of youth transition'.

In response, it is crucial to invoke two important distinctions. The first is between the empirically demonstrable 'smooth' transitions that fit the normative parameters and the category of scholarly activity known as the 'youth transitions tradition' – dominated as it has been by narrowly quantitative cohort studies. The second is between the concept of 'transition' and the 'transitions discourse'.[10] These distinctions determine how the continuing value of 'the youth transitions tradition' is to be evaluated. However, so do two more fundamental distinctions for theorising young people's fragmented and supposedly failed trajectories into non-participation. In the course of mounting their defence of transitions, MacDonald et al (2001, para 2.8) developed an insightful analysis of the bifurcation of youth studies into two separate fields: the youth cultural studies tradition and the youth transitions tradition – in which 'youth cultural studies remain marginal to the main (stream) thrust of the field'.

It is certainly the case that in the transitions literature, exploration of factors influencing young people's post-16 trajectories is almost invariably confined to material benefits and risks – reflecting the economism criticised above. As Cohen and Ainley (2000, p 80) argue, 'The youth-as-transition approach ... is premised upon the availability of waged labour as the "ultimate goal". The consequent emphasis on production has led to a limited research paradigm focused on 'transition' as a rite of passage between developmental stages.'

Most analyses in that tradition also neglect the centrality of young people's rationales, beliefs and subjectivities to the ways in which they navigate between activity categories.[11] One study concluded that:

> The critical role of leisure and culture in 'making up' young people is well established [in other academic traditions] ... What is of interest here is the way in which the pursuit of consumption becomes integral to other activities. ... Many of the young people who experience [fragmented transitions] are actively creating new subcultural spaces and new ways of defining themselves. Dislocation from the dominant parameters which describe progress as moving towards financial and social independence is counterbalanced by new forms of location in other modes of economic and cultural life. (Fergusson et al, 2000, pp 297-8)

These observations highlight the divisions between analyses premised on the material and those premised on culture. They also contribute to the deep schisms and rifts that separate those who focus on economic and institutional conditions from those who focus on the ontological and the symbolic; and that separate positivist-inclined empiricists from those for whom interpretation and meaning are central. In particular, drawing on MacDonald et al's (2001) analysis, these schisms imply a deep division between quantitative analyses of transitions, and the much more methodologically diverse approaches to transitions which recognise the complexity of their meanings and constructions. Some key aspects of these distinctions are summarised in Table 2.1.

To escape the failings and normativities of the empiricist quantitative tradition of transition studies by diverting attention to the cultural drivers of young people's choices would be to sidestep the contradictions they pose. However, by the same token, any attempt to deny the influence of values, beliefs, identities, practices and ontological positions that constitute cultures would be to ignore critical determinants of many young people's preferences. To adopt either course would be to treat 'the cultural and leisure lives of young people [as though they] were wholly detached from their lives as young workers, trainees, college students or the young unemployed' (MacDonald et al, 2001, para 2.7). But MacDonald et al also claim that transitions-based studies are capable of addressing the unpredictability, insecurity and contingency of young people's trajectories, of giving equal emphasis to personal agency and structural constraints, and of embracing cultural factors in analysing young people's choices and actions (paras 4.7–13).

Table 2.1. Youth transitions and youth cultural studies traditions

| Analytical tradition | Youth transitions | Youth cultural studies |
|---|---|---|
| Dominant disciplines | Economics/political economy<br>Labour market studies<br>Sociology of education | Cultural studies<br>Sociology of youth |
| Analytical focus | Work and labour markets<br>Employment/unemployment<br>Production<br>Structures and institutions | Youth culture<br>Leisure<br>Consumption<br>Agency and networks |
| Dominant metaphors and concepts | Transitions<br>Pathways<br>Trajectories | Diversity/unpredictability<br>Tactics<br>Adaptations |
| Epistemology | Empiricist/positivist | Interpretive/discursive |
| Assumed motivating criteria | Material gain | Meaning and interaction |
| Dominant categories of analysis of behaviour | Cognition and action<br>Objectivity and rational choice<br>Calculation of risks/benefits | Emotion and affect<br>Subjectivity and expression<br>Construction of personal identity |
| Critique of other approach | Underestimates centrality of material circumstances to cultural responses<br><br>Misrepresents and underestimates transitions tradition as narrow and homogeneous | Economism<br>Narrowness of analytical frame<br>Preoccupation with linear pathways<br>Subjects as victims<br>Under-recognition of agency |

These conflicted paradigms are partially aligned with some still more fundamental schisms that shape many important aspects of the analysis of young people's post-education trajectories and increasing levels of non-participation. They map onto aspects of binary divisions identified in Chapter One, founded in paradigms that afford precedence to the individual, the personal, the emotional, the affective, the therapeutic, the psychosocial, and that focus on endogenous factors and idiographic levels of analysis on one side; and paradigms that prefer structures, material conditions, power, rationality, cognition, the political-economic, and focus on exogenous factors and nomothetic levels of analysis on the other. They mark a prevailing axis of difference and contestation which is explored and critiqued in depth in Chapters Six to Eight.

## Section 2: The social exclusion discourse

Shortly after the Conservative party came to government in 1979, its monetarist-inspired efforts to reduce rampant inflation precipitated the 1980-81 recession that took the youth unemployment claimant count above 1 million for the first time (Bivand et al, 2011). A decade later, a second recession triggered a second peak in youth unemployment of 8-900,000. During the subsequent resurgence of 'New Labour', the devastating effects of endemic youth unemployment in some of the worst hit localities emerged as a defining political issue. New Labour's pledges in the run-up to the 1997 election listed a commitment to achieve a radical and lasting reduction in youth unemployment as its first priority (Labour Party, 1997). This was also inspired by a recognition during the closing years of the 1979-97 Conservative governments 'that child poverty had trebled between 1979 and 1995, that Britain had more children growing up in unemployed households than anywhere else in Europe, that it had the highest teenage pregnancy rate [in Europe], and that 80% of rough sleepers used drugs' (Muncie, 2015, p 259).

Embracing these and other sources of social and economic inequality and hardship, the concept of 'social exclusion' became a centrepiece of New Labour's 1997 election manifesto. The roots of the concept lie in the philosophies of French and wider European political traditions, which afford priority to social rights, citizenship and solidarity, and the pooling of social risk (Silver, 1994). New Labour definitions of social exclusion radically diluted and departed from this tradition in favour of a vague definition that identified social exclusion as 'a combination of linked problems such as unemployment, poor skills, low incomes, poor housing, high crime environments, bad health and family breakdown' (Social Exclusion Unit, 2004, p 3).[12] For New Labour, a re-versioned social exclusion policy was a necessary counterbalance to its preoccupation with economic globalisation and its ambitions for the UK economy to compete with the expanding low-cost economies of the global south, and with increased innovation and productive efficiency worldwide. The tensions between these priorities debilitated New Labour's ambitions to promote social justice through 'social inclusion' far more than they restricted its ambition to foster neoliberal wealth maximisation.

One of the first priorities of the new government was to establish its much-vaunted Social Exclusion Unit (SEU). It was hyperactive in its opening years. By 2002 it had researched and reported on four youth-oriented issues: rough sleeping; teenage pregnancy; school exclusion and truancy; and young people described as 'NEET' (not in education, training or employment).[13] A flood of new initiatives followed, including 'Youth Inclusion Projects' targeted at 'high risk' 13 to 16-year-olds, the 'New Deal for Young People' workfare programme, and the 'Connexions' service, charged with securing young people's transitions after school.[14] The defining publication in this field was *Bridging the Gap* (SEU, 1999). In his introduction to it, Prime Minister Tony Blair asserted that paid employment is the best defence against social exclusion (SEU, 1999, p 6). And this was to be the defining theme of the work of the SEU and of New Labour's approach to addressing social exclusion. It was also the basis of a discourse of social exclusion which asserted, embedded and reproduced in the public imagination a crucial range of beliefs about the causes of unemployment, poverty, non-participation and a range of other material, social and cultural inequalities. Despite prolific statistical modelling of correlations between socioeconomic conditions and outcomes that identified individuals as socially excluded, as Chapters Four and Five argue, many of the claimed causal connections lacked sound bases.

A substantial literature lent intellectual and political legitimacy to the SEU's assertions (e.g. Pearce and Hillman, 1998; Hills et al, 2002). Nevertheless, a considerable body of work also articulates a range of shortcomings in the intellectual and practical foundations of *Bridging the Gap*. Colley and Hodgkinson's (2001, p 335) influential critique, for example, argues cogently that:

> Despite appearing to re-instate a concern for the social, it locates the causes of non-participation primarily within individuals and their personal deficits. Yet it denies individuality and diversity by representing the socially excluded as stereotyped categories. In a flawed move, the Report presents non-participation not just in correlation to a raft of other social problems, but as cause to their effect. Deep-seated structural inequalities are rendered invisible, as social exclusion is addressed through a strongly individualistic strategy based on personal agency.

Whatever the rigour of the work of the SEU, flaws in the evidence and discourse began to plumb the limits of the policies they informed. By 2005, an adjusted relaunch of youth-oriented policies was needed. The Department for Education and Skills (2005) stepped in to publish the *Youth Matters* Green Paper, which acknowledged:

> [This] document starts from an understanding that, while existing services ... have made a crucial contribution, they do not amount to a coherent, modern system of support ... the various organisations providing services and help for young people do not work together as effectively or imaginatively as they should ... Not enough is being done to prevent young people from *drifting into a life of poverty and crime*. (DES, 2005, para 10, emphasis added)

The paper reprioritises targeted integrated support and interventions focused on 'personalised intensive support for each young person who has serious problems or gets into trouble' (DES, 2005, para 12). The commitment to joined-up services in the work of youth justice professionals, youth offending teams, social services, truancy and pupil referral units, and so on, was to be paramount in achieving integration, holism and the avoidance of gaps and overlaps. Every young person 'at risk' was to be allotted a 'nominated lead professional who will be a single point of contact and make sure support is provided in a co-ordinated, convenient and integrated way' (para 33) with a strong focus on early intervention. The document argues that 'The risk factors involved in many poor outcomes ... are often the same': non-participation, pregnancy, criminal activity and drug misuse are listed (para 31). Fifty pages on, these outcomes unaccountably metamorphose into risk factors in their own right, rather than manifestations of them: 'We know that, for many young people, problems multiply if they are not addressed. These problems are often caused by the same factors' (para 210). The ensuing list replicates that of paragraph 31.

In these ways, the concepts of non-participation, failed transitions, social exclusion and crime became empirically and discursively entangled: non-participation becomes the critical index of failed transition; failed transitions are presented as defining features of social exclusion; and social exclusion is identified as a predictor of future criminality. Much usage of these concepts and the discourses they carry deploys these tautologous meanings without query. The determinist tone of inexorability in these connections is typified by Bynner and Parsons (2002, p 209), for whom failed transitions, non-participation and social exclusion become entwined with 'poor physical and mental health, drug abuse, and criminality', while non-participation 'may well be not much more than a staging post on the downward path to the bottom of the labour market and social exclusion ... [and] predictive of later social exclusion outcomes' (p 302).

Using these entangled logics, the solution to social exclusion is to maximise participation in some form. Thus, from the late 1990s, the policies for achieving participation and for ensuring that opportunities were exploited began to change significantly. Rights of citizenship in the form of entitlement to welfare came to depend not just on attendance at youth schemes like YTS, but on 'responsible' conduct, in the form of positive responses to expectations of participation in prescribed provision. From the inception of the New Deal for Young People in 1998 onwards, new modes of securing participation were pursued in the form of ostensibly more client-oriented policies, operated through newly empowered and better connected local agencies.

A substantial literature highlights the many shortcomings of this approach. Craig (2008, p 329) argues that the contradictions of New Labour's conception of social exclusion inscribed in the work of the SEU

> excludes it from examining such basic questions as the adequacy of benefits ... or the causes of inequality. Further, it focuses not on the actions of those controlling the mechanisms and processes excluding the poor but ... on the poor themselves, thus implicating them in their own exclusion.

Consequently, as Fairclough (2000), Colley and Hodgkinson (2001) and Byrne (2005) point out, structural and other exogenous sources of poverty, inequality, non-participation and failed transitions are side-lined in analysis. 'The excluded' can then be portrayed as hapless victims of supposedly inexorable meta-forces of globalisation, modernisation and deindustrialisation. Such renditions circumnavigate politically contentious claims that 'the excluded' constitute an underclass, along the lines so clearly articulated and rebutted by Levitas (1996, 1998), and by MacDonald (1997), whose critical analyses query the centrality of waged labour to New Labour's conceptions of social cohesion and social integration.[15]

The resilience of the discourse of social exclusion was severely tested during New Labour's period in government. By 2006 the SEU had been closed down in the face of criticism of its ineffectiveness

(Muncie, 2015, p 261). The currency of the discourse had diminished significantly since the halcyon days of the 1997 landslide election, when it enjoyed temporary status as emblematic of qualified government commitment to social justice. Even before the onset of the 2007/08 global financial crisis (GFC), the stubborn persistence in the numbers of young people without jobs or places on courses gave the UK one of the poorest records of participation in the Organisation for Economic Co-operation and Development (OECD).[16] In response, for the first time in 30 years, this evidence of the limited impact on sustained levels of non-participation prompted recourse to the dominant historical solution to youth unemployment: the government raised the age threshold for compulsory participation, but with a difference. The 2008 Education and Skills Act established the phased introduction of compulsory participation in school, college or a job that includes a training element, for all 17 and 18-year-olds.[17]

## Section 3: The disengagement discourse

By the time of the election of the Conservative-Liberal Democrat coalition government in 2010, a new discourse had begun to supplant that of social exclusion.[18] Following the GFC and the worst multiple recessions in 70 years, in the name of austerity, several programmes to reduce youth unemployment were cancelled and others substituted.[19] At the same time, the discourse of social exclusion disappeared from official rhetoric and much media narrative, in favour of a 'disengagement' discourse. This rose rapidly in common usage and policy texts, in an attempt to re-narrate levels of non-participation that were reaching unprecedented heights.[20] The degree of the term's penetration into common parlance in a range of contexts (considered later) heralded a critically important shift in policy and practice as well as nomenclature and meaning. The increasing tendency to reconceptualise non-participation as disengagement embeds a radical move away from locating it in failures of transition or exclusionary provision, towards self-determined choices and failures of young people's performances and responsibilities. The outgoing conceptualisation of social exclusion recognised young people's experiences as products of social and economic environments that governments can improve; the incoming discourse of disengagement constructs young people primarily as individualised authors of their own fortunes in given environments which will improve only at the initiative of participants.

'Disengagement' has an extensive and revealing provenance. The concept of *engagement* entered the lexicon of management studies in the 1990s. Its penetration of the everyday vocabulary of managers and researchers of management has been extensive. It refers to the disposition of employees towards their work roles and responsibilities. The first focused deployment (Kahn, 1990, p 700) was embedded in social psychology and social interactionism:

> Personal engagement is the simultaneous employment and expression of a person's 'preferred self' in task behaviors that promote connections to work and to others, personal presence (physical, cognitive, and emotional), and active, full role performances. My premise is that people have dimensions of themselves that, given appropriate conditions, they prefer to use and express in the course of role performances. To employ such dimensions is to drive personal energies into physical, cognitive, and emotional labors.

What is crucial in this context is that the 'preferred self' that is on show in the workplace 'drives personal energies'. Here, a bridge is constructed between particular dispositions and behaviours of employees, and labour value to the employer that might accrue to employees. Just as some employee dispositions are engaged, there is a necessary antithesis that others are disengaged:

> Personal disengagement, conversely, is the simultaneous withdrawal and defense of a person's preferred self in behaviors that promote a lack of connections, physical, cognitive, and emotional absence, and passive, incomplete role performances. To withdraw preferred dimensions is to remove personal, internal energies from physical, cognitive, and emotional labors. Such unemployment of the self underlies task behaviors researchers have called automatic or robotic (Hochschild, 1983), burned out (Maslach, 1982), apathetic or detached (Goffman, 1961a), or effortless (Hackman and Oldham, 1980). To defend the self is to hide true identity, thoughts, and feelings during role performances. (Kahn, 1990, p 701)

On the basis of such definitions, the concept of disengagement has a notably mixed application and usage. It has been reproduced in ways that sensationalise, dramatise and in some cases technicise it. Disengagement is the focus of a government report on vocational courses in which the term is extraordinarily broadly defined as 'underachievement at Key Stage 3, having poor attitudes to school, aspiring to leave education and training at the age of 16, and playing truant' (Ross et al, 2011, p 5). In each instance, disengagement is represented as individual deficiency.

In a second example, the report on the August 2011 riots commissioned by the Cabinet Office is peppered with references to high levels of youth unemployment as associated with the riots. One of its findings is that 'there was a sense that too many young people were disengaged – for example, they were not part of their community in any positive way and they were uninterested in, or cynical about mainstream politics' (National Centre for Social Research et al, 2011, p 46). Once again, the inference is of lack of attachment, willed by the (unemployed) rioters themselves. Other examples abound.[21]

These illustrations mark a crucial discursive shift away from social exclusion and its partial recognition of exogenous influences on non-participation interpreted using nomothetic levels of analysis, towards a powerful and damaging discursive emphasis on endogenous determinants using idiographic levels of analysis.

## Political, social and employee disengagement

These uses of the concept of disengagement are strongly indicative of its problematic inferences and ambiguity. This may be partly attributable to its diverse provenances, in relation to political participation, social engagement and employee effectiveness. Many academic studies offer analyses of what constitutes political participation, of the sources of apparent disengagement from its formal constitutional processes, and of the conditions that support active participation (see, for example, Henn et al, 2005; Howe, 2010; Thomas and McFarland, 2010). Perhaps the most high-profile recent public expression of this position reads: 'I have never voted. Like most people I am utterly disenchanted by politics ... I don't vote because to me it seems like a tacit act of compliance ... it is a far more potent political act to completely renounce the current paradigm' (Brand, 2013, np).

Russell Brand's polemic relates this form of 'democratic refusal' to other forms of non-participation. Manning's (2010) analysis lends support to Brand's claims when it argues that the disengagement discourse arises from a narrow interpretation of regulatory and formal political engagement which 'does not reflect contemporary social conditions and actually militates against young people understanding themselves as political actors and beings' (p 1). Other scholars have identified an important distinction between apathy and cynicism: Bhavnani (1991) argues that 'cynicism requires a level of political analysis and critique and thus, a modicum of engagement', such that choosing to be disengaged can be a political act, and 'may even act as an *impetus* for political activity' (quoted in Manning, 2010, para 2.4, emphasis in original). Similarly, Coleman's (2007) chapter on 'How democracies have disengaged from young people' disrupts the negative associations with a title that purposively inverts the locus of responsibility which is implicit in the vocabulary of disengagement.

The origins of these uses of disengagement are grounded in social-psychological and social-cognitive paradigms that date back half a century. 'Disengagement theory' is attributed to Cumming and Henry (1961), who postulated an inevitable process of disengagement from a range of forms of social participation and interaction associated with the ageing process. As this approach took hold, extensions of this conceptualisation emerged. The most striking and controversial are the social cognitive theories of 'moral disengagement' as explanations for terrorism developed by Bandura (1991, 2004). This version has since infused interpretations of youthful criminality, deviancy and delinquency, and a range of their supposed associated social pathologies (Bandura et al, 1996; Barnes et al, 1999; Hymel et al, 2005; Kiriakidis, 2008). The theoretical analysis of non-participation in Chapter Six considers the significance of these applications of the concept.

The psychological and managerial study of employee engagement and disengagement in the workplace is relatively recent (see, for example, Saks, 2006; Macey and Schneider, 2008). Kahn (1990, p 694) defines employee disengagement as 'the uncoupling of selves from work roles; in disengagement, people withdraw and defend themselves physically, cognitively, or emotionally during role performances'. More recent claims perceive a major shift: 'the phenomenon of employee disengagement is increasing but that the methods for its identification are inadequate ... the majority of managers seem unwilling or unable to halt the rising tide of employee disengagement' (Pech and Slade, 2006, Abstract, first page).

Whatever the grounds for such dramatic claims, the Department of Business, Innovation and Skills initiated a substantial investigation. Drawing on a wide range of psychological and management studies, MacLeod and Clarke's (2009) report stresses the value of engagement by employees, and the ways in which managers can secure it as a means to improve performance. Nonetheless, the report is replete with references to engagement deficits. It goes so far as to argue that 'disengagement may also be a factor behind Britain's continuing lag in the international productivity league table ... Senior private sector HR managers believe that the top challenge they face now is maintaining employee engagement' (MacLeod and Clarke, 2009, para 48).

The report cites data which suggests that in 2008 'the cost of disengagement to the [UK] economy was between £59.4 billion and £64.7 billion' (para 51). The framing of this remarkably precise quantification apparently neglects the cost of employer failures to engage staff. For all the references to the ways in which managers can improve engagement, this typifies the ways in which the report leaves the lasting impression that the presenting problem is grounded in individual employees much more than in the environments in which they work.

Overall, disengagement emerges as an ambiguous, contestable and contested concept for explaining and interpreting reduced participation and non-participation in a range of contexts. Most have strongly negative associations, ranging from lack of opportunity, failure to seize opportunity, apathy and indifference, alienated incapacitation, and limitations of social and cognitive competence, to moral failure and criminal pathology. Almost all locate disengagement within the social, cognitive or behavioural characteristics of the individuals identified, reinforcing the shift to an emphasis on endogenous factors derived from idiographic levels of analysis. What began as a concept used to explain characteristics associated with human ageing has been reworked as a discourse through which non-participation has been reconstructed as personal failure, and often reinterpreted as non-compliance with socially approved behaviours.

Aspects of this provenance are visible in contemporary endeavours to interpret young people's non-participation in education, training or employment (DeLuca et al, 2010; Sheehy et al, 2011; Upton, 2011). Much of this usage is unreflective and uncritical of the concept of disengagement.[22] Importantly for what follows, some commentators assert direct connections between this form of disengagement and offending (Stephenson, 2007), paralleling similar claims in relation to social exclusion in the 2000s.

These reinterpretations freight the concept of disengagement with such prejudicial, negative and normative discursive connotations as to render it unusable for analytic purposes. As Chapter Seven will argue, the discourse is infinitely more pertinent to a critical understanding of strategies for the governance of burgeoning cadres of problematised young non-participants than it is for explaining their circumstances. Whatever its discursive impact in reinterpreting the legacies of interrupted transitions from the 1980s and 1990s, and those of social exclusion from the 2000s, it has been immeasurably more successful in reframing policy analysis than in reducing non-participation. Many more young non-participants may have internalised the claims that they are responsible for their own misfortunes, but the UK also has many more of them to convince. Significant proportions of young people who are not in school, college, work or training are unequivocally victims of lack of opportunities. Five years after the onset of the GFC, the UK was bottom of the league of the world's 29 most advanced economies, with only 73% of 15 to 19-year-olds participating in further education of any kind (UNICEF, 2013, Figure 3.1 b).

## Concluding comments

This chapter began from a brief historical contextualisation of the emergence of mass non-participation in education, training and labour markets by young people, at an unprecedented scale in modern UK history. It has charted the gradual emergence of a discourse that purported to explain non-participation, just as historically-dominant trajectories of progression and participation were fragmenting. It has reviewed the literature of weakening and collapsing trajectories from schooling to adult independence for many young people, and offered critical analyses of three discourses that have sought to account for these transformations in young people's prospects.

As a concept, transition has little to offer as the basis for the analysis and interpretation of the experiences of a substantial minority of young people. As a discourse, its normative assumptions about life-stages and pathways to adult independence display some tendencies to view interrupted trajectories and periods of non-participation as aberrant, in ways that turn attention towards individuals and their shortcomings, and away from the material circumstances and exogenous factors that have shaped their experiences. But what differentiates it from the discourses that succeeded it is its relative agnosticism on the causes of such shortcomings, and its implicit acceptance of arguments that mismatches of supply and demand for places in schools, colleges and jobs are relevant considerations for analysis.

In place of the transitions discourse, the social exclusion discourse acknowledged the importance of exogenous factors and nomothetic levels of analysis for understanding the unprecedented levels of mass non-participation its exponents inherited. It had some success in providing the conceptual basis for an extensive set of policies for driving down the proportion of young people who were not studying, training or working, despite propitious economic circumstances. These policies identified impoverished groups that were reconceptualised as excluded. They thereby avoided analysis of their circumstances based on underclass theories, and they acknowledged some of the political-economic drivers of inequality. But they also sought to make 'the excluded' jointly responsible for their own fortunes, offering some support only if they were willing to accept the imposed terms of increased opportunities for participation, while never succeeding in reducing non-participation to the levels they aspired to.

The concept of disengagement, in turn, has mixed and highly contested origins, most of which are associated with apathetic withdrawal, or failures of responsible participation and deviant or even pathological behaviour. By commuting its conceptual base into a discourse for representing contemporary non-participation among young people, disengagement has emerged as the most individualising of the three discourses. It is most inclined to place the responsibility for non-participation with those most adversely affected, and least inclined to acknowledge overwhelming macro-economic and political-economic determinants of mass unemployment and non-participation among young people, despite the exceptional conditions of GFC-driven national and global economic instability under which the use of the discourse proliferated. Explanations based on exogenous factors have thereby given way to a focus on endogenous factors, and idiographic levels of analysis marginalise nomothetic approaches.

It follows from these critiques that 'non-participation' is, despite some negative implications, the least problematic and least freighted nomenclature for supporting unprejudiced inquiry into the causes of the obstacles faced by young people in their efforts to attain social and economic independence as autonomous adults. Unprecedentedly high proportions of 16 to 24-year-olds have experienced extended periods of non-participation during and after the GFC. Large-scale non-participation by young people is a phenomenon that now has some claim to being endemic, ubiquitous and transnational. The next chapter charts its changing profile in and beyond the UK since the late 1970s, and considers the specific context of the employment, wages and the forms of welfare and social security that create the conditions in which young people experience – and sometimes choose – non-participation. It does so as a first step towards a reinterpretation of the nature and drivers of mass non-participation.

## Notes

1  The National Child Development Study for the 1958 birth cohort; the British Birth Cohort Study, for the 1970 cohort; the Millennium Cohort Study for the 2000-01 UK birth cohort. The Youth Cohort Study which began in 1984 is based at the National Centre for Social Research (NatCen).

2  See Barker (1972) and Simon (1974) for well-documented descriptions.

3  During the debates prior to the approval of Fisher's Education 1918 Act, for example, Labour MPs, the Parliamentary Labour Party and constituency parties were deeply divided on compulsory attendance up to the age of 14 (Barker, 1972, p 32-3 ). Richard Johnson's (1976) summation of English working-class education between 1780 and 1850 also captures some of these tensions and ambivalences succinctly (see especially pp 51-2).

4  Cunningham's (1990) use of census material from 1851 notes that in the most industrialised counties, more than half of boys were employed, while in rural counties and the London conurbation barely one in five worked. Predictably, gender difference is most manifested in the two-to-one ratio of girls staying at home.

5  The reliable, systematic collection of unemployment data by the state apparently began in 1886 as reflected in Great Britain Department of Employment (1971) *British Labour Statistics: Historical Abstract 1886–1968.*

6  High unemployment rates in the late 1910s informed recommendations for compulsory attendance up to the age of 14. The ensuing 1918 Act legislated this extension, but was immediately followed by the post-war recession and unprecedented levels of recorded unemployment. It was implemented at the height of the adverse labour market effects of the recession in 1922, but still resulted in a temporary dip in unemployment. The Wall Street crash and the 1930s depression produced the highest levels of unemployment ever recorded in the UK, prompting the 1936 Act. This legislated a further increase to include children aged 15, was cancelled at the onset of the Second World War, then revived before the end of the war when the 1944 Act made provision for the school-leaving age to be raised to 15 as soon as possible (implemented in 1947), and to 16 at a later date (in the event, 1973) (see Fergusson, 2014a).

7  See Bynner's (2004) encapsulation of the findings of the differentiated cohorts of the National Child Development Study (NCDS).

8  The Conservative government's introduction of the YTS was described as a 'bolt from the blue' by Sir Geoffrey Holland, then director of the newly created Manpower Services Commission. (Audio-interview with Roger Dale for the Open University course 'Society, Education and the State' (E353), 1981).

9  Specifically on the relationship between academic attainment and ceasing full-time education, Roberts et al's (1989) and Beherens and Brown's (1991) work had found particularly strong competition for places on the employer-based option of the Youth Training Scheme, manifested in higher aggregate qualifications among successful applicants.

10  For the first distinction, what is disputed is the value and relevance of the quantitative tradition of cohort-based transitions studies and other methodological premises of the youth transitions tradition. The post-16 trajectories of a substantial minority of young people are sufficiently irregular and unpredictable to place them outside the scope of the word 'transition' as measured by such methods. The transitions discourse fuels normativity and lines of analysis that are incomplete and partial,

and may misrepresent the experiences of particular groups of young people (see Fergusson et al, 2000, Fergusson, 2004, for evidence of 'churning' affecting up to a third of age cohorts).

[11] In the transitions literature, it is rare to find any discussion of the influence of cultural (and social) changes of the kind researched by, for example, Hebdidge (1979), Clarke and Critcher (1985), Hollands (1990), Redhead (1993), Rojek (1985), Fornas and Bolin (1995), Back (1996), Cohen (2003); or of culture and its relationship to youth crime, notably Presdee (2000), Hayward (2002) and Webster (2007).

[12] Béland and Hansen (2000) and Atkinson and Davoudi (2000) have pointed to prior dilution of these principles within the European Union, particularly in respect of fiscal policies, and neglect of social and cultural exclusion. Levitas (1996) explains this revision in terms of a Durkheimian approach whereby the division of labour – and paid employment – is the principal axis of social cohesion. In this conception, material inequalities are overlooked in favour of engagement with the labour market as proof against social fragmentation. See also Fergusson (2002) for a fuller discussion regarding youth unemployment.

[13] The SEU commissioned several literature reviews directly concerned with young people's social exclusion, including Coles et al (2002), Bradshaw et al (2004) and Bynner et al (2004).

[14] See Muncie (2009, pp 263-6) for a fuller account.

[15] Levitas (2006, p 147) also provides 'some cause to think that paid work can have an inhibiting impact on inclusion in social relations' and that 'economic inactivity' does not necessarily result in 'social exclusion' (p 148).

[16] In the late 2000s, the UK ranked as having the fifth highest rate of youth non-participation among the world's wealthiest 29 countries (OECD, 2008), after Turkey, Mexico, Greece and Italy.

[17] This was not the only response to the GFC: the Future Jobs Fund, initiated in 2009, represented the most progressive version in the long history of youth training schemes. 100,000 newly created waged jobs for 18 to 24-year-olds were established. Almost half of participants remained in employment after the six-month requirement (Bivand et al., 2011). As later chapters show, the 2008 Education and Skills Act has yet to be implemented in its original form.

[18] The processes by which ideas and concepts achieve influence in policy making are addressed in the literature. On policy ideas and discourse, see for example Beland (2007) in relation to social policy and social exclusion, and Schmidt (2008) in relation to wider political contexts. On how knowledge and ideas work in the wider context of policy making in government see Loader (2006) in relation to criminal justice policy, and see Freeman and Sturdy (2014) on the forms that influential knowledge takes in the formation of education and health policy.

[19] The principal causalities were the Education Maintenance Allowance and the Future Jobs Fund (see note 17). For a critical analysis of the schemes substituted by the coalition government in the wake of the GFC (the Work Programme, the Work Experience Scheme, the Youth Contract and 'Help to work'), see Muncie (2015, pp 241-2).

[20] There are well over half a million hits for 'disengaged young people' on Google, and the term is widely used by non-governmental organisations, government departments and agencies (see, for example, Ford, 1998; Adams and Smart, 2005; Scottish Government, 2005; Institute of Welsh Affairs, 2010; Sodha and Margo, 2010; Ghosh, 2011).

[21] A major report from Demos (Birdwell et al, 2011, p 13) made dramatic predictions of youth unemployment rates as a source of 'disengagement and lost dreams'. By the time of a report from the House of Commons Work and Pensions Committee (2012)on the Youth Contract, the language of disengagement was in prolific use among the many witnesses called.

[22] The work of Simmons and Thompson (2011, 2013) and Strathdee (2013) provide notable exceptions. See also Fergusson (2013).

THREE

# Non-participation, wages
# and welfare

The world's youth, more than 1 billion aged between 15 and 25, comprise the largest youth cohort in history, a majority in developing countries. The world may be ageing but there are a very large number of young people around, with much to be frustrated about. Although many other groups make up the precariat, the most common image is of young people emerging from school and college to enter a precarious existence lasting years, often made all the more frustrating because their parents' generation had seemingly held stable jobs. Youth make up the core of the precariat and will have to take the lead in forging a future for it.

*Guy Standing (2011) The precariat: The new dangerous class, pp 65-6*

## Introduction

Mass non-participation among young people now has some claim to being endemic, transnational and ubiquitous. In 2013 just over 3 million of the 7.2 million young people aged 16 to 24 in the UK were in full-time education, 637,000 were unemployed[1] and 664,000 were classified as economically inactive[2] (House of Commons Library, 2014). This suggests that 18% of the young population are non-participant, as defined in Chapter One. Youth unemployment in the UK has been in excess of half a million since the early 1980s, fluctuating between 10% and 20% of 16 to 24-year-olds. Troughs and peaks in total numbers and the unemployment rate coincide precisely with the global financial crisis (GFC), but with no recovery visible in the sustained maximum 13% rate. In several European countries (see Chapter One), many more than half of young people were unemployed. These figures do not include young people who are invisible to systems of recording, who avoid them or who work without pay.

This chapter charts the changing profile of mass non-participation in and beyond the UK since the late 1970s. The first three sections locate profiles of non-participation in conditions that are shaped by growing gaps that separate levels of youth and adult unemployment;

55

the mean incomes and minimum pay which young people receive; and the established forms of welfare benefits and social protection to which they are entitled. Section 1 considers the scale of unemployment among young people, and the claim that it is now nationally endemic and internationally ubiquitous. Section 2 addresses the relationship between skills and unemployment, and provides associated evidence of dual labour markets and declining youth wages. Section 3 outlines the withdrawal of state welfare provision for a range of young people. Section 4 is concerned with the interaction of these factors and their consequences for young people's choices. It begins by locating young people at the confluence of three major forces that frame their participation decisions, and argues that many young people's choices not to participate in recognised forms of economic and educational activity are economically rational.

## Section 1: The scale of unemployment among young people

### Endemic: sustained and growing mass youth unemployment in the UK

*Recession and youth unemployment: a very brief history*

The antecedents of contemporary levels of mass non-participation in education, employment and training by young people have a lengthy provenance, and a complex profile. On most accounts, the emergence of mass youth unemployment in the UK can be dated to the 15-month recession following the election of the Conservative government in 1979. The exponential increase in the numbers of non-participant young people in 1981 and 1982 saw youth unemployment rates quadruple to more than 1.2 million. However, seen in context, this was preceded by other unprecedented increases. The longest recorded period of sustained 'full employment' in the UK began in 1941 and ended in 1969, during which period the mean combined youth and adult rate hovered around 2%.[3] Double-quarter recessions in 1956 and 1961 had barely discernible impacts on the unemployment rate. In 1960, the number who received unemployment benefit is recorded as a now-extraordinary 5,100 young people (Deacon, 1981, p 69), and began to increase only in the late 1960s. But appreciable increases that began in 1970 rose sharply around the time of the early 1970s recessions, and continued to do so throughout most of that decade. Immediately before the 1980-81 recession, unemployment among young people aged under 20 had already reached 0.5 million (Loney, 1983, p 27).

From 1981 onwards, the short history of youth unemployment can be summarised in a sentence. Youth unemployment peaked dramatically in every recession, and only partially recovered after each recession, bottoming out at higher levels than before the previous peak, when the rising trend towards the next recession began.

Figure 3.1 depicts the history with as much clarity as constantly changing bases for the calculation of youth unemployment allow.[4] It shows clearly the impact of five recessionary periods to 2009. Beyond this, in 2011 the unemployment rate among 16 to 24-year-olds reached its highest ever level at 22%, exceeding the 20% level of 1984 (Mizra-Davies, 2014).

**Figure 3.1:** Youth unemployment since 1969

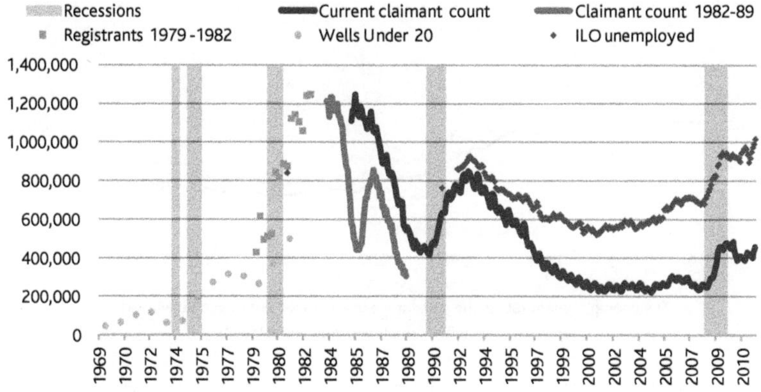

Source: Bivand et al (2011)

## The divergence of youth and adult unemployment

From virtual parity with adult unemployment rates in the 1960s, young people were almost twice as likely to be unemployed by 1980.[5] This was a significant marker in two respects. First, in the long history of tensions between the employment of young people and adults, struggles concerning the duration of school attendance requirements turned on the cheap, dextrous labour of young people, in competition with adults (see Chapter Two). Second, the disproportionate growth in youth unemployment led to an established wisdom that the rapid and accelerating decline in primary and manufacturing industries was the principal cause of major reductions in the demand for unskilled and under-educated labour.[6] This claim has long since outlived its relevance, but its continued currency misleads and confuses much contemporary analysis of youth unemployment.

Recessions have a major impact on youth unemployment, much greater than their impact on adults, as part of a continuing pattern of divergence (Verick, 2009). Figure 3.2 highlights this.

**Figure 3.2:** Unemployment rate and proportion by age group, 1984–2013

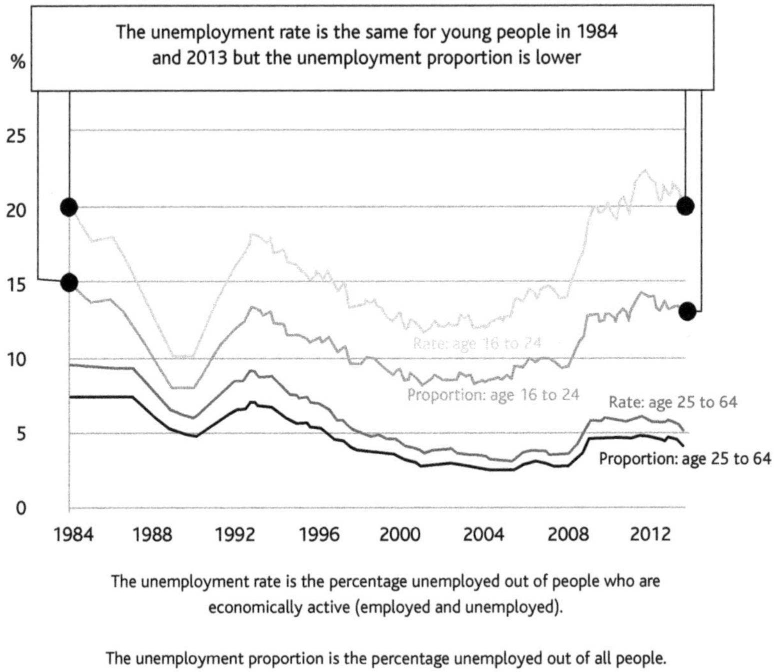

The unemployment rate is the percentage unemployed out of people who are economically active (employed and unemployed).

The unemployment proportion is the percentage unemployed out of all people.

Source: Office for National Statistics (2014b)

The divergence that began in the 1970s is shown by Figure 3.2 to have become greatly magnified by 1984. As both unemployment rates fell in both age groups following the period of recovery from the early 1980s recession, youth and adult rates re-converged, while still remaining several percentage points apart. Following the 1990-91 recession, both rates climbed again and the previous divergences were restored, with the unemployment rate for 16 to 24-year-olds quickly reaching double that for 25 to 64-year-olds. It is of considerable significance for the analysis which follows that the separation between the unemployment rates of the two age groups did not re-converge at any point throughout the economic boom years that began in the late 1990s and continued for a decade.

As Figure 3.2 has shown, the impact of the first recessionary wave of the GFC in 2008–09 on the younger age groups was far greater than on the older age groups.[7] The divergences between youth and adult unemployment rates expanded to unprecedented extremes, and the signs of recovery reflected in the declining proportion of adult unemployment from late 2011 onwards are not matched among 16 to 24-year-olds. While some small signs of decline in the rate of the younger age group mirror that in the older age group in the most recent data shown, of far greater significance is the 15 percentage point difference that separates the two. By 2013, the recovery in adult employment was not mirrored at all among young people.

Any doubts about the longer history of age differences in unemployment rates are dispelled by Figure 3.3. It confirms the earlier evidence of divergence. The most striking observation is the relatively long-run stability of unemployment rates for the population as a whole over 24 years of age, which contrasts dramatically with that of 16 to 17-year-olds in particular.

Being classified as 'not in education, employment or training' (NEET) does not fully describe the extent of non-participation. There have never been secure ways of confidently counting the numbers of school-leavers who are non-participant in the early years after leaving school. As Table 3.1 shows, in almost all English regions, at ages 16, 17 and 18 years, the proportion of young people whose post-school destination is recorded as NEET is exceeded by the proportion whose destinations are not known. Among 18-year-olds the destinations

**Figure 3.3:** Unemployment rate by age group, UK, 1975–2010

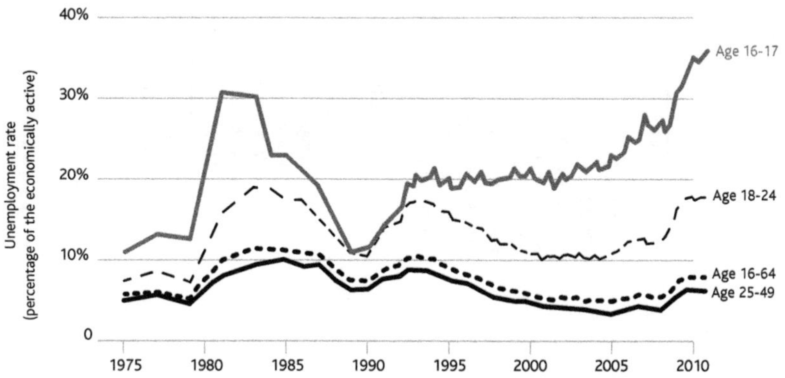

Source: Petrongolo and Van Reenan (2011)

Table 3.1: Proportion of 16 to 18-year olds NEET and 'not known' by English regions and selected local authorities, 2014

| | Age 16 | | | Age 17 | | | Age 18 | | |
|---|---|---|---|---|---|---|---|---|---|
| | Number NEET* | % NEET | % not known | Number NEET* | % NEET | % not known | Number NEET* | % NEET | % not known |
| ENGLISH REGIONS | | | | | | | | | |
| SOUTH EAST | 1,660 | 1.8% | 4.4% | 3,740 | 4.0% | 9.7% | 6,590 | 7.4% | 23.9% |
| LONDON | 1,270 | 1.5% | 3.5% | 2,650 | 3.1% | 6.8% | 5,090 | 5.9% | 20.8% |
| EAST OF ENGLAND | 1,200 | 2.1% | 1.7% | 2,520 | 4.3% | 4.8% | 4,170 | 7.4% | 13.4% |
| SOUTH WEST | 1,060 | 1.9% | 3.8% | 2,520 | 4.3% | 6.6% | 4,370 | 7.8% | 18.4% |
| WEST MIDLANDS | 1,730 | 2.8% | 4.2% | 3,150 | 4.7% | 9.6% | 5,590 | 8.8% | 22.7% |
| EAST MIDLANDS | 1,030 | 2.0% | 2.6% | 2,150 | 4.1% | 5.1% | 3,620 | 7.1% | 9.9% |
| YORKS & THE HUMBER | 1,470 | 2.5% | 1.2% | 3,040 | 5.1% | 5.2% | 4,690 | 7.9% | 13.5% |
| NORTH WEST | 2,190 | 2.7% | 2.1% | 4,040 | 4.8% | 6.7% | 6,550 | 8.1% | 14.0% |
| NORTH EAST | 890 | 3.1% | 0.9% | 1,830 | 6.1% | 3.8% | 3,510 | 11.8% | 10.2% |
| SELECTED LOCAL AUTHORITIES | | | | | | | | | |
| Portsmouth | 70 | 3.4% | 2.1% | 150 | 7.7% | 13.7% | 240 | 12.5% | 47.5% |
| Islington | 40 | 2.4% | 5.2% | 90 | 5.1% | 9.9% | 160 | 9.1% | 42.0% |
| Lewisham | 40 | 1.2% | 2.3% | 110 | 3.4% | 7.4% | 220 | 7.4% | 42.0% |
| Waltham Forest | 40 | 1.4% | 6.0% | 80 | 2.6% | 11.3% | 180 | 6.1% | 47.1% |
| Southend | 40 | 1.8% | 5.2% | 110 | 4.9% | 8.5% | 250 | 11.3% | 44.0% |
| Bath & NE Somerset | 20 | 1.3% | 4.8% | 50 | 3.1% | 21.1% | 100 | 6.3% | 55.7% |
| S. Gloucestershire | 30 | 1.1% | 17.7% | 80 | 2.6% | 24.8% | 240 | 8.0% | 74.5% |
| Wiltshire | 70 | 1.4% | 7.5% | 210 | 4.1% | 9.4% | 360 | 7.8% | 57.4% |
| East Riding | 50 | 1.4% | 2.3% | 70 | 2.0% | 10.7% | 140 | 3.7% | 45.3% |
| Liverpool | 330 | 7.0% | 4.8% | 330 | 6.4% | 21.0% | 580 | 11.3% | 43.7% |

* Estimated

Source: Department for Education, 2015

of between one in five and one in ten are not known. In 10 local authorities the destinations of at least two in every five 18-year-olds are not known.

The difficulties of estimating NEET numbers have been exacerbated significantly by two new factors. First, as Maguire (2015) points out, the closure of a number of facilities – notably the Connexions service – substantially limits tracking capacity, as does the erosion of local authority funding for staffing it. Second, the age threshold definition of NEET changed in 2013, when the 2008 Education and Skills Act was implemented to require the 16+ age cohort to participate in school, college, training programmes or work that included specified training elements.[8] Ostensibly, this had a significant effect on NEET numbers.[9] However, the data gives a misleading impression, because in its 2011 Education Act, the coalition government suspended the clauses of the original legislation that required monitoring of participation.[10] In particular, there can be no clear basis for confidence that those in training and employment meet the requirements of the 2008 Education and Skills Act. In 2015, in addition to the 148,000 who were known to be non-compliant, 'figures appeared to show that a further 100,000 were unaccounted for'.[11] Statistics for the proportion of young people who are 'NEETs' are significant underestimates.

In summary, non-participation rates among 16 to 24-year-olds have fluctuated between at least 12% and 22% since the early 1990s and have not been below 10% since the early 1980s. For 16 to 17-year-olds the proportions are much higher. This overview and the clear evidence that most of these representations of non-participation substantially undercount non-participation suggest that mass non-participation among many hundreds of thousands of 16 to 24-year-olds is endemic in the UK.

## Ubiquitous: global youth unemployment

Globally, youth unemployment has ranged between 70 and 78 million since 2000, representing 12-13% of the world's 16-24-year-olds(ILO, 2015a, Figure 1 – reproduced below as Figure 3.4). Since the mid-1990s, the underlying trend of global unemployment among 16 to 24-year-olds has been one of major increase, from a low of about 65 million, to a high of 78 million, typically affecting between 11% and 13% of young people. Figure 3.4 shows that a brief period of recovery from those peak levels in the mid-2000s was quickly reversed by the effects of the GFC.

**Figure 3.4:** Global youth unemployment and unemployment rate, 1995–2015

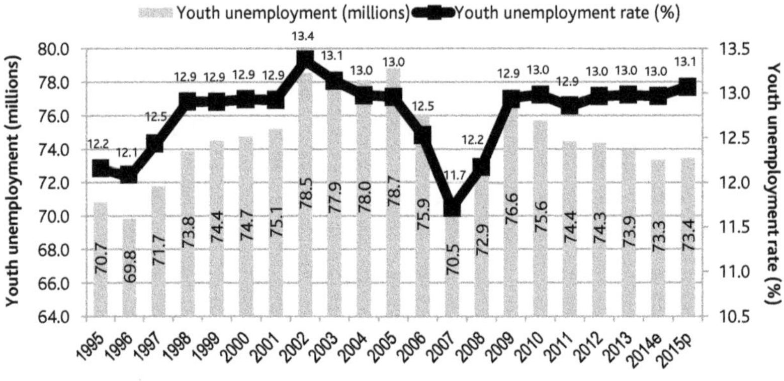

e = estimate; p = projection.

Source: © International Labour Organization (2015)

By 2010, the rate had returned to its historical peak of 13%, on an upward trend predicted to reach 13.2% in 2018-19 (ILO, 2015, Table A2). Historically, the Middle East and North Africa have the highest rates at around 25-30% (40-46% for young women)(ILO, 2015, Table A2). Remarkably, these regions apart, between 2009 and 2013 the wealthy countries of the Organisation for Economic Co-operation and Development (OECD) and European Union had the highest rates in the world, including some countries with record-breaking youth unemployment: Bosnia and Herzegovina (61%), followed by Greece (58%) and Spain (57%), which outstripped South Africa (54%) and Libya (51%).[12]

Figure 3.5 provides more detailed trends in European countries. Furthermore, the underlying trend of continuing increases in mean youth unemployment levels globally tends to be greatest in those regions in which the youth unemployment rate is already highest – as noted, the Middle East and North Africa.[13]

Divergences between UK youth and adult unemployment rates shown in Figure 3.3 are also reproduced internationally. Figure 3.6 shows that the OECD and EU28 countries have youth unemployment rates that are at least double those of the adults. Great Britain (GBR) has youth unemployment rates fractionally below four times those of the adult rate, among the highest in the OECD/EU28, exceeded only by Sweden and Italy.

Drawing on global data for the period between 2007 and 2013 and projected to 2015, the ratio of youth to adult unemployment rates has continued to increase, hovering just below the 3.0 level (ILO, 2015, Table A1). The phenomenon of sustained major difference and/or

**Figure 3.5:** Youth unemployment rates, European countries, 2008, 2013 and 2014

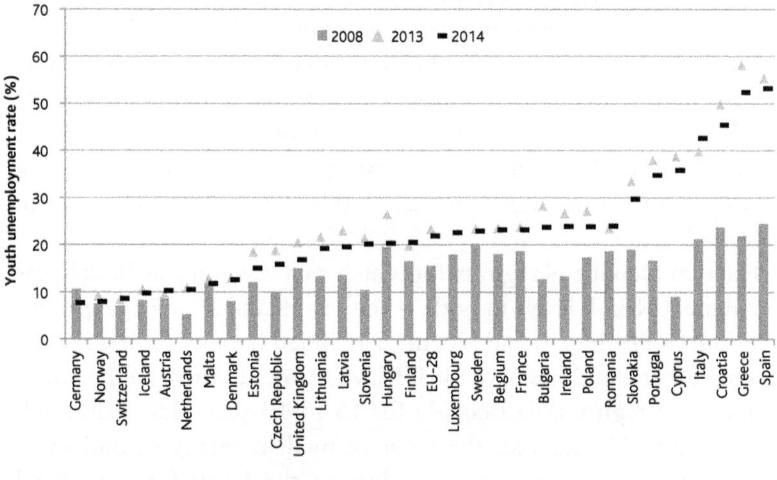

Source: © International Labour Organization (2015)

continuing divergences between youth and adult unemployment rates is now internationally ubiquitous.

The international differences in the ratio of youth to adult unemployment in Figure 3.6 are also of particular significance for the discussion in later chapters. Pemberton (2015) classifies 31 OECD countries according to seven regime types, which include 'Neoliberal',

**Figure 3.6:** Youth vs adult unemployment, OECD/EU28 countries, 2013

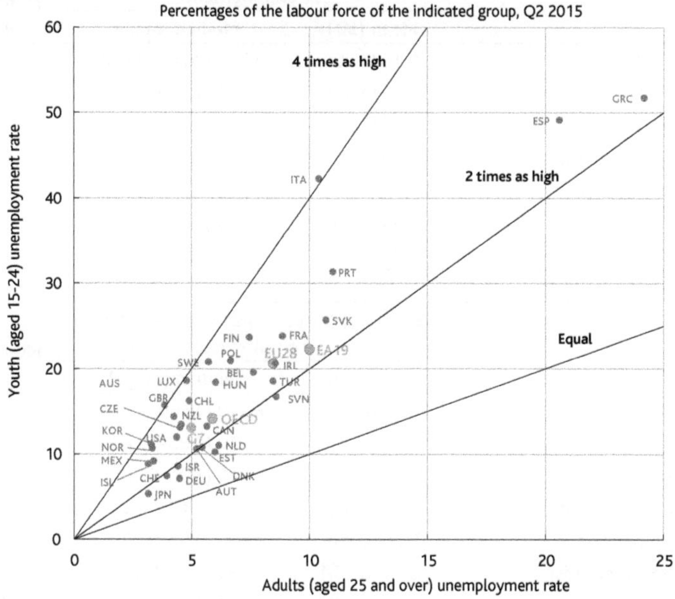

Source: Gregg (2014) / Based on data from OECD (2015). DOI: http://dx.doi.org/10.1787/data-00046-en

'Liberal' and 'Social Democratic' (plus four categories of corporatism). The Neoliberal group comprises four countries. The UK is included in the Liberal group, alongside Ireland, the US and three others. The Social Democratic group comprises four Scandinavian countries. [14] Pemberton's modelling compares the proportions of young people classified as NEET in each country across the seven categories (drawing on dataset indicators mostly for 2008-09). The results are shown in Table 3.2.

The two Neoliberal regimes for which data was available have by far the highest NEET levels in both of the 15-19 and 20-24 age groups. The four Social Democratic regimes included have by far the lowest. The six Liberal regimes have NEET levels closer to those of the Social Democratic regimes, particularly for 15 to 19-year-olds – although among 20 to 24-year-olds the range of median data is exceptionally wide, with some countries very close to the levels for Neoliberal regimes. For Pemberton's purposes, these findings are of interest as a 'proxy indicator of harm' (Pemberton, 2015, p 124) (and this will be of relevance in Chapter Seven). But in this context, it is important to note

**Table 3.2:** Proportion of young people who are NEET, by regime type (OECD countries)

| Regime | % of 20 to 24-year-olds not in education or employment | | Number obs |
|---|---|---|---|
| | Mean (SD) | Median (range) | |
| 1 Neoliberal | 35.15 (12.09) | 35.15 (26.60–43.70) | 2 |
| 2 Liberal | 17.98 (4.41) | 18.85 (11.20–24.30) | 6 |
| 3 Post-socialist corporatist | 17.77 (5.35) | 19.60 (9.30–22.40) | 6 |
| 4 Southern corporatist | 23.13 (5.22) | 24.35 (16.40–27.40) | 4 |
| 5 Meso-corporatist | 23.50 | 23.5 | 1 |
| 6 Northern corporatist | 14.54 (4.96) | 13.70 (7.80–20.60) | 5 |
| 7 Social democratic | 12.80 (2.95) | 13.20 (9.00–15.80) | 4 |

| Regime | % of 15 to 19-year-olds not in education or employment | | Number obs |
|---|---|---|---|
| | Mean (SD) | Median (range) | |
| 1 Neoliberal | 22.10 (4.95) | 22.10 (18.60–25.60) | 2 |
| 2 Liberal | 9.12 (1.28) | 9.10 (7.60–10.40) | 6 |
| 3 Post-socialist corporatist | 4.32 (1.04) | 4.20 (3.20–6.10) | 6 |
| 4 Southern corporatist | 9.23 (3.09) | 7.50 (7.40–12.80) | 3 |
| 5 Meso-corporatist | 9.20 (0.99) | 9.80 (8.50–9.90) | 2 |
| 6 Northern corporatist | 5.90 (2.15)) | 5.90 (3.70–8.20) | 5 |
| 7 Social democratic | 4.88 (0.93) | 5.25 (3.50–5.50) | 4 |

Source: Pemberton, 2015, Table 5.5

that the highest NEET levels are statistically significantly associated with regimes characterised as having the weakest forms of social solidarity (see Pemberton, 2015, Table 3.1), while those with the lowest NEET rates have the strongest social solidarity. Social solidarity characteristics of Liberal regimes, including the UK, are identified as being very similar to those of Neoliberal regimes. In all, these findings suggest that high NEET levels are closely associated with other manifestations of high levels of social and economic inequality.

Major international governmental organisations (IGOs) such as the OECD, the International Monetary Fund (IMF), and the World Economic Forum (WEF) have warned national governments about the risks of continuing mass youth unemployment. As noted, ILO projections suggest that levels will continue to rise until at least 2019 globally (ILO, 2015), and much of that mean upward trend is a consequence of continuing projected increases in much of Asia, and across the Middle East, North Africa and non-EU Central and Eastern Europe(ILO, 2013a, 2015). It is a striking indication of the seriousness of the situation that two IGOs as politically disparate as the IMF and the ILO joined forces to comment:

> Giulianio and Spilimbergo (2009) find that individuals who have experienced a recession in the formative age of 18–25 years tend to believe less in personal effort, perceive stronger inequalities, and have less confidence in public institutions. This finding, which is based on data prior to the current crisis, *sheds alarming light on today's situation of high long-term and youth unemployment rates.* In fact, due to population aging, the youth cohort in Europe today forms the largest share of total population at least for the next 20 years. Considering the effects of recession and unemployment on personal beliefs, this means that *the labour market experience of today's youth will have deep adverse impacts on the faith in public institutions of future generations.* (IMF/ILO, 2010, p 21, emphasis added)

The resonances with the concept of disengagement – economic, political and social – are strong. In a similar vein, the OECD comments:

> Investing in youth and giving them a better start in the world of work should be a key policy objective. Otherwise, there is a high risk of *persistence or growth in the hard-core*

*group of youth who are left behind,* facing poor employment and earnings prospects. (OECD, 2011, emphasis added)

Discussion in a range of documents from IGOs brought particular attention to major demonstrations of social unrest in a number of countries – notably Greece and Spain – as exemplars of the risky consequences of continuing mass youth unemployment (see Chapter Five, Section 3).

On the basis of this brief overview, non-participation is endemic in the UK and ubiquitous globally, as are the exceptionally high ratios of youth to adult unemployment, by up to a factor of four. There are indications that non-participation and unemployment rates are undercounted or underestimated in a number of contexts. It is also clear that within the OECD the UK has one of the poorest rates of participation in education among 15 to 19-year-olds, and one of the highest ratios of youth to adult unemployment. Both are associated with high levels of social and economic inequality more generally. As the following sections argue, this data offers a preliminary indication that young people have emerged as the quickest, easiest, least costly and least resistant fractions of the labour force to bear the burden of economic shocks resulting from recessions.

## Section 2: Skills, wages and labour markets

### Low skills, unemployment and mistaken labour market orthodoxies

It is well established that people with higher skills and qualifications are least likely to be unemployed. To differing degrees, the social exclusion and disengagement discourses apply this logic in reverse: if high skills fuel economic stability and growth, inadequate skills contribute to economic decline. Certainly, high unemployment rates among young people tend to ratchet up qualification thresholds as a means of efficient selection when the supply of would-be workers greatly outstrips demand. This fuels the belief that higher skills and qualifications are the route to improved employment prospects. Emanating from this reasoning, and from a wide range of epochal commentaries on work, employment and labour markets in late modernity (for example Beck, 1992), two important beliefs now circulate widely as orthodoxies. First, work will be increasingly fragmented, casualised, insecure, uncertain and lead to frequent job changes. Second, the skills and knowledge required to sustain the economy, employability and secure jobs will change frequently, demand recurrent enhancements of skills and knowledge, and lead to the eventual erosion of demand for low-skilled and unskilled labour. As a corollary, those with poor skills and qualifications will fare badly. By these accounts, persistently rising levels of youth unemployment are already partly attributable to mismatch with the demands of changing economies.

There is a good deal of evidence that both beliefs are anachronistic, and at best only partially valid in advanced economies.[15] MacDonald's (2011) work marshals a range of research that queries the orthodoxy that up-skilling is the solution to youth unemployment. Shildrick et al's (2012, p 106) study found that 'levels of educational attainment did *not* straightforwardly predict improved labour market fortunes ... In listing the things they looked for in new employees, very rarely were particular types or levels of skill, qualification or educational background mentioned [by employers].'

There is also strong support for the obverse argument that demand for skilled workers frequently falls short of supply. Projections indicate that by 2020 the numbers of jobs requiring no qualifications will grow to outstrip availability at a ratio of more than ten jobs to one unqualified worker.[16] These trends are already evident. In the UK the recorded incidence of workers whose educational qualifications outstrip the requirements of their job increased dramatically amongst 15-24-year olds from 9% to 21% in the ten years to 2012, while the incidence of qualifications below job requirements declined equally sharply from 45% to 25% over the same period (ILO, 2015, Table A.10, p 92). The same data also shows that in 2012, well into the supposed 'economic recovery' period, apart from Ireland, the UK and Spain had by far the highest levels of over-education of 15 European countries, and a mid-range level of under-education. It is also clear that the exceptionally high ratios of youth to adult unemployment in the UK noted above, compared to equivalent levels in the OECD and EU28 countries are, at least in part, attributable to causes other than skills deficits (ILO, 2013a, Figure 10).[17]

## Low-skilled labour, declining youth wages and bifurcated labour markets

These findings substantially limit any claims to attributing the dramatic rise in youth unemployment in the UK to deficient skills and qualifications. Rather, for employers, finding sufficiently low-skilled or uneducated workers to take low-skill, low-pay jobs may be the more significant issue, in aggregate terms. Since rising levels of over-education and declining levels of under-education in the UK substantially exceed comparable rates of change in most of the rest of the OECD and the EU28, it is likely that the exceptionally high ratios of youth to adult unemployment compared to equivalent levels in those countries are primarily attributable to reasons other than skills deficits. Some consideration of the nature, causes and consequences of the use of low-skilled labour in changing labour markets is needed.

It is widely established that one major source of the mismatch between the rhetoric of up-skilling and deficient demand for better skilled and educated labour - as outlined in Chapter One (see Figure 1.1) – can be traced to the growing demand for person-to-person care and service work. The shift to ever more frequent, intimate and minute forms of personal service in combination with the needs of an ageing population extend the need for low-skilled work, much of which is unpleasant, exhausting and potentially degrading. This shift is under-recognised in much influential public discourse about education, skills, work and unemployment.[18] As MacDonald (2011, p 435) points out, major questions arise about 'who will do the abundant low-skilled work that will remain in the UK economy ... in this mythical vision of a high-skill, knowledge economy'.

Shildrick et al's (2012) Teesside study of the deindustrialised labour market built around low-quality work, low pay, low skills and insecurity (to which Chapter Seven returns) perfectly illustrates these arguments. Similarly, McDowell et al's (2014, p 850) interpretation of the development of precarious work captures them well:

> The UK now has a two-tier workforce in which millions of young people are trapped in low paid part time jobs. In 2013, more than one in three 16 to 30-year-olds (2.4 million) are low paid compared with one in five in the 1970s (1.7 million at that time) ... Among the fastest growing jobs in the last two decades are retail assistants, catering workers and hotel workers. More than a quarter of all 18 to 21-year-olds in employment in 2010 worked in the retail sector (Department for Education, 2011), many on a part time basis.

Here, the implication of the emergence of a dual labour market is critical. The fundamental axis of division is not between unemployed young people and employed adults. Rather, it is between a precariat which undertakes insecure low-paid, low-skilled and unskilled service work and those (notably the salariat) whose work has potential for career progression (Standing, 2011; Shildrick et al, 2012; Gregg, 2014).

Figure 3.7 makes very clear that recessionary conditions fall most heavily on the wages of young people. Between 1999 and 2007, the median earnings of all three age groups increased in step by around 4%. After the GFC in 2007, annual increases slowed for all three age groups but adult increases were least affected. By 2011-14, the median earning of 16 to 17-year-olds almost ceased to grow, implying recurrent real-terms income decreases over three years, while slow growth continued for those aged 18 and above. At the same time the national minimum wage for both younger age-groups failed to keep pace with the increase for older workers.

Figures 3.8 and 3.9 show the cumulative effects of six years of recurrent decline on the real values of median earnings of 16 to 20-year-olds, up to 2014. The Low Pay Commission (LPC) calculates that between 2009 and 2013, the real earnings of 16 to 17-year-olds fell by 17%, and those of 18 to 20-year-olds by 12% (LPC and Department for Business, Innovation and Skills, 2014).

Figure 3.10 shows that the proportions of younger people who were being paid at or below the minimum wage for their age range doubled between the start of the 2008-09 recessions that followed

**Figure 3.7:** Growth in the minimum wage and median earnings, by age, UK, 1999–2014

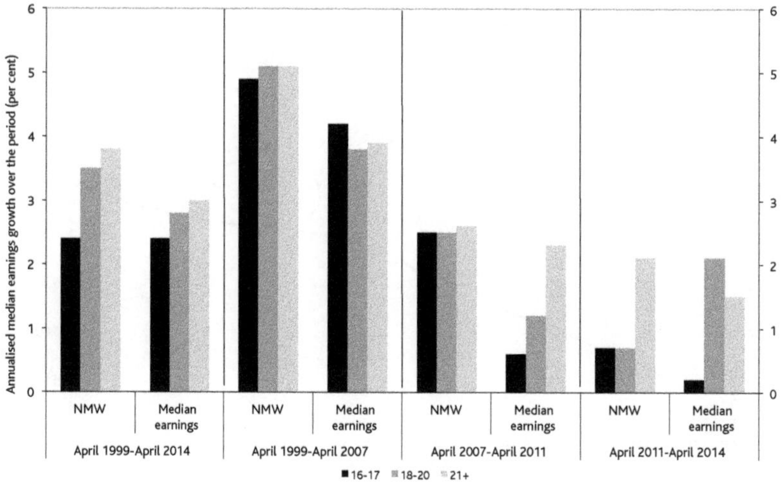

Source: Low Pay Commission (2015)

**Figure 3.8:** Nominal and real median earnings for 16 to 17-year-olds, by Price Index, UK, 1999-2014

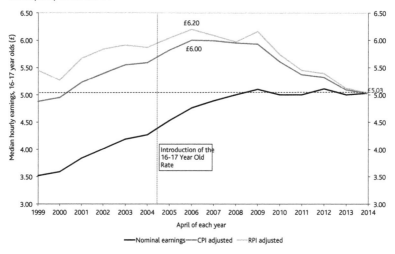

Source: Low Pay Commission (2015)

**Figure 3.9:** Nominal and real median earnings for 18 to 20-year-olds, by Price Index, UK, 1999-2014

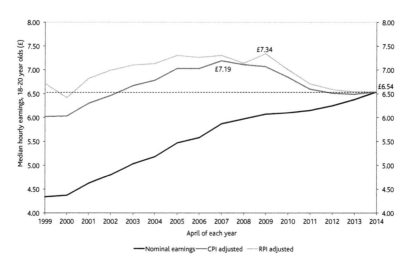

Source: Low Pay Commission (2015)

GFC in 2007/08 and 2013, to 14% of 16 to 17-year-olds and 16% of 18 to 20-year-olds. This contrasts sharply with the consistently low proportion of adult workers paid at these (sub)minimum rates.

**Figure 3.10:** Percentage at or below minimum wage rates, by age, UK, 1999-2013

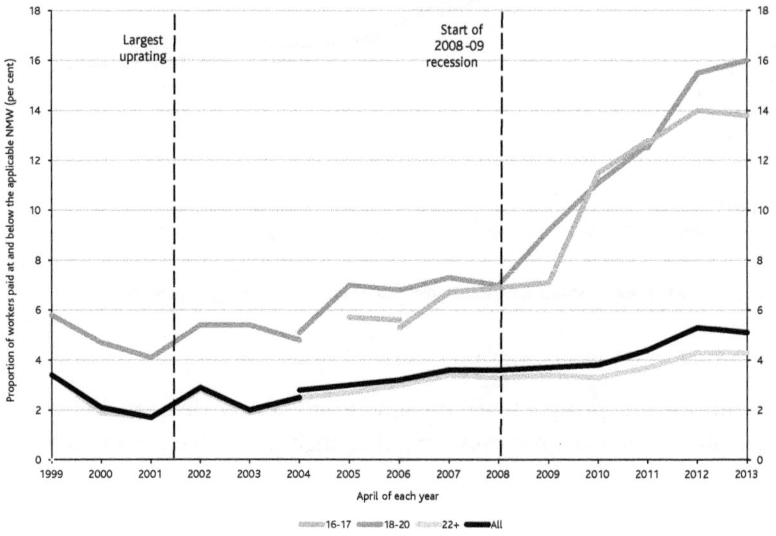

Source: Low Pay Commission (2014)

Figure 3.11 shows that, by the end of 2014, the median weekly earnings of 22 to 29-year-olds had fallen to 89% of their 2008 level, several percentage points below that of all older age groups, as part of a trajectory which shows that, overall, seniority was associated with a lower decline across all age groups (Cribb and Joyce, 2015).

This data provides a stark account of age differentiation in pay rates, and of the pronounced recurrent pattern whereby the heaviest reductions in pay resulting from recession fall most acutely on the youngest age groups, while adult rates tend to be sustained.

The combined effects of the erosion of rates of pay for young people and of low levels of demand for their labour are of course related. Following classical expectations of the functioning of labour markets, oversupply of labour and the resultant increase in competition for jobs drives wages down, and more are admitted to the labour market as a result. Since the GFC however, reductions in mean earnings among young people have continued alongside unprecedented levels of youth unemployment. Understanding this combination of conditions, and

**Figure 3.11:** Changes to real median weekly earnings since 2008, by age group

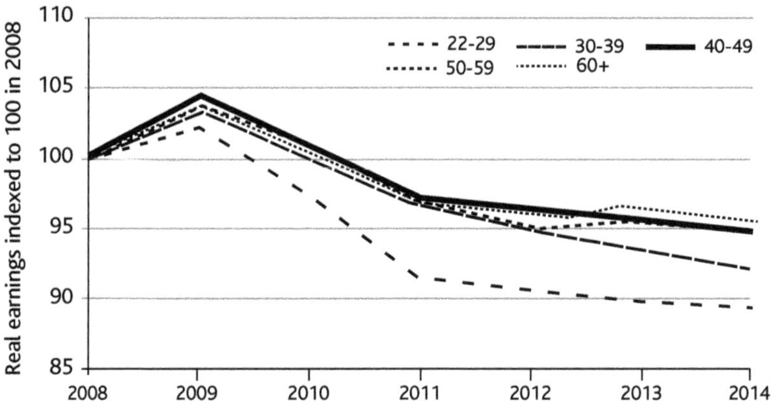

Source: Cribb and Joyce / Institute for Fiscal Studies (2015) http://www.ifs.org.uk/publications/7530

examining the prospect of an increasingly sharp division between dual labour markets, requires a parallel analysis of changes in welfare entitlement for young people.

## Section 3: Dismantling entitlement: the withdrawal of social security

Since the early 1980s, almost without exception, the trajectory of state-provided social protection for young people without work, education or training has been one of steady withdrawal. This has culminated in a conjuncture at which 16 and 17-year-olds who are not in employment are now defined by default as students or trainees, or as continuing dependants of their parents or carers, while 18 to 24-year-olds receive reduced and increasingly conditional benefits that are generally inadequate to support subsistence as an independent adult.

### Dismantling entitlement: a brief history

A full account of the erosion of entitlements enjoyed by young people up to the ages of 18 and 24 since 1985 throws into sharp relief the extent of the withdrawal of state provision. Surprisingly, there has been no focused economic analysis of how losses in social protection intersected with the withdrawal of other provisions that smoothed the passage from youthful economic dependence to adult independence during the post-war period. However, a brief history gives a clear picture of the fundamental repositioning of young people's entitlements to social protection.

Harris' (1989) detailed history of post–war social security provision is a salutary antidote to Golden Age renditions of the social protection assured by the welfare state. Harris concludes his review of provision from 1911 to 1980 by commenting on the lack of a coherent policy, the denial of young people's independent status as unemployed adults, significantly reduced benefit rates, the exclusion of school-leavers from entitlement, and vacillation between treating 16-year-olds as dependants and as independent claimants, 'as convenient' (Harris, 1989, p 66). He highlights the partial invisibility of young people as an ambiguous category trapped in an undefined territory between familial dependence and work-enabled independence according to the ebb and flow of labour market demand and the extension of compulsory and post-compulsory educational provision. His dispassionate conclusion is that in the face of complacency and indifference, 'intervention only occurred *when there was a threat to social order*, a massive drain on the insurance fund, or suspected "idleness" on the part of the unemployed' (Harris, 1989, p 66, emphasis added). The long provenance of these themes places contemporary developments in an informative perspective. Until the 1970s, young people who were above the school-leaving age had automatic entitlement to unemployment benefits.[19]

As independent members of households they were in effect 'poor by proxy' and hence the rightful recipients of direct benefits. While children remained in education, benefit entitlement accrued to their parents. Once they became employed or unemployed, entitlement generally switched from parents to young people. It was not until the early 1980s that young people were demoted to the unambiguous status of dependants with reduced entitlements.[20]

The emblematic moment of redefinition came in the Social Security Act of 1988 – one of the key monetarist-inspired measures of the Conservative governments of 1979-97.[21] It became increasingly evident that large numbers of young people in this age group were experiencing significant financial difficulties. The deregulation of young people's wages (1986) and of the working hours of school-aged children up to 18 years (1989) compounded the downward pressure on young people's means. By 1993, the campaigning organisation Youthaid estimated that 76,700 16 to 17-year-olds lacked a job, a place on a Youth Training programme or access to any form of benefit – with resultant poverty and homelessness for many.[22] The use of sanctions for failure to meet the complex requirements of Jobseeker's Allowance (JSA) that affected the entitlements of 18 to 24-year-olds were especially controversial.[23] So also was the underlying erosion of the value of JSA, which declined during the 2000s compared to pensions and child tax credits.[24] During this period, the sole exception to the pattern of curtailing and eroding the value of benefits to young people was the introduction of the Education Maintenance Allowance (EMA).[25]

JSA replaced unemployment benefit for young people in 1996 and was subsequently conditional on taking up appropriate options on the New Deal for Young People. Successive changes to housing benefits severely limited entitlement for those aged under 18, and in 1997, young people under the age of 25 were restricted to renting a single room in a shared property.[26] In 2015, the Conservative government removed automatic entitlement to housing benefit for 18 to 21-year-olds.

By 2013/14, the core basic entitlements for 18 to 24-year-olds were set at £56.80 per week – an unaccountable £15 below the rate for adults (Child Poverty Action Group, 2013). One indication of their inadequacy is that the government's own poverty measures set the poverty threshold at £128.[27] For 18 to 24-year-olds, at 44% of the adult rate, JSA and Income Support provides considerably less than half of the weekly income which defines the poverty threshold. In high-cost localities where weekly housing costs exceed the £56.80 allowance, the shortfall and the numbers affected were much greater. In 2015 the Conservative Government committed itself to a 'Youth Obligation' for 18 to 21-year-olds from 2017 which includes 'an intensive regime of support', followed by apprenticeship or traineeship, or mandatory work placement.[28] It is likely to attract an allowance equivalent to half the national minimum wage for this age-group.

A number of indicators have suggested that the benefits system may be underused by young people, resulting in serious financial hardship. For 16 to 17-year-olds, JSA conditions of exemption and entitlement are extremely stringent.[29] Sanctions for breaching regulations and conditions are widely applied. In 2012/13, sanctions were extensively and often erroneously over-applied for JSA as a whole, and young people were heavily overrepresented among the half million sanctions made every year.[30] From the onset of the GFC, the rate of adverse sanctions decisions increased each year, as shown in Figure 3.12.

Figure 3.12 makes clear the progressively intensifying focus on young people. Ten per cent of claimants were wrongly sanctioned for minor infringements, and in almost a third of cases there is clear evidence that the delays involved resulted in severe hardship (Miscampbell, 2014; see also Manchester Citizens Advisory Bureau, 2013). One survey found poverty levels that actively impeded finding employment.[31] At

**Figure 3.12:** Monthly adverse decisions as % of all JSA claimants

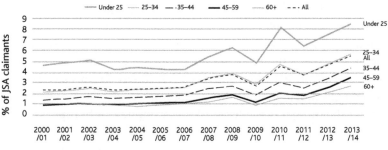

Source: Watts et al (2014) / Joseph Rowntree Foundation

the same time the pressures on young people to work in return for an 'allowance', or to take on full-time work without pay continue.[32] In other ways too, the effects of the GFC fell heavily on the poorest, including young people.[33] The contentious changes to post-compulsory education funding that began with contributions towards higher education tuition fees in 2006, culminated in the shift to an approximation of full-cost tuition fees up to £9000 per annum in 2010, and the imposition of student loans for personal maintenance for students from low-income households after 2015. The EMA was discontinued in 2010, save for a residual hardship fund,[34] while the legislation to raise the 'participation age' in 2013 and 2015 effectively forced 16 to 17-year-old would-be employees into school or college if they could not find a job,[35] or to 'disappear' as missing non-participants (see above and Maguire, 2015). It is not known how many young people turned away from a further year or two years in school or college after 2010 as a result. However, in more favourable labour market conditions, Gregg and MacMillan (2010) indicate that the EMA had previously increased school and college rolls by up to 7%.

This brief history of the erosion of entitlements describes the progressive displacement onto parents and carers of the costs of young people's loss of financial support from the state. The combined effect of changes in welfare provision and the legislation requiring participation is to define official recognition of non-participation out of existence, despite its evident mass endemic presence. Those 16 to 17-year-olds whom the state deems sufficiently vulnerable to be classified as minors for the purposes of criminal justice now enjoy fewer rights of welfare protection than adults. Obversely, 18 to 24-year-olds who are subject to the full force of law no longer have full rights to be enabled to subsist independently as the equals of adults – the age threshold of which has shifted incrementally, unacknowledged and undebated, to 25.

The circumstances in which young non-participants strive to subsist independently or are forced to remain dependants with few or no financial means is well expressed in the findings of one comparative analysis of young workers' security in seven European countries. The exclusivity of the UK's low-level rights for 'traditional' workers combine with its exceptional levels of flexibility in terms of labour market regulation to indicate that young workers in the UK experience some of the most extreme levels of precariousness in Europe.[36]

## Section 4: Rational actors: choosing non-participation

The first two sections of this chapter show a sharp division between young people and adults, in terms of young people's increased susceptibility to being unemployed, particularly in conditions of economic duress, and of their vulnerability to declining wages. Section 3 has described the erosion and almost complete withdrawal of state welfare for young people in the UK who are not employed, studying or training. This section is concerned with the interaction of these effects and their consequences for young people's choices in the face of unviable options and irresolvable dilemmas. It begins by locating the trends observed earlier in the confluence of three major forces that frame young people's decision-making in relation to work and non-participation. It then briefly explores the operation of those forces, to argue that many young people's choices not to participate in recognised forms of economic activity are economically rational.

## Three forces of non-participation: the 'wage rate suppression dynamic'

Three interacting forces determine levels of unemployment in youth labour markets. The first derives from every young person's individual prerogative to predetermine a personal reservation wage threshold. The second arises from the existence of a permanent pool of surplus labour. The third is the product of one of the founding principles of the provision of poor relief, that of 'less eligibility'. All three concepts and the forces they describe are fundamental to (neo)classical and welfare economics. However, literature that explores the interaction between them is surprisingly rare.

Conceptually, it is useful to consider the interactions between the three forces as three sets of interacting pairs. Reservation wages are those levels of pay which individuals determine are the minima they will accept to justify entering into a contract of employment.

Many factors influence how they are set, but essential elements are the size, composition, structure and location of all those inactive potential employees who lack employment primarily because there is a permanent pool of surplus labour, whereby the supply of would-be employees always exceeds the demand for their labour. The readiness of each would-be employee to compromise on wage expectations, to travel the required distance to work, to take undesirable work, and so on, contributes minutely to establishing his or her personal reservation wage threshold. To the extent that the size, mobility or flexibility of the pool of surplus labour is such that some of its members are willing to work below the prevailing market rate for the job to gain competitive advantage, it will force others to lower their reservation wage rates if they wish to work. Alternatively, if the pool of surplus labour is small, unadaptable and immobile, the reduced competition for jobs that results allows would-be workers to maintain higher wage expectations and to have those expectations met if appropriately experienced local labour is scarce. This describes the interaction between reservation wage thresholds and the pool of surplus labour.

Reservation wage thresholds are also determined by an interaction with the principle of 'less eligibility'. This specifies that the monetary benefits of receiving state support in the absence of an earned income must always be less than the monetary gains of being employed.[37] This means that employment should always be more attractive than benefit-supported unemployment, that personal reservation wage thresholds will always be credible if they exceed benefit levels, and that benefit levels will be detrimental to the profit-maximisation functions of labour markets, if they approximate to or exceed prevailing reservation wage levels.

The third paired interaction, then, is between the less eligibility principle and the pool of surplus labour. It is a precept of state-provided welfare that benefit levels should be high enough to secure a minimum subsistence floor, however much the size of the pool of surplus labour exceeds the level of market demand for labour; and that when the pool of surplus labour is small, benefit rates should, nevertheless, continue to be low enough to maintain a functional gap between entitlement rates and minimum wages, sufficient to incentivise labour market participation.

The points of confluence of these three forces are central to assessing the rationality or otherwise of myriad decisions made by individual young people whether or not to participate in recognised forms of economic or educational activity. The essential precondition for unimpeded interaction between the three forces is that of free labour:

that individuals participate (or decline to participate) in labour markets of their own volition, in adherence to a fundamental tenet of the liberal state. In turn, this precondition of free labour is contingent on the assumption that the liberal democratic state will in all circumstances secure the basic conditions of subsistence of its citizens.

This balance in the three-way interaction between the less eligibility principle, individual power to set a personal reservation wage threshold, and the dynamic effects of the size, composition, structure and location of the pool of surplus labour is inherently complex and profoundly difficult to chart and govern. One way of illustrating this complexity is to ask how would-be new entrants to the labour market might determine their personal reservation wage thresholds and make rational decisions about whether to work, to seek benefits in lieu of work, or to refuse both options as irrational – whether economically or according to a range of other considerations. Figure 3.13 depicts the complexity of this task. Each force interacts with two other forces, both by exerting power over each element and by being subject to the force of both of the other elements.

The clockwise arrows (1–3) represent the ways in which reservation wage thresholds (RWTs) bring pressures to bear on benefit rates through the less eligibility principle (LEP), to ensure that benefit rates do not disincentivise paid employment (1); the LEP operates to influence the size/composition/structure/location of the pool of surplus labour (PSL) by ensuring that benefit levels maintain the surplus of labour (2); and the PSL helps determine sustainable RWTs by securing sufficient competition for work to hold down wages (3). The anti-clockwise arrows (6–4) represent the reverse forces whereby RWTs influence the size/composition/structure/location of the PSL by making available labour scarcer or more plentiful according to would-be workers' wage expectations (6); the PSL signals the need to adjust benefit rates without breaching the LEP, by bringing pressure to bear on prevailing rates according to conditions of labour surplus or shortage (5); and the rate at which benefits are set in conformity with the LEP incentivises adjustment of personal RWTs, such that employment at the lowest acceptable RWT exceeds those rates (4).

The elementary model in Figure 3.13 is a basic schematic representation of the complex dynamics between these three forces, based on the two-way interactions between each pair. They operate cyclically in continuous dynamic tension in ways that cause recurrent adjustment and readjustment of wages, benefits and the size of the pool of available labour, in repeated attempts to reconcile the competing

**Figure 3.13:** The wage rate suppression dynamic

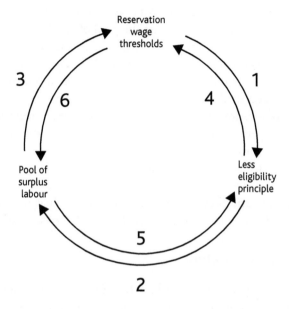

pressures of changing economic conditions, political priorities and the decisions of quasi-autonomous individual actors in labour markets.

Viewed as a whole, this constitutes what might be termed a *wage rate suppression dynamic.*[38] How this dynamic is played out (in extremis at the margins of disequilibrium) differs significantly, however, in specific sections of the population. Because the one million-plus young people who found themselves in the pool of surplus labour during and after the GFC had much weaker benefit entitlements than adults, their power within the dynamics of the model meant that many of them could secure only the lowest wages, if they could gain employment at all. As the data in Sections 2 and 3 showed, it is to be expected that they would have responded differently to their circumstances, compared to the adult population. To the extent that young people tried to maintain unrealistic and unrealisable reservation wage expectations, the effects of the less eligibility principle continued to depress available wage levels so as to limit or nullify any accommodations they could make. The worst-placed young people were trapped in a pool of surplus labour by the exaggerated effects of a less eligibility principle that resulted in benefit levels that do not sustain independent living, and squeezed out of oversubscribed labour markets if they were unwilling to set personal reservation wage thresholds that were insufficient to provide basic subsistence.

In this way, the wage rate suppression dynamic exerted the strongest downward pressure on the personal reservation wage thresholds of the youngest age groups, both because the pool of surplus labour of those age cohorts was disproportionately large, and because the less eligibility principle applied with greatest vigour in relation to 16 to 18-year-old and 18 to 24-year-old segments of the potential labour force, in the ways described in Section 3. Yet however powerfully the dynamic of wage suppression is felt in such circumstances, it cannot achieve equilibrium between the three forces: the contradictions of accepting wage levels insufficient to sustain basic subsistence requirements inevitably drive a significant proportion of would-be participants to remove themselves from the reach of the dynamic and the economic contradictions and social injustices it embodies. That is to say, *young people in such circumstances make rational choices to become non-participant.*

## The research literature

As was noted earlier, research literature related to this model of the wage rate suppression dynamic is sparse. A small number of studies consider the relationship between two of the three dynamic factors in adult labour markets, but have no direct relevance here (see for example Morris, 1998; Alcock et al, 2003; Jones and Novack, 2012; Seabrook, 2013).However, some other studies provide broadly confirmatory evidence of aspects of the dynamic in operation. Harris' (1988) historically focused analysis takes into account the centrality of the less eligibility principle for asserting the work ethic, and the pool of surplus youth labour that emerged during the 1920s and 1930s recessions.[39] Rankin and Roberts' (2011) contemporary analysis of young people's reservation wage rates in South Africa explores the extent to which unrealistic reservation wage expectations account for extreme unemployment rates, particularly in relation to small-scale employers. In Australia, Hui (1991, p 1349) noted that the 'reservation wage is found to decline with elapsed unemployment, albeit at a decreasing rate'. Obversely, Kelly et al (2012) found evidence in Ireland that young women's propensity to endure long-term unemployment is influenced by the number of benefits they are able to claim.

These variants point to the context-specific nature of young people's responses to extreme labour market conditions that are nevertheless broadly consistent with the expectations of the proposed wage rate suppression model. However, other studies suggest that young people's decisions in the face of some of the irreconcilable tensions and pressures fostered by the model produce outcomes that are not consistent with its expectations. Here, two UK-based studies are informative. Lynch's (1985) London study in the run-up to peak 1980s youth unemployment found that the very substantial difference between average benefit levels and average reservation wage thresholds indicated that, contrary to the model, high unemployment rates may *not* greatly depress reservation wage thresholds. Lynch (1985, p 82) concludes that the study demonstrates 'the insignificance of unemployment income as a determinant of the duration of unemployment'.

The other study also indicates the variable operation of the model. Consistent with its expectations, Petrolongo's (2009) study of job search requirements (covering both youth and adult samples) anticipated that increased requirements following reforms of the JSA in 1996 would reduce reservation wage levels and drive more unemployed people into work. However, contrary to the model, the study also anticipated that increased requirements might in some cases 'raise exits into non-claimant non-employment, even when the actual level of benefits received remains unchanged' (Petrolongo, 2009, p 1235). In concluding, Petrolongo (2009, p 1252) offers an interpretation of her findings, that:

> tighter [job] search requirements implied by the JSA indeed *moved claimants off unemployment benefits, without really raising job finding rates* ... those who left the unemployment register without finding a job might have in general *become detached from the labor market — for example by no longer perceiving themselves as 'workers,'* as they were not covered by labor force welfare.

It is particularly notable that Petrolongo (2009, p 1252) also comments that 'overall, all the estimated effects [that were observed] tend to be stronger for the 16–24 than the 25–64 year old sample'.

From these two studies alone, it is clear that extreme labour market conditions like those of the GFC do not reliably result in accommodations of the three dynamic factors of the model along the lines proposed above. Instead, where equilibrium cannot be achieved, even by accepting reservation wage rates that approximate to benefit levels, such conditions have the capacity to propel young people out of the ambit of job placement agencies, workfare programmes and conditional welfare allowances into *non-claimant* unemployment. Once again, this clearly implies that, in unsustainable market circumstances, young people make rational choices to become invisible non-participants.

## Concluding comments

The prospective limitations of models that predict connections between benefits, wages and pools of surplus labour are clear from this brief overview. The imperfections of their application to actual stratified diverse labour markets, and the importance of specificities of locality and demographic variation partially determine these limitations. Nevertheless, the power of the proposed wage rate suppression dynamic continues to be a force that is worthy of further dedicated empirical assessment. Provided that weak labour market demand drives down pay rates to levels that approximate benefit rates, those rates inevitably establish one important benchmark for the individual determination of reservation wage thresholds that are low enough to inhibit labour market entry. Among young people alone, the size of the pool of surplus labour now hugely exceeds its functional value for exerting downward pressure on wages. In such conditions, the option for young people to depress their own wage expectations in order to secure a survivable income has vanished for a very substantial minority of those least well placed to find or compete for work. For them, in effect, there is no rational choice to be made in favour of joining the race to the bottom of the going rate of wages; or of settling for poverty-level and sub-poverty-level state allowances that require involuntary job placement. Neither option offers any hope of independent living; neither is likely to result in competitive advantage in a local market that is permanently massively oversubscribed.

In effect, positive options are closed off for what is often a very substantial minority. Rational choice encourages non-participation in favour of some other unrecognised activity, work in the informal labour market, or inaction. While for some this may take the form of resentful refusal, for others it is experienced as a hopeless and imposed condition of an exclusionary and inequitable labour market, as Chapters Four and Five will show.

Such impasses in young people's pathways to employment have significant consequences. They create the preconditions of worklessness and welfare ineligibility that are frequently claimed to result in crime. One ostensibly powerful illustration of the credibility of such claims concludes:

> It is instructive, for instance, that in their longitudinal study of the NDYP [New Deal for Young People] in Sheffield, Hoogevelt and France (2000: 121) found that after 18 months nearly half (16 of the 35) of the cohort that were

disengaged from it 'were either in prison, on probation or waiting to go to court – all of them after incidents that had occurred since we had first interviewed them, and all but four of these were recorded burglary or other property offences'. (Grover, 2008, p 76)

On the face of it, this example is emblematic of the consequences of the impasses which this chapter has identified. But this inference raises some important questions about the relationship between unemployment, welfare benefits and property crimes committed by young people. As the next two chapters argue, establishing causal links of this kind in the quest to understand the consequences of young people's non-participation is at best difficult to achieve and at worst misleading, prejudicial or mistaken.

### Notes

[1] The internationally accepted International Labour Organization (ILO) definition of unemployment refers to the number of jobless people who want to work, are available to work and are actively seeking employment, irrespective of whether they are registered as unemployed or claiming unemployment benefits. The percentage figure represents the total number of unemployed people, divided by the sum of total employed and unemployed.

[2] The Office for National Statistics' definition of 'economically inactive' is 'people without a job who have not actively sought work in the last four weeks and/or are not available to start work in the next two weeks', Barham /ONS, 2002.

[3] Great Britain, Department of Employment (1971)

[4] Exclusion of young people on training schemes, and those in some form of education, means that from the 1980s onwards these figures are widely regarded as undercounts of youth unemployment – as a result of which, data using the ILO definition is also presented Figure 3.1.

[5] Hirsch (1983, p 31) reported adult unemployment rates of 7% and youth unemployment rates of 12% in 1980.

[6] See, for example, Atkinson and Rees, 1982.

[7] The GFC produced multiple recessions: from the second quarter of 2008 until the third quarter of 2009; from the last quarter of 2011 until the second quarter of 2012. The UK was in recession for almost half (eight quarters) of the period between 2008 and 2012. Only the first of these two recessions is represented in Figure 3.1.

[8] A similar requirement for those aged 17+ came into force in 2015.

[9] The proportion of 16 to 18-year-olds in education increased by two percentage points between 2012 and 2013, and those in employment increased by four percentage points: www.gov.uk/government/uploads/system/uploads/attachment_data/file/346024/Quarterly_Brief_NEET_Q2_2014_FINAL.pdf

[10] For a full account, see Fergusson (2014a).

[11] UK Parliament, House of Commons Public Accounts Committee (2015). This places a more informative and realistic perspective on the record two percentage

points decrease in the numbers of young people counted as NEET at the end of 2013 in the immediate wake of the first year of implementation of the 2008 Education and Skills Act: www.parliament.uk/business/committees/committees-a-z/commons-select/public-accounts-committee/news/16-18-participation-education-training/

[12] Source: World Bank (2015). This data is not adjusted for national variations in census and recording capacities, which are likely to be considerable underestimates, particularly in conflict zones. http://data.worldbank.org/indicator/SL.UEM.1524.ZS

[13] For a full analysis see ILO (2013a). A graphic of these regionally differentiated growth trends is also available at: www.ilo.org/global/about-the-ilo/multimedia/maps-and-charts/WCMS_212431/lang--en/index.htm

[14] The Neoliberal group comprises Chile, Mexico, Russia and Turkey. The Liberal group comprises Australia, Canada, Ireland, New Zealand, the UK and the US. The Social Democratic Group comprises Denmark, Finland, Norway and Sweden. For the full classification, see Pemberton (2015, Table 3.4).

[15] For a general overview, see, for example, Gleeson (1986); Moore (1988); Avis et al (1996); Hyland and Johnson (1998); Payne (2000). In addition, Auer and Cazes (2003), Cam et al (2003) and Hutton (2005)evidence declining job tenure during the 2000s.

[16] For a fuller account, see Lawton (2009), Keep and Mayhew (2010), and Payne and Keep (2011).

[17] It should also be noted that the ILO argues that the basis for calculation of the youth-to-adult unemployment rate is now partly exaggerated as a result of the declining size of the whole active labour force (ILO, 2015, Box 3, p 18).

[18] A major report from Demos (Birdwell et al, 2011, p 67) which designates much of the employment taken by young people as 'dead-end jobs' displays a profound misunderstanding of the structure of labour markets, and the growth of personal care and service work, in this regard.

[19] In 1975, for example, 25,000 16 and 17-year-olds were still in receipt of Supplementary Benefit in their own right, because their parents too were receiving Supplementary Benefit (Harris, 2008, p 65).

[20] In 1983-84, for example, 10,000 young people who did not join the Youth Training Scheme had their benefits reduced by 40% (Harris, 2008, p 56).

[21] See Craig (1988 pp 10-14, 70-73) for a full account. The eligibility criteria for young people to receive benefits were largely conditional on physical and moral danger, risk to physical or mental health, or effective severance of contact with parents/carers (Centre for Economic and Social Inclusion and Bateman, 2009, pp 53-6).

[22] Ball, 1993, p vii. Ball's guide also demonstrates the highly restrictive complexity of young people's entitlements as radical policy changes sought to find the 'middle ground' between enforcing participation while also maintaining the state's legal responsibility to protect minors (see pp 7-25).

[23] Sanctions can be applied for misconduct, including outside of the workplace or working hours, refusal to work overtime, negligent or inefficient work and 'arguing' (Centre for Economic and Social Inclusion and Bateman, 2009, p 74). Severe hardship payments apply if JSA has been stopped, but this was not defined in law and there are no published criteria (p 79).

[24] Grover (2008, p 18), for example, shows that in 2005, 'JSA increased only by 1% … compared to the state pension which rose by 3.1% … and the Child Tax Credit that rose by 4% … Average earnings were increasing by about 4.4% at the time.'

[25] The EMA began as a pilot in 16 English LEAs in 1999 (see Chatrick, 1999, pp 107-9). From 2004 it was fully available to young people between the ages of 16 and 19 who had completed compulsory education and were on a full-time course of further education or training. Full eligibility resulted in a general maintenance allowance of £30 per week, conditional on household income below approximately £21,000 (£23,000 in Wales, Scotland and Northern Ireland). See later in this chapter (see also Note 34).

[26] Research undertaken in London in the late 1990s indicates a substantial shortfall between housing benefit and the rent paid by young people (London Research Centre, 1999, cited in Kemp and Rugg, 2001).

[27] A household is in poverty if its income is below 60% of the median income for all households of similar composition. The median income for a single person household with no children was £213 after housing costs (DWP, 2010, Table 2.4ts). The poverty threshold for such a household is therefore £128 after housing costs.

[28] https://www.gov.uk/government/publications/summer-budget-2015/summer-budget-2015

[29] Eligibility is conditional on estrangement, physical or sexual abuse, handicap or illness, not having parents or carers, or parents who are in custody/chronically sick/mentally or physically disabled/excluded from UK (Child Poverty Action Group, 2013, p 61); or severe hardship following refusal of all support allowances/JSA. Exceptions are dealt with by a specialist national support team (Child Poverty Action Group, 2013, pp 61-3).

[30] Under tougher sanctions introduced by DWP in 2012, 43% of sanctions were applied to 18 to 24-year-olds, although they comprised 27% of claimants (Hayes, 2013; Department for Work and Pensions, 2013).

[31] One indication is that 12% of young people aged 18 to 25 (over 500,000) and 21% of those who are unemployed and looking for work cannot afford appropriate clothes for a job interview (Poverty and Social Exclusion (PSE), 2013, p 6).

[32] A London-based pilot announced by the Mayor of London envisaged three months' unpaid full-time work for 18 to 24-year-olds who have had less than six months in employment since leaving full-time education, as a condition of benefit (see www.gov.uk/government/news/we-need-all-our-young-people-to-be-working-and-contributing-say-mayor-and-employment-minister).

[33] Gough (2011, Figure 3.4) has shown that, apart from the richest decile, tax and benefit reforms fall most heavily on the poorest decile, especially families with children, effecting a 6% loss of income.

[34] The original EMA was a discretionary means tested provision at local level, under the terms of the 1944 Education Act and the 1948 Education (Miscellaneous Provisions) Act (Educational Bursaries in Scotland, following the Education (Scotland) Act, 1946), to cater for young people who continued school or college beyond the compulsory leaving age. Substantial attempts were made to introduce allowances at national level in the face of increasing youth unemployment in the 1980s (Gordon, 1980; Rice, 1987). Under New Labour they were piloted from 1999 and established in 2004. Fiscal pressures were unambiguously the principal motivation for the cancellation of the re-introduced EMA in 2010, irrespective of the austerity campaign. In conjunction with the raised participation age for 16 and 17-year-olds, in the face of minimal employment opportunities and low pay, the weekly £30 allowance was likely to have been the deciding factor in favour of extended schooling for many eligible young people, with substantial costs to the exchequer (see also Note 25).

35  Unlike a series of previous legislative acts that have raised the school-leaving age in contested circumstances (see Fergusson, 2014a), the 2008 Education and Skills Act instead imposes a duty to take employment for those who wish to avoid an extended school career, with the caveat that full-time employment be accompanied by part-time education or training, (although this was provisionally suspended in the 2011 Education Act, removing the requirement to secure education and training for 16 to 17-year-olds in response to the UK's abysmal participation rates compared to those of other rich economies (see OECD, 2008; UNICEF, 2013).

36  Cinalli and Giugni (2013) assess provision across four ideal types for characterising the model of unemployment protection for young people in France, Germany, Italy, Poland, Portugal and Spain.

37  The principle is a fundamental precept of the Poor Law Amendment Act of 1834. Its continuing value for controlling reservation wage thresholds and benefits is exemplified by Grover's (2008, p 72) comments on ministers' intention that the Youth Training Scheme would suppress wage expectations among 'trainees'. For an extensive analysis of the less eligibility principle, the Poor Law and its current manifestations in income supplementation see Grover, 2016.

38  Wage suppression is of course only one dynamic outcome of the model – the one that reflects current prevailing conditions. In conditions of labour shortage and strong welfare provision the dynamic is capable of generating wage inflation.

39  See especially Harris (1989, footnotes, pp 61-3).

# FOUR

# Non-participation and crime: constructing connections

Finally, why do contemporary crime policies so closely resemble the anti-welfare policies that have grown up over precisely the same period? Because they share the same assumptions, harbour the same anxieties, deploy the same stereotypes, and utilize the same recipes for the identification of risk and the allocation of blame. Like social policy and the system of welfare benefits, crime control functions as an element of the broader system of regulation and ideology that attempts to forge a new social order in the conditions of late modernity.

*David Garland (2001) The culture of control: Crime and social order in contemporary society, p 201*

## Introduction

This chapter begins by tracing the construction of the discursive thread that has established a now widely accepted claim that significant connections exist between non-participation and unemployment, between unemployment and crime, and so between non-participation and crime. Of the three prominent discourses that have dominated discussion of non-participation since the 1980s, the social exclusion discourse has been by far the most explicit in identifying these connections. As Chapter Two noted, from the beginning of the use of the concept, New Labour identified a clustered link with crime (Social Exclusion Unit, 2004). *Youth Matters* (Department for Education and Skills, 2005) reasserted the connection, and its influence grew, including on the basis of research derived from longitudinal studies identified in Chapter Two.

This chapter examines the empirical connections between non-participation and crime identified in a range of studies, particularly in relation to unemployment among young people. These connections are important insofar as they provide powerful legitimacy for claims that the link between non-participation and crime is causal; and insofar as they have constituted a leading element of policy discourses since the rise of New Labour. Through an exploration of policy documents, official statistics and the 'Risk Factor Prevention Paradigm', Section 1 traces the construction of the unemployment-crime link, through major influential research studies and policy discourses. Section 2 examines the contributions of research to interpreting the claimed connections between them. Section 3 reviews the influence of welfare provision on the unemployment-crime relationship and considers in depth a number of studies that attempt to isolate causal factors that shape it.

This chapter and the next develop claims that any notion of an exclusively empirical approach to understanding connections between non-participation, unemployment and crime is not sustainable; that the empirical data on which they are premised can only be meaningfully interpreted through an explicit theorisation of the connections between them; and that the data itself, and the methods of its construction, are contested. More generally, a central argument of this and subsequent chapters is that the operation of the criminal justice system at the interface with young people's non-participation and unemployment needs to be interpreted in the context of fundamental shifts in the nature of youth labour markets, in the welfare system in relation to work, and in the governance of some groups of young people as problematised populations.

## Section 1: Constructing discursive connections

As the quotation from the 1816 'Report of the Committee' that opens Chapter Two demonstrates, historically, in popular discourse and published opinion, the connections between crime and 'idle hands', inactivity, indolence and street vagrancy have long been asserted (Chambliss, 1975; Pearson, 1984; Clarke and Critcher, 1985). The useful occupation of young people has infused thinking about education and criminal justice, particularly since the Industrial Revolution. Chapter Two demonstrated the tensions during the 19th century between the marketised value of youthful labour and the commitment to schooling young people as a means of control and providing skills of basic literacy. Public concern about youth crime was also prominent.[1] But historically, it was the growing affluence of young people that resulted from regulated fair-waged employment and relatively high disposable incomes in the 1960s and 1970s, not idleness, that particularised public concern about an expressly identifiable 'youth problem' (Hebdidge, 1979; Presdee, 2000; Hayward, 2002). It was not until the emergence of New Labour's approach to mass youth unemployment that, for the first time since the early 20th century, any serious empirical connection between non-participation and crime was being interpreted to indicate a causal link, or prompted efforts to connect youth criminal justice policies and education and employment policies.

## The risk factor prevention paradigm

The crystallising moment of contemporary connection between non-participation and crime can be traced to the antecedents of the 'Risk Factor Prevention Paradigm' (RFPP), which has its origins in the Cambridge Study in Delinquent Development.[2] Analysis of extensive longitudinal data identified a range of risk factors associated with crime among young people. By the early 1990s, these risk factors were attaining the status of predictors of delinquency and crime. Most were founded in family background and circumstances, in combination with some identified behavioural traits, and purported to identify prospective offenders with a high level of confidence by the time they reached the age of 10 (Farrington, 1994, 1996).

These analyses formed the basis of the RFPP. Its principal risk factors do not include unemployment, although low parental income was one element of the predictive model. Nevertheless, some years in advance of the full development of the RFPP, Farrington et al (1986) analysed the trajectories of 399 boys who left school in 1968-69. They found that their sample offended approximately three times as often during periods of unemployment as they did when they were employed. Their offences were heavily dominated by a range of property-related crimes which the authors suggested were strongly indicative of responses to 'financial need'. However, Farrington and his colleagues were at pains to point out that, although it is highly suggestive, their research 'does not prove unambiguously that unemployment causes crime' (Farrington et al, 1986, p 352). This cautionary note was heavily underpinned not just by reference to the foregoing analysis, but by some of the inferences the researchers pursued in additional statistical testing. At the heart of them was the central caveat of the study:

> The major problem of interpretation, as explained above, is that youths who have periods of unemployment may differ from those who have no such periods in many ways. Therefore, the higher crime rate during unemployment periods *may be caused by the association between unemployment and some other factor which causes offending.* (Farrington et al, 1986, p 345, emphasis added)

This in turn informed an investigation of those young people who other parts of the study identified as being more likely to offend by virtue of their past behaviours and family background. Using a method the team had devised to predict delinquency, they asked whether unemployment had a greater impact upon the identified group's propensity to offend by virtue of low income, large family size, low non-verbal intelligence, and the criminal records of their parents. Analysis of these indicators and other data led the authors to conclude that 'unemployment may have a criminogenic effect *especially on those with the greatest potential for offending in the first place*' (Farrington et al, 1986, p 347, emphasis added). This observation in turn prompted some remarkable comments:

> There was an interesting interaction between unemployment and *types of persons*, since the relation with crime was greatest for those who were the *most predisposed* towards offending. Unemployment, therefore, did not seem to cause *basically law-abiding youths to commit crimes*. It also had a stronger relation with crime when it occurred in the context of a lower status job history*, possibly because this was characteristic of the most delinquent-prone youths.* (Farrington et al, 1986, p 351, emphases added)

This binary essentialist view of the research subjects as inherently law-abiding or criminally predisposed embodies a form of deterministic stereotyping that is now widely discredited. The two final sentences draw tendentious inferences that apparently lack material support in the analysis. The findings of the study identified an increased incidence of offending during periods of unemployment by young people who are implicitly labelled as delinquent by virtue of their family background and behaviour. But even if this conjectural link between a particular construction of 'delinquency' and future criminality had any empirically demonstrated foundation (and this is not available within Farrington et al's article), it is by no means the case that people who did not match the supposed delinquency indicators were exempt from offending during periods of unemployment. To the contrary, it was not known whether the supposedly 'law-abiding' youths had clean criminal records previously, but nonetheless offended during periods of unemployment.

These constructions of delinquency and law-abidingness add nothing to the analysis or its empirical base, but disclose the palpable assumptions of the researchers, including in an apparently gratuitous addendum that 'there have been many social changes in the last 14 years, including a great increase in divorce and one-parent families, which may affect the relation between youth unemployment and crime' (Farrington et al, 1986, p 352).

This provides further indication that the researchers looked first to essentialist understandings of personality and endogenous characteristics, as well as to family histories and other exogenous factors, to explain propensity to offend during periods of unemployment. Consistent with this observation, the authors suggested that future research should develop a more comprehensive theoretical model by reference to the criminological literature on psychological and psychiatric effects of unemployment (Farrington et al, 1986, p 351), further substantiating indications of potential bias away from endogenous influences and nomothetic levels of analysis.

## Birth cohort studies

Much of the work of other researchers in related fields continues the trajectory of Farrington et al's (1986) study. Some of the most significant contributions have emerged from two other major government-funded cohort studies referred to in Chapter Two: the National Child Development Study of the 1958 UK birth cohort and the British Birth Cohort Study of the 1970 birth cohort. Four decades later a single paragraph (written by the one-time director of the Centre for Longitudinal Studies which housed both studies ) crystallised the chain of logics that Farrington and his colleagues' work had helped articulate:

> Though the [social] exclusion process in no way defines a criminal career, most offenders have gone through the process of disaffection and alienation from education on the route to the alternative lifestyles and survival approaches that crime offers. As their schooling proceeds, truancy and school exclusion become increasingly common, restricting further the prospects of rectifying basic skills deficiencies, and increasing the risk of criminal outcomes. The consequence is typically young people leaving school ill-equipped to meet the demands that employers are going to make on job applicants. Exclusion from mainstream routes into employment forces young people towards casual unskilled jobs and unemployment. Reinforced by the values of the peer group, *this unsatisfying work experience may in turn lead to criminal activity* in which drug taking and alcohol abuse are often involved. The vicious circle continues, with contact with the police and criminal convictions reducing

the prospects of employment and mainstream life chances even further. (Bynner, 2009, pp 17-18, emphasis added)

It is difficult to imagine a more succinct encapsulation of the discourse that constructs the logic connecting non-participation to crime. Bynner's portrayal of trajectories to offending reads as a litany of risk factors and serial events reputed to lead to 'criminal careers'. For all its pre-emptive opening remarks to the contrary, its rendition of the causes of crime reproduces the proto-determinist belief that certain combinations of conditions and circumstances exhibit a material link to criminal behaviour that is to be expected. It also reinforces the stereotype that most offenders are poor, disaffected, unemployed, poorly educated and/or drug or alcohol dependent.

## The non-participation–crime link in policy discourses

As noted earlier, the RFPP and the birth cohort studies became a driving force of some transformative policies built around the new discursive rendition of the unemployment-crime relationship. Risk analyses and the RFPP exerted enormous influence over policy. In the late 1990s the Social Exclusion Unit (SEU) contributed much to the acceptance of the claim that there is an inherent link between non-participation and crime, mediated through substantial periods of unemployment.

### Bridging the Gap and Youth Matters

The Prime Minister's foreword to *Bridging the Gap* (SEU, 1999, outlined in Chapter Two) establishes the link from the outset. He proposed that solving the problem of (a comparatively very modest) 160,000 16 to 17-year-olds who were not in employment, education or training would lead to 'a better life for young people themselves, saving them from the prospect of a lifetime of dead-end jobs, unemployment, poverty, ill-health and other kinds of exclusion'.[3] It was also predicted to lead to 'a better deal for society as a whole that has to pay a very high price in terms of welfare bills and crime for failing to help people make the transition to becoming independent adults' (SEU, 1999, p 6).

The opening paragraphs of the report itself explicitly assert non-participation-crime links:

> 1.5 At worst, these years for those aged 16 and 17 involve no education or training, but some combination of short-

term, poor quality jobs with no training, a lack of any purposeful activity and, all too often, a descent into the hardest end of the social exclusion spectrum – a variety of relationship, family and health problems, including homelessness, persistent offending or problem drug use. (SEU, 1999)

The report goes on to acknowledge the absence of any clear evidence of a link between non-participation and crime, but undermines this by citing the evidence of the large proportion of 16 to 17-year-old offenders who are NEET (SEU, 1999, para 4.9).

Other broad indicators of association are cited to try to cement the link:

6.30 By the age of 18, one in every hundred young men will have experienced some time in custody … and in the last five years the custodial population for 15–17 year olds has increased by 55 per cent, from 1,526 to 2,370. There is serious concern about their level of education and training. (SEU, 1999)

In the absence of any demonstration of causality, speculative inferences are invoked:

6.28 Responses to the consultation exercise frequently mentioned offending. In many cases, the lifestyle and income available through criminal activity, especially dealing in drugs, may appear far more attractive than any legitimate alternative. (SEU, 1999)

*Youth Matters* (Department for Education and Skills, 2005) extended this approach. As Chapter Two noted, the consultative document argued that too many young people were 'drifting into a life of poverty and crime' (DfES, 2005, para 10), and were 'at risk' of 'getting into trouble'. This narrative develops later in the document. The reduction of youth crime and the reduction of the number of young people who are NEET was part of the commitment to 'develop with the Inspectorates revised performance indicators that reflect Local Authorities' responsibilities' (DfES, 2005, para 215). This reference to performance indicators is followed up in a series of elaborations on the managerialisation of activity in local authorities to address the supposed link between non-participation and crime.[4]

At the centre of this approach, building on the work of the Cambridge Study, is the basis of a policy framework that became New Labour's hallmark risk assessment and intervention paradigm. Intensive efforts to managerialise interventions through partnership between key agencies began to take as read the existence of an objective connection between non-participation and crime. Both *Bridging the Gap* and *Youth Matters* exhibit a bimodal discourse that attributes crime to non-participation, and non-participation to crime. By keeping both options open, they sidestep the fundamental question of sound empirical evidence of causality. As with all discourses, the appeal to the reader's imagination invites prejudicial interpretations of the nature of the connection.

### Applying the Risk Factor Prevention Paradigm

The critical discursive connection between non-participation and crime became substantially consolidated through the work of the Youth Justice Board (YJB). It began to combine the logics of the RFPP and the birth cohort study analyses with the discourses of the key policy documents detailed above, as the basis for a practical application of risk assessment methodologies to the everyday practices of youth justice workers. The YJB commissioned the Centre for Criminological Research at the University of Oxford to design an assessment tool that would enable youth offending teams (YOTs) to profile young people's risk of offending (Roberts et al, 1996). As one of 12 domains comprising what were termed 'dynamic criminogenic factors', the 'Asset' tool included 'education, training and employment'. Using the tool, YOT workers scored young people against these domains. If they were thought to be at risk of offending because of a lack of involvement in education, training or employment, the resultant score would contribute to determining the level and focus of an intervention plan. The same system was subsequently used for the 'Onset' assessment framework, which focused on prevention and early intervention.

These developments constitute the final link in the discursive chain, and the first systematic consequence of the construction of connections between non-participation and criminality. Since many of the other 11 domains associated with dynamic criminogenic factors concern young people's domestic and other circumstances, it would in principle have been possible for a young person to come to the attention of a YOT if their NEET status coincided with living arrangements, family relationships, a neighbourhood or a lifestyle that were deemed to put them at substantial risk of offending. Irrespective of their own past behaviours and personality characteristics, the conditions into which they were born came to be treated as risk factors judged to be capable of being or becoming determinants of offending.[5] In effect, this approach meant that being categorised as NEET could, alongside other risk factors, result in a *pre-emptive* intervention with a young person who had no previous contact with the criminal justice system.

During later New Labour administrations, it became commonplace to assert the existence of such connections as matters of empirical fact. Stephenson, for example, acknowledges that evidence of the association between unemployment/non-participation and crime is more plentiful than evidence of a causal connection between them, but offers largely unsupported speculation of the sources of causality, including 'the greatly increased amount of time that young people have on their hands ... Conflict within families already under severe pressure ... The absence of positive socialisation effects of participation ... And the relationship between unemployment and poor qualifications' (Stephenson, 2007, pp 87-9). He also asserts that evidence indicates that offending for personal material gain increases particularly during periods of unemployment, without citing sources (p 90).

### The precarious evidence base for intervention policies

These developments constituted a momentous shift in the way the criminal justice system engages with young people, and established some of the critical groundwork for later policies that began a steady trend towards the underlying *criminalisation* of non-participation (see Chapter Eight). In view of their significance for understanding how non-participation is interpreted by a key agency of state, it is important to review the studies that were already in place, mostly undertaken by criminologists and economists, in pursuit of the unemployment-crime relationship.

The discourse that connects non-participation to crime among young people is in large measure the product of the copious modelling of birth cohorts, and the RFPP. These studies stand in stark contrast to a dearth of official data capable of demonstrating the scale and extent of the purported connection in the UK. By way of illustration, one government-commissioned study to estimate the costs of young people's non-participation, including costs associated with crime, was unable to derive any official or independently validated data with which to proceed (reported in Godfrey et al, 2002).[6] The tenuous proxy-data suggested that barely 10% of non-participant 16 to 17-year-olds were offending in key crime categories. While this underestimates total crime, it leaves no doubt that the overwhelming majority of young people classified as 'NEET' do not offend. It is also telling that Godfrey et al's complex projections concluded that, taking into account the underestimate, the costs of crime on the part of this cohort seem 'relatively low' (p iii) compared to the current and projected costs of the educational underachievement of the cohort and of its status as unemployed.

The only other source of dedicated relevant UK data about crimes committed by non-participants is the self-report Youth Lifestyles Survey (YLS) (Flood-Page et al, 2002). It sampled almost 5000 12 to 30-year-olds, distinguishing between young people who were participating in education, training or work and those who were not. It found miniscule and entirely insignificant differences between the proportions of each group who had offended in the last year. Only in the case of serious or persistent offending do small but significant differences appear among younger men (and none among younger women).

Although the self-report methodology limits the validity of this data, the minimal differences between the unemployed group and the remainder substantially weaken claims of an unemployment-crime relationship in this age range.

In all, this scant data provides little support for any claim of a systematic link between non-participation and crime. The hazards of drawing inferences across very different studies conducted several years apart and using very different methodologies and sampling methods need no elaboration. Nonetheless, these two studies provide a prima facie case that the statistical modelling techniques that drove the RFPP and the Asset and Onset tools do not constitute convincing evidence of a clear connection between non-participation and crime. Still less do they demonstrate that any such connection is causal. These observations prompt important questions regarding how a belief about the connection between non-participation and crime can have attained such purchase over policy discourses and policies themselves.

## Section 2: Young people and the 'economic causes of crime' thesis

One explanation for the advance of these poorly evidenced policies is that much of the thinking that gave rise to the policy discourses connecting non-participation and unemployment to crime among young people flowed from a single theoretical source. The 'economic causes of crime' (ECC) thesis has a remarkable provenance in criminological thinking.[7] Gary Becker's (1968) major advancement of the thesis triggered a huge literature that used econometric modelling to demonstrate the relationship between the incidence of crime and income, poverty or unemployment. Increasingly sophisticated models sought to establish the prima facie case that those who were poor or unemployed were more likely to commit crimes. For all their attempts at quasi-scientific impartiality, the studies were driven by the quest for a causal link. To some, such a link was a demonstration of the desperation and destitution caused by poverty and worklessness, consistent with some of the basic precepts of rational choice theory and instrumental rationality.[8] Others sought to disprove the validity of the connection and its prejudicial imputation of an inherent connection between 'the poor' and 'the criminal', whereby the causal connections were seen to denigrate the moral standing of an impoverished and exploited working class. In turn, underclass theorists in particular sought support for claims that the poor and workless were prone to property crimes. For others still, this was an opportunity to argue the moral standing and resilience of those who could desist despite poverty – and hence to demonstrate that deficiencies of personality and morality were the determining factors of criminality.[9]

Numerous meta-studies have sought to synthesise these studies. A majority concluded that if there is a demonstrable unemployment-crime relationship, it is highly inconsistent and weak (Long and Witte, 1981; Chiricos, 1987), leading to the 'consensus of doubt' thesis (Chiricos, 1987). Nevertheless, others continued to show that crime rates rise and fall in line with improving and declining economic conditions.[10]

## At and beyond the limits of aggregate statistical modelling

It is notable that in studies that have sought to disaggregate populations by age, gender, region and ethnicity, stronger patterns of association have qualified the supposed 'consensus of doubt'. In particular, a strikingly large number of contemporary studies have claimed a positive statistical relationship between young people who are without work and some categories of criminal activity.[11] But many are largely or wholly confined to statistical modelling of the relationship. Many lack sufficient variables or controls to allow anything more than speculative inferences about it. Most lack any qualitative element that might encompass the agency and intentionality of young people.

If the point of academic studies of the relationship between non-participation or unemployment and crime is to move beyond the risk assessment and intervention targeting policy mind-set described in Section 1, and to progress from predicting who might offend to understanding common factors that prompt unemployed young people to commit crimes, a sound contextualisation of unemployment and the crimes committed is required to assess claims of causality. Seven studies provide this.

Carmichael and Ward's (2000) research in England and Wales is remarkably frank on the limitations of aggregate studies like their own for isolating causality in demonstrated statistical relationships between crime and unemployment. Their findings from an extensive study are largely consistent with those of the meta-studies summarised earlier:

> Youth unemployment and adult unemployment are both significantly and positively related to burglary rates. Youth unemployment is also consistently and significantly related to robbery and criminal damage rates … It appears that while youth unemployment motivates robbery and criminal damage, rising adult unemployment is more likely to lead to a higher incidence of theft … criminal damage and robbery can be seen as crimes committed by those who are more risk-loving and who perceive themselves as having less to lose from committing a criminal act. In this light a positive link between youth unemployment and both robbery and criminal damage might be expected … This interpretation … implies that acts of robbery and criminal damage are disproportionately committed by young unemployed males. (Carmichael and Ward, 2000, pp 569-70)

However, the authors go on to recognise the problems of assigning causality – not by merely querying the motivations that connect unemployment to crime, but by highlighting the methodological limitations of aggregate data analyses. Their concluding comments acknowledge that:

> All we can say is that our evidence supports the existence of a positive unemployment-crime relationship that is conditional on both type of crime and the measure of unemployment. *Whether it is the unemployed themselves that are committing the crime is another question.* (Carmichael and Ward, 2000, pp 569-70, emphasis added)

Carmichael and Ward's recognition of this inherent limitation of modelling highlights a key incapacity of methodologies of this kind to cast light on causality. They offer no proof that a single unemployed person committed a crime, still less that it was motivated by the effects of being jobless.

Farrington et al's (1986) study in Section 1 places their work above such criticisms. It drew on biographical case-based data that was appropriate for profiling supposed indicators of delinquency. But the information about the circumstances and biographies of the individuals was limited to coding cases according to three indicators of bad behaviour, a range of aspects of parental and child-rearing behaviour, low non-verbal intelligence, parents' criminal convictions, and 'social handicap' defined as low income, poor housing and large family size. The authors report that 'The results showed that unemployment was significantly related to crime only for those with the highest prediction scores' (Farrington et al, 1986, pp 347-8). However, detailed case-specific biographical profiles were not available. Indicators that may have been predictive of future propensity to offend unrelated to delinquency were apparently absent from the analysis. The basis for claiming an association between periods of unemployment and crime appears to be inherently selective. It takes no account of a range of contextual factors bearing upon poverty (as an exogenous socioeconomic condition) rather than delinquency (as a supposedly endogenous personality trait) as triggers to property-related crime in particular.[12]

Grönqvist's (2011) study exemplifies the potential value and scope of a different approach. In some respects it is methodologically similar to Farrington et al's. The strength of both is that they move beyond aggregate data to case-based data. However, in the case of Grönqvist's study, the dataset is hugely enlarged, and takes account of highly pertinent exogenous factors. Grönqvist sampled more than 700,000 Swedish 19 to 25-year-olds with at least one period of recorded unemployment that would have brought with it an entitlement to welfare benefits. This was compared to the profiles of the entire Swedish working age population of over 5 million, for observations between 1992 and 2005. Grönqvist's study includes case-by-case data on high school graduation, family size, marital status, age, immigrant status, disposable income and annual earnings, and several crime categories.

Grönqvist's dataset means that statistical significance levels are exceptionally high. His principal finding was that the youth sample had criminal convictions twice those of the adult population. Being unemployed for more than six months increased the likelihood of 19 to 25-year-olds committing theft by about 33%, compared to the adult population (and only by 2% in terms of the probability of committing a violent crime). Grönqvist suggests that this much larger effect, compared with other studies, is likely to be attributable to the use of case-based large-sample data.

Importantly, Grönqvist's further analyses suggest that differences in disposable income across the sample do not have the expected effect of reducing propensity to offend during extended periods of unemployment, contrary to the ECC thesis. Long-term unemployment was associated with 17% lower disposable income and 73% lower annual earnings. However, Grönqvist suggests that this data should be treated with caution, particularly because the relatively generous welfare benefit entitlement of young people in Sweden during the observation period would very probably mean that disposable income was not as significant a factor as in other countries. Attempts to differentiate between social groups in terms of correspondences between unemployment and crime found no significant differences across a range of variables – notably previous convictions, migrant status, school performance or parental social class. There is a strong implication that unemployment has a largely undifferentiated impact on increasing young people's propensity to one type of property crime (theft), irrespective of almost all social and socioeconomic differentials.

Not only does this raise important questions as to why such a case-specific large-sample longitudinal study produces results so heavily differentiated by age and so little differentiated by all other social/economic variables, it raises questions about the ECC thesis in contexts where state welfare provision guarantees basic forms of material security. This suggests that in the UK, the low pay, negligible welfare benefits and generally minimum financial means of many young people may indeed influence propensity to offend – a point to which the next chapter returns.

## Section 3: Welfare and the unemployment–crime relationship

These observations draw attention to a further limitation of many studies of the unemployment–crime link that do not take account of state welfare and social security provision. One of the effects of welfare reform and the shift to conditional benefits in advanced neoliberal states has been to alter the proportions of working-age people of all ages who are registered as unemployed and are required to participate in welfare-to-work programmes. Therefore, it is not only changes in the unemployment rate that may be found to correspond to increases in property crime: more stringent benefit regimes stand to have a similar effect. In the UK, Machin and Marie (2006, p 163) analysed these effects across all age ranges:

> The introduction of the Jobseekers Allowance (JSA) in the UK in October 1996 enables us to implement three complementary research approaches to look at connections between crime and the toughening of the benefit system. We first consider a quasi-experimental research design to study crime rates in areas more and less affected by the policy before and after JSA introduction. In the areas more affected by JSA introduction, where the outflow from unemployment rose by more, crime also rose by more. These were also the areas with higher outflows from unemployment and particularly to people dropping off the register but not into work or onto other benefits. Second, we consider qualitative survey evidence which suggests crime was high on the thinking of individuals who lost benefits and/or were sanctioned. Third, studying the relation between area crime rates and sanctions after JSA introduction also confirms that areas where more people were sanctioned were those where crime rose by more. *As such these results seem to reflect that the benefit cuts and sanctions embodied in the stricter JSA regime shifted people off the benefit system and raised crime.* (Emphasis added)

Important aspects of this study are corroborated by Petrongolo's (2009) study, cited in Chapter Three, which also considered the switch to the JSA regime, and looked at more long-lasting consequential effects. Petrongolo's conclusions begin with the observation that more stringent requirements for eligibility for unemployment insurance in the form of JSA would normally be expected to result in reduced reservation wages, and increases in the proportion of unemployed people who withdraw from the benefit system. However, as was noted above, one explanation she offers for her findings is that claimants move off unemployment benefits into unsupported economic inactivity and potential detachment from the labour market. She also found that many adults were able to withdraw from JSA in favour of other benefits that were not search-related, but were conditional upon means testing that took account of incapacities and dependants in particular, but that far fewer young people, particularly in the 16 to 19 age range, were likely to be eligible, as reflected in the observed stronger effects of the changes on the 16 to 24 than the 25 to 64-year-old sample noted in Chapter Three.

Machin and Marie's findings and Petrongolo's analysis recall Grönqvist's observation that the distinctive nature of the Swedish welfare state was likely to mean that the minimal moderating effects of higher disposable income on propensity to commit crime cannot be generalised to other national contexts. It follows that the UK's minimalist and highly conditional benefit regime and the lack of disposable income among unemployed young people of the same age range should result in an increased probability of committing property-related crimes.

Fougère et al's (2009) study offers corresponding results. It is extensive in its longitudinal coverage of 95 French departments between 1990 and 2000, producing 1045 separate sets of observations, based on aggregate datasets. The authors claim to be able to identify causal effects, and are confident in concluding that:

> Youth unemployment has a clear (positive) effect on most economic crimes: robberies, burglaries, car thefts, thefts from cars, pickpocketing, drug offenses, and damage to vehicles. However it has a negative effect on four types of violent crimes, namely blackmails and threats, family offenses (including violence against children), illegal weapon ownership, and violence against the police. The effects are often extremely large and significant. (Fougère et al, 2009, pp 932-3)

In relation to state protection, Fougère et al (2009, p 924) report that:

> Results show that not receiving Unemployment Insurance (UI) benefits appears to be positively associated with some economic crimes (for instance, burglaries, thefts of objects from cars) and only those ... *[Receipt] of benefits appears to decrease the incentives to commit economic crimes, conditional of course on unemployment.* (Emphasis added)

It is clear from these findings that there is scope for considerable refinement of the key elements of the ECC thesis. Complications arise when attention is given to what might constitute disposable income, especially in contexts of relative poverty and deprivation. Of particular relevance are the faltering efforts in and beyond the UK to reduce welfare expenditure under neoliberalism. The impact of these factors on young people's marginal decisions to work, to register as unemployed, to accept minimal benefits, to become invisible non-participants, or to commit property-related or survival crimes has yet to be a focus for research.[13] In the light of the propositions of the wage rate suppression dynamic set out in Chapter Three, these observations draw attention to a potentially highly significant limitation of that overwhelming majority of studies that are not able to take into account the dynamic interactions between the effects of the pool of surplus labour, the less eligibility principle, and the scope for individuals to determine personal reservation wage thresholds within specific limits.

The closest approximation to a study that attends to such issues is Baron's (2006, 2008) study of the impact of unemployment on crime among street-homeless young people in a large Canadian city. It represents a potentially important advance.[14] It gathered responses from 400 young people aged under 25 who had curtailed or completed their school careers, were currently unemployed and had been without a fixed address or shelter in the previous 12 months of 2000 and 2001. Baron's key findings were as follows:

> First, those who reported greater monetary dissatisfaction were more likely to be involved in property crime. Second, those who indicated that they felt relatively deprived were more likely to report greater property offending, violent offending, and total offending. … Unemployment was significantly related to total crime while homelessness was related to property crime. The results also showed that street youths with strong monetary goals were more involved in violent crime, drug dealing, and total crime. Deviant peers and deviant attitudes were related to all four offenses. Respondents who made external attributions for their strain also engaged in more violent offending. (Baron, 2006, p 217)

> The current findings suggested that *objective measures of deprivation were not strong consistent predictors of crime.* While the findings showed that objective measures of deprivation, in particular homelessness and unemployment, can be related to crime, it appeared that most of their influence emerged when they conditioned perceptual measures of deprivation. (Baron, 2006, p 219, emphasis added)

Baron (2008) develops this theme in a subsequent paper. Commenting on the limited availability of individual-level research, he is critical of the restrictive tendency of such research to focus on objective information about respondents' employment status and history, because 'similar to aggregate-level work [it] *tends to ignore the more subjective aspects* of the theoretical foundations' (Baron, 2008, p 401, emphasis added). Interestingly, given the impoverished positions of his respondents for at least part of the year in which they were studied, differentiation still emerged as essential to understanding whether and how it is unemployment itself and not associated factors that triggers acquisitive and other crimes. Baron (2008) comments:

> Those who feel more deprived relative to others and express more monetary dissatisfaction also express more anger over their unemployment. Further, it appears that those with a greater commitment to employment are more likely to express anger over their unemployment. Those who reported a stronger work ethic and reported looking for work more regularly also reported more anger. Moreover, contrary to expectations, it was those who felt that they lacked the proper qualifications to gain employment, or made an internal attribution for unemployment, that reported greater anger. (p 414)

> The findings suggest unemployment is more likely to have an impact on crime when people are unhappy with their monetary situation. Thus, *the subjective interpretation of one's economic condition when unemployed is vital ...* Having a strong work ethic leads indirectly to violent and drug crime through its effect on anger and has a direct effect on violent crime. Further, those who searched actively for employment but were persistently rebuffed were more likely to be angry, and this led to violent crime and drug dealing. (p 421, emphasis added)

These summaries show that these young people's experiences of deprivation were more strongly related to offending when they were most resentful of and angered by its consequences. Taken together, they signal an important distinction between the kinds of factors that appeared to be associated with offending among this group of homeless young people. Baron's first summary (2006, pp 217, 219) places a strong emphasis on the material drivers of crime, founded in unemployment and homelessness – and so on the importance of exogenous factors and nomothetic levels of analysis (typically associated with cognition and rational choices). His second summary (2008, pp 414, 421) stresses the subjective interpretation of those factors as critical differentiators of whether or not the material consequences of unemployment and homelessness result in anger, frustration or disappointment – and so stresses endogenous factors and idiographic levels of analysis (associated with emotion, expression and affective domains of action). This exemplifies the broader distinction between *instrumental* and *expressive* crime in which the former is typically associated with property crimes and the latter with violent crime and criminal damage.[15]

## Differentiating causality: instrumental and expressive crime

These categories of differentiation that were first referred to in Section 1 of Chapter Two (exogenous/nomothetic/instrumental/cognition versus endogenous/idiographic/expressive/affect) raise fundamental issues about the ways in which the supposed unemployment–crime relationship is to be understood. They also open up important distinctions about the ways in which non-participation, welfare and crime are theorised. Chapters Six and Seven focus on theorisations of these phenomena that use but also work across the boundaries they embody. The distinction between instrumental and expressive crime, for example, is often in practice too rigid and restrictive to be equal to the complexities of the analysis of crime. Many violent crimes have acquisitive purposes, while others such as domestic violence constitute purposive assertions of control over others that have material consequences, including those of intra-household distribution of resources (Tedeschi and Felson, 1994). Obversely, some acts of theft are clearly conceived by actors as retributive, restorative of entitlements or symbolically reassertive of the just distribution of goods. In effect, such hybrid motivations typify the complex admixture of cognitive and affective drivers of decisions and actions that characterise much human behaviour.

This distinction-blurring complexity significantly affects possible claims of causality in both Baron's studies. Overall, they are exceptionally well placed to make such claims. The rich data, focused sampling and analysis of key variables, particularly with regard to the profound deprivations of homelessness alongside unemployment, appear to construct a highly conducive set of conditions for establishing causality. Nevertheless, what triggers engagement in property crime, violent crime and other crimes remains surprisingly unclear in Baron's analysis. Following the ECC thesis, it might reasonably have been expected that among this distinctive group, of all possible samples, unemployment in combination with homelessness would have produced a preponderance of property-related crimes. And while this would have left uncertainty as to whether unemployment or homelessness was the principal driver, there would be little doubt that material privation was the immediate cause. But no such clarity emerges. The significant incidence of violent and drug-related crime actively disputes the presumption that material need is the principal trigger of crime. However, it is certain that, for this exceptionally strained sample, perception, emotion and interpretation of their own circumstances are critical factors in their responses to homelessness and unemployment; that they constitute critical points of *intersection* between the cognitive and affective determinants of behaviour; and that they are as significant in shaping individuals' decisions about whether or not to break the law as are basic material needs.

Baron's research design and methodology are at the opposite end of the spectrum from aggregate whole-cohort studies of mass undifferentiated populations with which this chapter began. His sample of some of the most strained groups to experience the vicissitudes of unemployment is supported by broadly based profiling, alert to exogenous and endogenous influences, nomothetic and idiographic levels of analysis, socioeconomic context and local specificity. Despite this, Barons' studies have been unable to make a clear contribution to an understanding of the ways in which the crimes of some young people may be a direct result of their unemployed status. It is therefore something of a paradox that his second study (Baron, 2008), which was attentive to young people's interpretations, was fundamentally lacking in scope for self-generated subjective interpretation. Opportunities for Baron's sample of young people to offer their own open-ended narrative account of how being unemployed and homeless lead them to acts of theft or violence were apparently beyond the reach of the research design. Subjectivity was largely missing, thereby significantly limiting the insights the study could provide.

## The welfare–crime relationship

The work of Grönqvist (2011) and Machin and Marie (2006) above laid some groundwork for the importance of giving attention to welfare provision to understand the unemployment-crime relationship. One key element of the financial and other pressures on young people derives from successive withdrawals and real-terms reductions in welfare benefits and forms of support for education and training described in Chapter Three.

The cumulative effects of these changes should allow a focus on those subsets of younger populations for whom the privations of non-participation might trigger property-related crime. In other contexts, reduced welfare provision has been correlated with increased offending. As Chapter Five will show, extensions to the unconditional unemployment benefits programme following the global financial crisis (GFC) in the US may have had a beneficial effect on crime rates, though further investigation is needed to establish this (Lauritsen et al, 2014). More generally, the adverse effects of rising income inequality on the incidence of crime is well established in transnational statistical analyses. The strongest correlations are between levels of income inequality and violent crime and murder (Green et al, 2003; Wilkinson and Pickett, 2009). Broadening this assessment finds a general pattern of association between the size of state/private police forces and inequality levels across countries (United Nations Crime and Justice Information Network, 2000). There is also clear evidence that nation states that imprison higher proportions of their populations spend less on welfare, and some evidence that reduced welfare rates are associated with penal expansionism (Wacquant, 2004/09; Downes and Hansen, 2006). These correspondences in turn have strong resonances with some of the findings of Pemberton's (2015) transnational regime-type analyses outlined in Chapter Three.

Demonstrations of the directions of causality in these correspondences are less clear. Some studies specifically verify the connection between increased welfare spending and reduced levels of violent, serious or lethal crimes. Worrall (2005) categorised 19 studies that demonstrated an inverse relation between welfare spending and serious crime. Most studies were at national level, but Savolainen (2000) analysed two datasets that captured social protection levels and lethal violence rates covering more than 30 countries across four continents. In both sets, he concluded that nations that addressed the effects of economic inequality by means of substantial welfare provision successfully offset the incidence of murder that is associated with inequality.

It is surprising in these analyses that the strongest associations between welfare provision and crime are in relation to serious and violent crimes. Property crimes are less commonly reflected in comparable associations. Most of the exceptions arise from studies in the US. Hannon and DeFronzo (1998) identified links between increased welfare benefits and reduced rates of burglary, larceny and vehicle-related crime. Beckett and Western's (2001) study of differing state policies found substantial evidence of a progressively intensifying relationship between declining welfare provision and increasing rates of incarceration, when comparing states with contrasting welfare policies between the 1970s and 1990s. The authors conclude that, since the inception of neoliberal governance regimes in the US, 'penal and welfare institutions have come to form a single policy regime aimed at the governance of social marginality' (Beckett and Western, 2001, p 55) and that this is evident in differing state policy regimes which variously place emphasis on welfare and incarceration as responses to poverty-related crime.[16]

UK-based studies of the relationship between welfare and crime are scarcer. Jennings et al (2012) used Home Office data on recorded property crime between 1961 and 2006, alongside official government data on unemployment rates and state welfare spending. Theirs is an unusually broad-based review, incorporating political-economic analyses alongside statistical modelling of changing crime rates. Their analysis traced concurrent trends in unemployment, income inequality, welfare expenditure and incarceration rates. Their simple visual analysis (Figure 4.1) conveys a strong sense of the extent to which these trends map on to one another.

**Figure 4.1:** Unemployment, income inequality, welfare spending and incarceration in Britain, 1961-2006

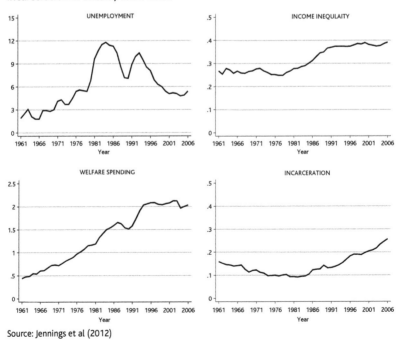

Source: Jennings et al (2012)

Their findings led the authors to propose that economic causes of crime are likely to be time-variant according to conditions and policy regimes. They concluded that:

> It is evident that the growing magnitude of the effect of unemployment on the rate of property crime in Britain during the 1970s and 1980s coincided with the monetarist revolution, and the policies of successive British governments directed at economic liberalisation and labour market reform. While monetarist policies brought the inflation so problematic during the 1970s under control, subsequent upturns in the national level of unemployment were associated with increases in the rate of property crime and strengthening of the link between unemployment and property crime. (Jennings et al, 2012, p 207)

Jennings et al also found that an increase of £10 per person spent on welfare was associated with a 0.03% reduction in the number of property crimes, the scaled effect of which is that, for a notional population of 50 million people in England and Wales, each additional £10 per person spent on welfare would be expected to be associated with a reduction of £14,000 in reported property crimes (Jennings et al, 2012, p 196).

Machin and Marie's (2006) study, outlined earlier, provides strong evidence of increases in crime resulting from the reduction in welfare benefits following the introduction of the JSA in 1996. The study focused on property crimes and violent crimes in more than 40 police force areas in England and Wales. The stricter JSA regime altered the proportions of claimants who continued to claim benefits, to be refused benefits, to take work, or to disappear from records. Under new rules, monthly data showed that an average of 2% of claimants who would previously have been eligible for benefits were refused JSA. The authors calculate that this affected more than 60,000 claimants per quarter (Machin and Marie, 2006, p 161). In the highest risk groups, the change between the quarter-year data following the introduction of JSA showed an increase in property-related offences of 1.2 per thousand people, at high levels of significance. For the same group, the increase in violent crime was less than a tenth of that for property crimes, at much lower levels of significance. As was noted earlier, Machin and Marie conclude that crime increased most in areas where claimants withdrew from the register, did not claim other benefits and did not become employed; and in areas where benefits sanctions were highest. Their qualitative data appeared to confirm a causal link. Their findings regarding differentiation of property crime from violent crime are revealing:

> The results for property crime remain robust and this is in line with the idea that the altering of economic incentives brought about by the JSA may well have caused individuals previously on the margins to engage in property crime. The violent crime results are much weaker when placed into this framework. … *the hypothesis that benefit sanctions and a tougher benefit regime may raise crime is only relevant for property crime.* (Machin and Marie, 2006, p 160, emphasis added)

A third study also makes an important link between changes in social protection benefits and crime rates specifically among young people. Chapter Three described the history of the Education Maintenance Allowance (EMA). Government-sponsored research showed that it had increased participation rates among 16 and 17-year-olds by up to 7% (Institute for Fiscal Studies, 2005). Feinstein and Sabatés' (2005) study across 15 Local Education Authority (LEA) areas during the pilot phase of the EMA found that burglary rates were significantly reduced by about one per thousand pupils in the 16–18 age range, and theft rates by two per thousand, compared to other areas. In the same period no such reductions were evident among 19 to 21-year-olds, who were outside the scope of the EMA. No significant difference in the incidence of violent crime among 16 to 18-year-olds was identified in the pilot LEAs.

These studies offer clear evidence of an association between changes in welfare entitlements and propensity to commit property-related crimes. Jennings et al (2012) stressed the temporality and regime-specificity of this association. Machin and Marie's (2006) study supports this, inasmuch as it shows sharply defined change in rates of property crime between two successive quarters following a change in welfare entitlements. Importantly, two of the three studies emphasise the distinction between increased property crime alongside much smaller and less significant increases in violent crime associated with welfare improvements, in contrast with Baron's (2008) findings.

It appears that once the focus of analysis shifts from a broad concern with unemployment and crime to a specific interest in the relationship between crime and welfare provision, the association with property crime is clearer. The importance of this in respect of young people is that, insofar as they are more financially vulnerable than adults, even minor reductions in benefit rates can precipitate crises of subsistence that may trigger minor property crimes.[17] Nonetheless, for the most part, studies focused on the relationship between welfare and crime are unable to provide persuasive generalisable evidence of a causal relationship between the two.[18] In contrast, Gould et al's (2002) study of the records of young less-educated men in the US substantially strengthens claims that extreme financial duress is causally linked to property crimes and violent crimes. It found that:

> From 1979 to 1997, the wages of unskilled men fell by 20%, and, despite declines after 1993, the property and violent crime rates ... increased by 21% and 35%, respectively ... these analyses control for county and time fixed effects, as well as potential endogeneity using instrumental variables. We also explain the criminal activity of individuals using microdata ... *allowing us to control for individual characteristics that are likely to affect criminal behavior.* Our ... analysis using annual data from 1979 to 1997 shows that the wage trends explain more than 50% of the increase in both the property and violent crime indices over the sample period ... *These results are robust to the inclusion of deterrence variables (arrest rates and police expenditures), controls for simultaneity using instrumental variables, both our aggregate and microdata analyses, and controlling for individual and family characteristics.* (Gould et al, 2002, pp 57–8, emphases added)

This is a substantial advance in understanding the relationship between reduced income and crime using aggregate data analysis, in that it claims to have controlled for several critical variables that are usually hidden in large dataset analyses.

## Reverse causality in the unemployment–crime relation?

For many social scientists, these findings would substantiate the claim that reduced income brings pressures upon unemployed people that are likely to result in crime. For others, as noted earlier, the major limitations of aggregate data analysis inhibit any such interpretation, supported by other findings. Some studies invert the claimed relationships between crime and unemployment. The working premise of discussions about the relationship thus far has been that unemployment causes crime. But some research also suggests that crime increases unemployment.

One version of this argument is well summarised by Grönqvist (2011, p 3):

> One problem is that potential employers may react adversely towards individuals with a criminal record (Grogger 1992, 1998; Kling 2006). A related issue is that firms might choose to relocate as a consequence of rising crime rates (Cullen and Levitt 1999). If crime raises the risk of unemployment instead of the opposite this will bias the results in past studies upwards. Third, due to data limitations most investigations have relied on aggregated measures of unemployment and crime. In these models any effect of unemployment on criminal behaviour is likely to be confounded by general equilibrium effects. For instance, in areas with high unemployment rates there may be fewer resources available to steal and fewer potential victims on the streets (Mustard 2010). Although some studies have tried to account for these problems, no single study has been able to properly address all issues.

Fougère et al (2009, p 927) echo this view: 'If crime in a region induces firms to stop investing or even to start relocating their activities to less crime-prone regions, then unemployment and crime will be positively correlated because crime causes unemployment.'

This position is also supported elsewhere (Papps and Winkelmann, 2000; Narayan and Smyth, 2004). In effect, it signals the classic upward spiral of increasing unemployment and crime that becomes the centrepiece of blighted localities and neighbourhoods abandoned by commercial enterprises and placed outside the operation of the market. Nevertheless, by close analogy with the 'broken windows' thesis,[19] while the plausibility and logic of the reasoning is clear, the incidence of a spiral of economic degeneration in which one (employed) population's criminal activity is demonstrably directly contributory to another population's unemployment is difficult to establish.

## Concluding comments

This survey of the relevant research does more to demonstrate the paucity of academic understanding of the unemployment–crime relationship among young people than to cast any confident light on its interpretation and analysis. At the levels of specificity and detail that these studies provide, most are capable of informing practice or influencing policy but none provide reliable and confidently-replicable conclusions about the nature of the unemployment-crime relationship.

Nonetheless, all the studies considered here have implications for future research in this area – some of which are negative. A number of summary prescriptions for appropriate choices of method and research design as well as substantive focus can be adduced. For example, the limitations of Farrington et al's (1986) study demonstrate several needs: to illuminate category-based analyses with case-specific biographies to test inferential interpretations of emergent patterns of association; to avoid preconceived hypotheses of causality; to consider both exogenous and endogenous influences on outcomes; and to give particular attention to socioeconomic contexts specific to time and place. Carmichael and Ward's (2000) study is a clear reminder that aggregate data analysis is at best indicative of the range of factors that might help direct and focus case-based analyses. Baron's (2006, 2008) studies strongly indicate that research design must at minimum include young people's subjective interpretations of their criminal actions. And so on.

More broadly, to gain an understanding of how non-participation and unemployment trigger or inhibit crime, some priorities that promote an holistic approach to research can also be identified. The value of understanding the importance of welfare provision for unemployed young people when making claims about propensity to offend is clear from Carmichael and Ward's (2000) study, Machin and Marie's (2006), Fougère et al's (2009) and Grönqvist's (2011). All four studies, along with Petrongolo's (2009), also demonstrate the need to take into account the impact of changes in welfare arrangements, particularly those concerning workfare conditionality. This need is further demonstrated by the work of Beckett and Western (2001), Gould et al (2002), Feinstein and Sabatés (2005), the Institute for Fiscal Studies (2005), and Jennings et al (2012), all of which demonstrates ways in which welfare provision affects outcomes. Similarly, understanding variations in disposable income is shown to be potentially critical to informative analyses by Grönqvist's (2011) and Baron's (2006, 2008) research.

In different ways, all these studies point to the need for a significant refinement of some of the key elements of the ECC thesis. Alongside this, the work of Grönqvist and of Fougère et al demonstrates ambiguity in the direction of causality between unemployment and crime which should not be neglected.

Seen in the round, the cumulative uncertainties from this critical review nevertheless indicate limited confidence in understandings of the nature of the unemployment-crime relationship among young people. Although some recurrent tendencies emerge, irrespective of whether or not the impact of welfare provision is taken into account, significant ambiguity remains as to whether unemployment causes crime, in any meaningful and interpretable way.

Despite some qualified claims to the contrary, then, the 'consensus of doubt' concerning the ECC thesis retains its currency almost three decades after its articulation. The RFPP and birth cohort methodologies considered in Section 1 fall far short of demonstrating causal connections. The uncertainties about the relative importance of adequate welfare provision and survival-level disposable incomes in shaping the unemployment-crime relationship in different national contexts have reinforced questions about the value and credibility of any generalised thesis that purports to explain the economic causes of crime. The absence of clarity arising even from Baron's sophisticated and insightful study concerning the effects of material privation and its interpretation through instrumental *and* expressive motivations confirm the inconclusiveness of attempts to arrive at an empirically robust explanation for the contingent and contextually highly variable nature of the unemployment-crime relationship among young people.

After considering an exhaustive literature, and despite attempting to focus on elements of it that are particularly pertinent to understanding young people's involvement in crime in ways that take into account the welfare context in particular, the inconclusiveness of this review invites a negative if not resigned summation. It is important to recognise, however, that, despite its lengthy provenance, all of the research this chapter has reported is based on data and policies that predate the GFC. Nor has it given attention to the specific effects of economic recession on the unemployment-crime relationship. The next chapter offers such a focus, and affords the conditions of the GFC special attention, for three particular reasons. First, it would be reasonable to expect that short-cycle recurrent recessions are likely to throw any relationship between unemployment and crime into its sharpest relief. Second, the GFC offers an opportunity to examine some important claims that, despite (or because of) the distinctive and extreme conditions it imposed, it has coincided with youth crime rates that are the antithesis of those normally associated with recessionary conditions. And third, some well-established cross-national responses to the GFC open up important questions about expressive and emotional reactions to exceptional levels of economic strain on low-income households, and about what kinds of responses to such expressions are to be counted as crimes.

# Notes

1. An extensive historical literature provides competing analyses of the relationship between the demand for and management of the labour of young people, their 'civilisation' as god-fearing subjects and responsible citizens, their preparation as literate and numerate labour, their containment as an idle and unruly mass, and their supposed criminality (see for example Magarey, 1978; Rush, 1992; Hendrik, 1997; May, 2002; Shore, 2002).

2. This major study at the University of Cambridge by Donald West and David Farrington was funded by the Home Office for more than two decades, beginning in 1961. Its precursor in the 1930s was the Cambridge-Somerville Youth Study.

3. This reference to dead-end jobs is typical of the casual use of terminology in reports of this sort, as noted earlier. As part of a survey of the weakness of youth labour markets, Birdwell et al (2011, p 18) draw attention to the doubling of the proportion of young people entering 'labouring and other elementary occupations', and comment that 'These shifts in employment patterns for 16–18 year-olds suggest that those who are entering the labour market are doing so in dead-end jobs…'. The underlying implication is that dead-end jobs are the product of shortcomings of young people. As the analysis in Chapter Three indicates, short-life, low-skill, flexible labour remains the staple of the profitability of UK labour markets. Chapter Seven picks up this theme.

4. The connection is reiterated in relation to commissioning arrangements to secure integrated planning through Children's Trusts (Department for Education and Skills, 2005, para 234), and in the Annual Performance Assessment of Local Authorities, and the star rating for children's services as a whole in the Comprehensive Performance Assessment (para 241). See also Farrington (1994, 1996) as noted in Section 1.

5. In 2006, the Prime Minister suggested that it was now possible to identify prospective criminals before birth, using risk factor calculation techniques (http://news.bbc.co.uk/1/hi/uk_politics/5301824.stm).

6. Faced with the possibility of excluding this strand from their study, the researchers were left with no alternative but to rely upon unpublished, untested and non-transparent estimates supplied by the commissioning department. The data supplied was limited and crude. It estimated that 157,000 young people were classified as NEET. Crime categories were confined to estimates of residential and commercial burglaries and car crimes, thus overlooking a range of acquisitive crimes, as well as violent crime (Godfrey et al, 2002).

7. In the same year that Cesare Lombroso and William Ferrero (1895) were expounding their profoundly deterministic theory of 'criminal types', Roscoe Barnes (1895) was writing his treatise on the economic causes of crime. It was followed by Willem Bonger's (1916) analysis of the effects of the social and economic order of capitalism on crime, including in relation to poverty and survival crime.

8. For an examination of the fundamental precepts of rational economic self-interest calculated around effort, risk and reward, see Becker(1968) and Clarke (1992). For a brief overview of instrumental rationality see Bottoms (2007) on the multiple dimensions of instrumentality and their possible tensions with the basic tenets of rational choice theory.

9. Aspects of the ECC Thesis are in themselves largely undermined by their one-sided focus on the poor, when analyses of the convicted crimes of the wealthy, the powerful and corporate entities might prove capable of demonstrating that the

correlations in these sectors of the population are stronger and more significant – see for example Tombs and Whyte (2003, 2015) on the substantial protective obstacles to the analysis of such crimes and the gains associated with them.

[10] Box (1987) reviewed 51 studies, of which two-thirds found a positive unemployment-crime relationship. Rosenfeld (2014) identified three studies that reached the same finding in contemporary circumstances (see also Arvanites and Defina, 2006; Rosenfeld and Fornango, 2007; Bushway et al, 2013).

[11] See, for example, Farrington et al (1986); Britt (1997); Nilson and Agell (2003); Bynner et al (2004); Narayan and Smyth (2004); Baron (2006, 2008); Buonanno (2006); Machin and Marie (2006); Fougère et al (2009); Bynner (2009); Grönqvist (2011); Phillips and Land (2012).

[12] The factors of 'social handicap' are at best crude. Some may indicate degrees of household poverty, but others may indicate cultural norms (family size) or limited geographical mobility (poor housing) more than poverty. There are no measures of parental unemployment. Although the analysis was undertaken when the boys were aged 18, in 1971-72, there is no indication of their own employment status or earning power, apart from periods of unemployment, and it is unclear whether the references to low income in the coding are restricted to parental income. During this period, the possibilities for boys aged 15 to 18 to earn a substantial part-time income were significant. The condition of the London labour market is also relevant, but no information is included. See Wikstrom and Loeber (2000) on the importance of the inclusion of such factors in comparable analyses.

[13] Some studies have touched on this view of survival crime without making the circumstances by which it is triggered a central focus of attention (see Carlen, 1988; Craine, 1988).

[14] Other research cited by Baron and Hartnagel (1998) shows that the economic marginality of street homelessness is by no means universally associated with acquisitive or other crimes (Hagan and McCarthy, 1997) – thus setting Baron's study in a new perspective.

[15] One useful basic working definition differentiates this distinction as follows:

> Expressive crime, which is sometimes termed affective aggression, involves violence that is not directed at the acquisition of anything tangible or designed to accomplish anything specific other than the violent outcome itself. Assaults, disorders, and domestic violence are examples of expressive crime. Instrumental crime, on the other hand, involves behaviour that has a specific tangible goal, such as the acquisition of property. Predatory crimes, such as theft, burglary, and robbery, are examples of instrumental crime. (Cohn and Rotton, 2003, p 352)

On the additional element of the youthful 'need for excitement' as a driver of expressive crimes see Katz, 1988; Bottoms et al, 2004; Hayward, 2004.

[16] Chapter Seven takes up this question of the governance of the effects of unemployment, poverty and crime.

[17] The administrative category 'unemployed' encompasses professionals with high qualifications and others with transferable skills who work in industries in which frequent relocation is an expected feature of interrupted career profiles. Many in these groups have private insurance, financial and other reserves planned to withstand unemployment, along with creditworthiness and flexible loan and mortgage repayment arrangements. Those who are largely or wholly dependent on welfare often fall below minimal subsistence levels. The recessions of 2008/09 and 2011/12 resulted in recurrent levels of poverty (PSE, 2013; Taylor-Gooby,

2013), and these may have had an increased impact on the incidence of survival crime.

[18] The sole exception among the studies cited here is that of Machin and Marie (2006), which makes a gestural attempt to provide examples of welfare claimants who anticipated the prospect of committing a property crime to feed themselves or their children (see Vincent, 1998, p 30).

[19] Wilson and Kelling's (1982, p 2) famous theory is based on the proposition that 'Social psychologists and police officers tend to agree that if a window in a building is broken and is left unrepaired, all the rest of the windows will soon be broken'.

# FIVE

# Unemployment, crime and recession

The group that appears to be at the highest risk of being negatively affected by changes in the economy (primarily of becoming or remaining unemployed during periods of recession) is the same one that appears to be at the highest risk of committing property and violent offences: socially disadvantaged young males in urban areas as well as persons who have a criminal record ... This raises the possibility, already noted in the literature, that imprisonment is in effect being used as a method of segregating the surplus workforce – remarkably often aliens – from society. Although great variation was noted in this respect between countries, it was suggested that changes in the economy had an effect on the perception that practitioners in the criminal justice system had of the danger presented by offenders. Economic change may lead to changes in the cultural and ideological climate (as reflected for example in political rhetoric), which in turn affect the sentencing patterns.

*European Committee on Crime Problems (1994) Crime and economy, Strasbourg: Council of Europe, p 164*

## Introduction

Since the two-year Great Depression of 1930-31, recessions in the UK have been relatively infrequent and short-lived.[1] Uniquely, the recession of 2008-09 lasted for 18 months and was quickly followed by a second nine-month recession in 2011-12, which took the so-called 'double dip' form, in which renewed recessionary conditions were followed by a brief recovery and an immediate return to recession. To date, there is no detailed analysis of the effects of the global financial crisis (GFC) with regard to the unemployment-crime relationship among young people in the UK. However, the transformation of the economic landscape that followed provides a promising quasi-experimental basis for reviewing the claimed impact of unemployment on the incidence of crime in conditions of extreme financial duress for some households. There is also a reasonable expectation that established patterns of association and mooted causality between unemployment and crime will be more clearly manifested, and that the degree of welfare support available may be more clearly shown to be a significant factor in the relationship.

In this chapter, Section 1 draws on studies in the UK and beyond to assess the historical and recent effects of recession on the incidence of several categories of crime and their possible relationships to unemployment. Section 2 develops a critical review of the data that suggests that, contrary to the 'economic causes of crime' (ECC) thesis, crime rates among young people in the UK declined during the 2008-09 and 2011-12 recessions. Section 3 moves to a global perspective, regarding major widespread public and official concern about the effects of ubiquitous and endemic mass youth non-participation on social cohesion, and reviews the evidence of extensive social unrest and its claimed distinctive relationship to crime. The concluding section sets the frame for an entirely different approach to analysis that is developed in the Interpretive Review that follows this chapter.

Throughout the chapter, it is important to recall the opening caveats and the ambivalent conclusions of Chapter Four and expand on them with regard to the quality, validity and reliability of the data available to the researchers whose work is drawn upon here. All data that purports to record, model and differentiate crimes is, in the last analysis, a construction of highly variable socially, politically and economically determined circumstances. As Muncie (1996/2001) has demonstrated, official crime statistics are partially and subjectively constructed and subject to extensive contextual variation.[2] The critical analysis in Section 2 of flawed official UK government data that indicates substantial reductions in youth crimes during the GFC epitomises the significant dangers of uncritical uses of such data as though it were objective, valid and reliable.

## Section 1: Crime and recession

Contemporaneous studies that catch the ephemeral moment of recession are very rare.[3] Using data beginning in 1933 crossing nine complete business cycles in the US, Cook and Zarkin (1985) found that recessions increase the rate at which robbery and burglaries are committed. This preliminary analysis is consolidated with a study of employment and unemployment rates during the same period, which also coincide with increases in burglaries and robbery. The authors conclude that 'recessions appear to cause increases in these two crimes' (Cook and Zarkin, 1985, p 126). They interpret this claim of causality in terms of the reduced opportunity costs of time spent in criminal activity, and reduced funds for policing over this historical period (p 117), but provide no evidence of either.

Of potentially greater significance, Bushway et al's GFC-related study using data extended to 13 business cycles is more precise in its findings that 'the first year of a typical recession (immediately following the peak) will result in a 9% increase in robbery and 5% increase in burglary relative to the trend during the preceding expansion' (2012, p 445). The authors conclude that 'there now should be little doubt about the contemporaneous effect of the business cycle on rates of robbery and burglary, or the likely effect on auto theft' (Bushway et al, 2012, p 444).

Nonetheless, Bushway et al's claim is, ultimately, no more than a claim that the cluster of conjunctural conditions is closely aligned with conditions of economic strain that are often cited as causes of property crime, not least by those who commit those crimes.[4] At best this lends plausibility to the authors' claim; at worst it means that they are generalising from individual offenders' interpretations of their own actions to universal patterns of responses to specific recessionary conditions.

Following closely behind Bushway et al's (2012) study, Rosenfeld's (2014) collective overview of the effects of the GFC on crime rates also provides some initial indications of the importance of conjunctural differences in the ways in which recessions play out. Through four studies, Rosenfeld and his co-contributors endeavour to explain why, contrary to previous trends, the most serious economic crisis since the Great Depression did not apparently result in increased aggregate crime rates across the full age range in the US. Among other explanations offered by Lauritsen et al (2014), on the basis of a study of violent crime rates between 1973 and 2011, is the finding that changes in welfare provision may have reduced levels of financial hardship since the onset of the financial crisis. The number of people eligible to receive assistance for the purchase of basic foods increased by a remarkable 70% between 2007 and 2011, to benefit almost one in seven US citizens (US Department of Agriculture, 2013, p 22). Similar extensions to the unconditional unemployment benefits programme between 2008 and 2014 may also have had a beneficial effect on crime rates, as suggested by previous studies (Hannon and DeFronzo, 1998), from which Lauritsen et al (2014, p 23) conclude that 'Further research is necessary to determine whether changes in social welfare benefits during the recent period are potential moderators of the recent null relationship between macroeconomic conditions and serious violence'.

Buonanno et al (2014) add another dimension of the conjunctural that is highly pertinent here. Their transnational study covered the 15 European Union countries, plus Norway, Canada and the US, using data beginning in 1970 and covering all years until 2010, well into the period of the full recessionary effects of the GFC. In order to highlight factors that can be expected historically to significantly influence the visibility of the unemployment effects of recessions on crime levels, the researchers differentiated young men aged 15 to 29 as a demographic variable within their model – noting in justification one finding from a US study that 18-year-olds are five times as likely to be arrested for property crime as 35-year-olds (Levitt and Lochner, 2001).

Buonanno et al's (2014) study is the first substantial cross-national assessment of the effects of the GFC on crime rates on both sides of the Atlantic. Their analysis found that 'A one percentage point increase in unemployment increases total crime by 3.6% and 'homicide rate' by 2.7%, while unemployment does not exert any effect on robbery and burglary rates. On the other side, a one percentage point decrease in the unemployment rate lowers total crime rate by 4.4% and homicide rate by 2.9%' (Buonanno et al, 2014, p 31). While the match of increases and decreases in unemployment to rising and declining crime rates is consistent with the findings of other recession-focused studies, the absence of an effect on robbery and burglary of increased unemployment is atypical. More typically, though, young men in Buonanno et al's (2014) study contributed to the general in-step increases and decreases in crime rates at the highest levels of significance in most of their models.

It is informative to note that the authors do not view the absence of an overall effect on burglary and robbery rates as a challenge to the ECC thesis. Rather, they recognise the apparent anomaly by commenting that:

> Our cross-country approach has the advantage of allowing interesting comparisons between developed countries but admittedly, using aggregate crime rates, we lose within-country variation that is useful for the identification and estimation exercise. *The lack of variation might partially explain the reduction in the significance of the coefficients of the unemployment variables on robberies and burglaries* that are theoretically the kind of crimes more [sensitive] to variations in unemployment rates. (Buonanno et al, 2014, p 38, emphasis added)

The sceptical response to this comment recalls the observations in Chapter Four about the significant limitations of high-volume aggregate studies across highly differentiated populations. These criticisms could reasonably be expected to apply with greater force to cross-national studies. Perhaps more important in this context, though, is that Buonanno et al's concluding remarks resonate strongly with Bushway et al's recognition that recessions constitute highly variable 'bundles of events', and with Rosenfeld's (2014, p 6) conclusion that future research should:

> evaluate the impact of changing economic conditions on demographic subgroups; it should determine whether improving conditions have the same or differing effects on crime as deteriorating conditions; it should identify the mechanisms linking crime to economic change; and it should encompass all types of crime, not just the street crimes that have dominated criminological research.

These recommendations match those identified in the concluding section of Chapter Four, which advocated special attention to the experiences of young non-participants, as one of the groups most adversely affected by economic shocks.

The differentiation of young people in Buonanno et al's study supports this argument. The particular location they occupy as semi-dependent, semi-independent 'first victims' of recessionary conditions puts the value of their inclusion beyond doubt. The historical association with crime suggested by the almost universal recognition of the late teens as the 'peak age of offending' adds a further confirmatory dimension.[5] It is necessary only to compare the extreme unemployment rates of young people in Greece and Spain with those in Sweden (see Chapter One, and Grönqvist, 2011, in Chapter Four) to recognise why Buonanno and his colleagues suggest that the conflated inclusion of the 15–29 age cohorts across all 18 countries in the model may be the prime cause of their anomalous finding that the increase in crime rates was not reflected in increased rates of theft and burglary.

Chapter Three argued that eligibility for welfare benefits is a key driver of the ways in which deprivation, poverty and exclusion are experienced in contexts of instability and changing welfare regimes. Lauritsen et al's (2014) recognition of the historically exceptional responses to food poverty and long-term unemployment in the protracted GFC-driven recession in the US illustrates the dangers of research that attempts to interpret the unemployment–crime relationship in isolation from state welfare provision. These dangers are evident in the limitations that Buonanno et al recognise in their study. To conflate in one analytical model countries as diverse in their welfare regime types as the still broadly social democratic Scandinavian group, and the advanced neoliberal US is more apt to conceal than to reveal the differentiated influence of critical factors through which deprivation might result in increases in property crime.

The outcome of this brief review of a sparse recession-based literature is ambivalent. Two longitudinal studies (Cook and Zarkin, 1985; Bushway et al, 2012) demonstrate a powerful relationship between recession and increased crime, and assert a causal connection, but are unable to demonstrate it. Two studies demonstrate the absence of any such relationship (Hannon and DeFronzo, 1998; Lauritsen et al, 2014) and attribute it to welfare interventions. The fifth study (Buonanno et al, 2014) produces ambiguous results. Unsurprisingly, this prompts similar conclusions to those in Chapter Four with regard to the limitations of aggregate historical data analyses to offer any understanding of a possible causal relationship between unemployment and crime in the distinctive conjuncture of recession. At most, these analyses provide some tentative evidence of a correlation between recession and increased property crime.

Nonetheless, there could be no more graphic illustration of the importance of variation, differentiation, conjuncture and national and local specificity to analyses of the unemployment–crime relationship than the effects of recession in the US and the UK. The contrasts between a US Democratic government response to recession that prompted major state-provided food programmes, and a UK Conservative-led coalition austerity programme that bore down hard upon welfare provision, especially for young people in poverty (as Chapter Three argued) are striking.

This is perhaps the most useful single response that can be made to Rosenfeld's (2014, p 4) overall conclusion that 'What may be responsible for the absence of crime increases during the Great Recession remains a puzzle', and that in some ways the most recent findings 'deepen the mystery'. For despite the stark contrasts between the welfare responses to the GFC in the US and the UK, there is substantial statistical evidence that crime rates in the UK fell during the recession, just as they did in the US. The next section offers a critical assessment of this finding.

## Section2: Reduced youth crime in the global financial crisis?

The full gamut of studies of the unemployment–crime relationship based on aggregate data analyses have established an expectation that the effects of the GFC in the UK would be reflected in increased offending among young people. However, official data regarding the involvement of under-21-year-olds in recorded crime between 2002 and 2013 adds to the uncertainties surrounding the dominant approach to analysis by suggesting that this expectation is mistaken.

Figure 5.1 shows the 11-year trend for the total number of sentences for indictable offences to 2012/13 for young people, young adults and adults. The cumulative 'top-line' figures between 300,000 and 350,000 between 2007/08 and 2010/11 are broadly indicative of a trend consistent with the expectations of the ECC thesis. However, the age differentiation within each bar of the chart indicates a countervailing trend for under-18-year-olds dealt with in the youth justice system, and young adults (18 to 20-year-olds).

**Figure 5.1:** People sentenced for indictable offences, by age, 2002/03-2012/13

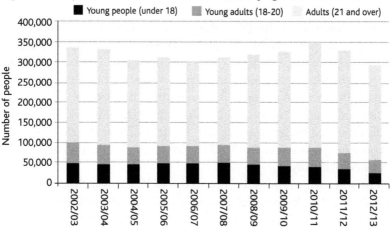

Source: Youth Justice Board / Ministry of Justice (2014)

The unusually sharp decline in numbers of young people sentenced in both age groups over the same period from 2007/08 onwards is even clearer in Figure 5.2, which records sentencing of 10 to 17-year-olds only. The total numbers sentenced is more than halved in the six years to 2012/13. The differentiation between custodial, community and other sentences appears to be roughly proportionate to the overall decline over this period.

**Figure 5.2:** Trends in the number of young people sentenced, by sentence type, 2002/03-2012/13

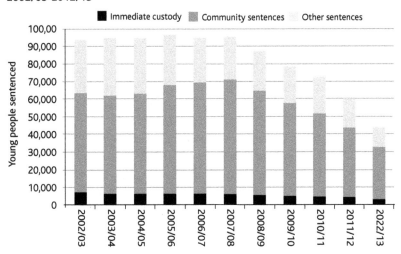

Source: Youth Justice Board / Ministry of Justice (2014)

In contradiction of the ECC thesis, these sharp downward trends among under 18-year-olds began in 2008/09, a year after the adult sentencing rate began its rapid rise at the onset of the GFC. The overall increase in the total number of people sentenced between 2007/08 and 2010/11 shown in Figure 5.1 was entirely attributable to increased sentencing among those aged 21 and above. There is some marginal indication that the sentencing rates for 18 to 20-year-olds remained broadly similar between 2007/08 and 2011/12, but they subsequently declined markedly.

The sole mitigation in defence of the ECC thesis is that, as Figure 5.3 shows, the sharpest declines in sentencing (proven offences) of under-18-year-olds were in non-property-related offences. But while robbery and burglary, in particular, declined less sharply over this period than other categories of crime, the rate of decline even among these offences remains substantial.

Taken together, most of the data in Figures 5.1–5.3 represents declines in youth offending rates of between 30 and 60 percentage points over the period indicated. On the face of it, this indicates a persistent and resilient medium-term trend that has continued through a major period of economic decline, in contrast with trends in the adult criminal justice system and the predictions of the ECC thesis.

**Figure 5.3:** Reduction in proven offences by young people, 2009/10-2012/13

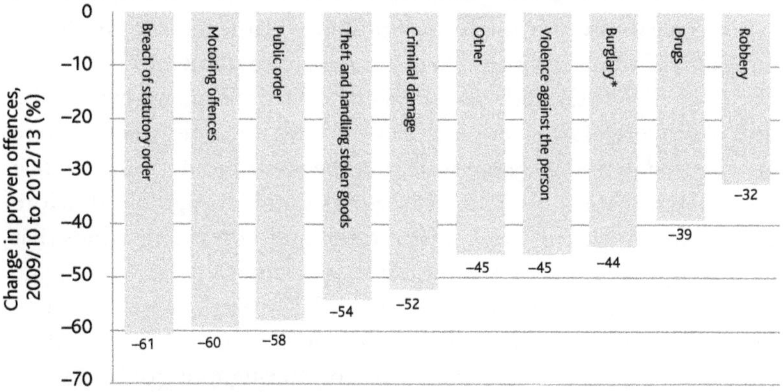

Note: * Burglary includes domestic and non domestic burglary
Source: Youth Justice Board / Ministry of Justice (2014)

A number of crucial caveats, however, substantially weaken the credibility of this data during the period covered. First, a number of general observations apply – in pursuit of the cautionary comments with which this chapter began. Most of the data referred to is taken from police and court records, and is thereby entirely confined to recorded crime which results in a conviction. This is widely acknowledged to be a significant undercount of actual offences. The Crime Survey for England and Wales (CSEW) has the major advantage of being based on a sample of victim-reported crime, but cannot be used in this context since it does not differentiate juvenile from adult crime. To juxtapose juvenile and adult rates, as Figure 5.1 does, is therefore to compare data based on significantly different methodologies.

Perhaps of greatest significance, in terms of the credibility of such data, unprecedentedly, in January 2014, the Office for National Statistics (ONS) completed an assessment of CSEW data that led to the removal of its official 'National Statistics' designation. This is tantamount to a withdrawal of recognition that the statistics collected meet statutory national standards for government-endorsed statistical data.[6] This substantially reduces the degree confidence that can be placed in CSEW data.

Furthermore, complications arise because of the age categories used in these figures, and the divided responsibilities for children, young people and adults across the criminal justice system. In terms of published data, as noted earlier, CSEW and Police Recorded Crime statistics do not differentiate within the 18 to 59-year-old age range. This is particularly pertinent since at least two studies demonstrate the importance in this context of offences committed by young adults aged

18-21. Historical evidence from the US shows that, 'unemployment has a greater motivational effect on property crime among youth and young adults' when compared to other age groups (Britt, 1997, p 405). Soothill et al's (2002) study also shows that the peak age for exactly the kinds of property-related crime associated with unemployment is more concentrated in the age range that spans the youth/adult administrative divide than for most other age categories up to the age of 40. More general official data on 'peak age of offending' consistently finds that young people aged 17 or 18 commit more crimes than any other age group, but that the 'tail-off' among 19 and 20-year-olds is slight. The significant step-change does not begin until the age of 21, and then continues at approximately the same rate throughout adult life (see Scottish Government, 2009; Palmer, 2010). A further complication is that the existing data for under-18-year-olds does not include minor property offences that were dealt with by means of non-criminal sanctions in the form of orders and injunctions.[7]

Adding further doubt, some specific policy changes undermine the validity of official statistics, at least insofar as they can illuminate the unemployment-crime relationship in recessionary conditions. One root of the changes in rates of prosecution is the changes to police performance indicators and their effects on police practices. As Bateman (2012a, p 6) explains:

> In 2002, the Government established a target to narrow the gap between offences recorded and those 'brought to justice' by increasing the number that resulted in a 'sanction detection', consistent with New Labour's determination to appear tough on crime. ... While the target applied both to adults and children, there was inevitably a disproportionate impact on the latter population ... between 2003 and 2007, the number of adults entering the criminal justice system rose by less than 1%, the equivalent figure for those below the age of 18 years was 22%. ... The introduction of the sanction detection target accordingly led directly to the unnecessary criminalisation of large numbers of children. In 2005, in an attempt to counter the inflationary impact of expanding sanction detections, the Youth Justice Board had already introduced a contrary target to reduce the number of children entering the criminal justice system for the first time.

Far from the fluctuations in detected youth crime since 2003 reflecting substantive changes in levels of criminal activity, it seems that they are a predictable outcome of the implementation of two contradictory targets set by central government. Bateman (2015, p 12) continues this line of analysis by arguing that the 2010 coalition government's stress on reducing first-time entrants to the justice system had the effect of

> encouraging the police to respond informally to children with no prior system contact. [The previous Labour administrations'] political commitments to formal early intervention were thus replaced by a focus on diversion and, predictably, this produced a deflationary impact on the overall volume of detected youth crime.

Bateman concludes that 'The ebbs and flows evident in recent youth crime statistics are expressions not primarily of changing patterns of delinquency but of shifts in the construction of, and responses to, children who transgress the law' (p 13).[8]

In summary, it is not possible to deduce from the data in Figures 5.1–5.3 that recent youth crime trends have 'bucked' the prevailing account of the unemployment–crime relationship among young people in recessionary conditions. It is beyond doubt that the published data substantially underestimates the number of crimes committed by young people in the age ranges most affected. Those aged 16–24 span two criminal justice systems. The offences of the youngest do not count in crime figures. Reliance on recorded not reported crime considerably adds to the underestimations. Age-differentiated data for those in the two to three years following the peak age of offending is unavailable, except from a source which no longer meets the required standard for government-published data. Changes in police targets and shifts in policy between governments result in ostensibly significant reductions in crime rates that are wholly attributable to how crimes and the recording of crimes are constructed politically. In short, there is no meaningful possibility of assessing the relationship between non-participation and crime among young people in the post-GFC recessions by reference to official crime data.

Although these circumstances may constitute an exceptional conjuncture of factors that prevent any valid quantitative analysis of the conditions that bear upon young people's offending, they are a salutary reminder of the perils of all such analyses that depend on crime data and its relationship to other factors. The pursuit of longitudinal econometric modelling using aggregate datasets seems certain to prolong the supposed 'mystery' Rosenfeld(2014) identified, in the conclusion to Section 1. Nevertheless, it is a mark of the paucity of alternative evidence and of the great international concern about the effects of the GFC on young people, referred to in Chapter One, that intensive analysis of similar evidence has also been a focus of attention among a number of international governmental organisations (IGOs).

## Section 3: The global financial crisis, social cohesion and social unrest

Chapter Three outlined the international scale and growth of youth unemployment in the wake of the GFC, and the major concerns among IGOs about its presence across some of the richest nations, as well as the poorest. The ways in which IGOs have become increasingly alert to the dangers of endemic and ubiquitous youth unemployment closely mirror the conflicted parameters and contrasting analyses and interpretations that prevail in this field across the social sciences. IGO analyses can be characterised schematically as broadly neoliberal versus broadly social democratic in approach. At their most elementary, neoliberal approaches focus on supply-side failures in terms of the skills of labour market entrants, alongside claims of welfare dependency. Social democratic approaches stress lack of labour market demand and young people's insecurity in terms of their needs for welfare provision. A number of IGOs' approaches straddle these categories. Nonetheless, past World Bank analyses have closely approximated the neoliberal model, while the International Labour Organization (ILO) and UNESCO have been closely aligned to social democratic analyses.[9]

More recently, the World Bank has moved towards a consideration of social as well as economic risks of endemic mass youth unemployment. Its World Development Report for 2013 devotes a chapter to the subject. It explains how having a job can manage social tensions, and provide social identities for young people. The Bank's Social Protection and Labour strategy stresses the importance of employment for ensuring social stability during periods of rapid structural change 'in the face of crises' (World Bank, 2012, p 2). In these accounts, social benefits are always reinforced by reference to associated economic benefits. Particular emphasis is given to an assumed association between unemployment and crime among young people, and the attendant risks of civil instability, unrest, disorder and violence – all of which are presented by reference to calculable economic costs. Examples of links between unemployment, gangs, drug use and firearms are cited to support these connections, and explained in terms of their capacity to compensate for unemployed young people's supposed lack of ties in economic and social life (World Bank, 2012, p 132).[10] By reference to events as diverse as the Arab Spring and the August Riots in England in 2011, social and even political considerations are brought to bear on the Bank's interpretations of the connections between unemployment and crime, violence and civil protest:

> Having, or not having, a job can shape how people view themselves and relate to others. While some jobs can be empowering, in extreme cases a lack of job opportunities can contribute to violence or social unrest. ... Frustration and even social unrest may develop when education and effort are not rewarded or when people perceive the distribution of jobs to be unfair. (World Bank, 2012, pp 126, 137)

These are remarkable concessions from an IGO whose previous analyses of youth unemployment repeatedly reverted to claims of welfare dependency and inadequate attention to preparations for working life as explanations for rising youth unemployment that firmly located responsibility with unemployed young people themselves.[11]

Even more remarkable is that these concessions to exogenous influences using nomothetic levels of analysis bear comparison with the analyses offered by the World Bank's politically polar opposite IGO, the ILO. Despite their historically conflicted alignments, both organisations have more recently drawn attention to similar risks, albeit with the support of somewhat differentiated analyses. The ILO's position is captured in three contemporaneous statements by its Director-General. At the Davos summit of 2012 he told the world's amassed leaders that more than a thousand cities across 82 countries had experienced youth protests during 2011 (Somavia, 2012). In a subsequent speech, he applauded what he described as 'a powerful reassertion of activism from young people who refuse to accept a future of unemployment, marginal work and expensive, poor quality education' (Somavia, 2012b). He later added '[T]here is a growing conviction of the need to change course stimulated by social movements and protests in many countries, themselves fuelled by the growth of inequality and intolerable levels of youth unemployment' (Somavia/ILO, 2012a).

The most tangible underpinning for some of these comments is the annual Gallup World Poll's Social Unrest Index.[12] ILO reanalysis of the Gallup data indicates that weak or negative economic growth and the unemployment rate in each contributing country are the two most important determinants of social unrest. Overall, youth unemployment levels and total unemployment levels are both associated with increases in the likelihood of unrest. For a subsample of 71 economies, the highest risk of social unrest was among the EU27 countries, where it had increased by 12 percentage points in five years, indicating a 46% risk in 2011/12 (ILO, 2013a, p 5).

The ILO (2013b, p 15) comments:

> This increase in the risk of unrest in the European Union is likely to be due to the policy responses to the ongoing sovereign debt crisis and their impact on people's lives and perceptions of well-being. The euro area economy has been in recession since the third quarter of 2011, the unemployment rate recently reached a record high of 12% and the youth unemployment rate is at 23.9%. Income inequality has also worsened in a number of euro area economies.

Between 2010 and 2012, the sharpest increases in the projected risk of social unrest occurred in Cyprus, the Czech Republic, Greece, Italy, Portugal, Slovenia and Spain, where unemployment affected between two–thirds and three-quarters of 15 to 24-year-olds (ILO, 2010, Table 7). Perhaps most disturbingly, commentaries have begun to identify links between terrorism, and the so-called 'radicalisation' of young Muslim men who live as third and fourth generation immigrants in Europe, and who endure jobless poverty and poor prospects, in contrast to the fortunes of their parents and grandparents who prospered through the post-war boom years .[13]

Some of these risk assessments are confirmed by demonstrations that have involved violent clashes with the police – for example in Greece, where young unemployed people have no benefit entitlements (Papadopoulos and Roumpakis, 2012) and in Spain, where young people's employment security as temporary workers was low even during the decade of economic boom which preceded the GFC (Ramos-Diaz and Varela, 2012). A number of other studies identify a connection between unemployment, social unrest and demonstrations beyond Europe, including among young people.[14] Elsewhere, extensive ILO analysis draws on a number of other studies examining determinants of social unrest outside war zones (ILO, 2011; see also Arezki and Bruckner, 2011). Anti-government demonstrations and riots in a number of countries have been associated with income inequality, austerity measures, food prices, and general social dissatisfaction, particularly in countries with large educated young populations facing poor job prospects.[15]

By shifting the focus to a transnational overview of unemployment and social unrest in conditions of recession, this discussion has highlighted expressions of resentment and anger that might broaden understandings of expressive crime referenced in Chapter Four. Crimes associated with social protest are by definition both instrumental and expressive in character. Chapter Four's discussion about different expectations and thresholds for demonstrating causality in the unemployment-crime relationship referred to the epistemological and methodological differences underpinning each version. It also alluded to conflicting social science paradigms that prescribe fundamentally different requirements. Both are a focus of discussion in Part Three.

## Concluding comments

This chapter has provided an assessment of the relationship between non-participation and crime under specific conditions of recession. It has also begun a tentative assessment of what more might be required to demonstrate that recurrent patterns of association between unemployment and crime might be causal.

It is now apparent that efforts to interpret young people's offending from an empirical base, through the lens of data on the material effects of unemployment, continue to be without clear conclusion. Certainly, several studies find evidence of motives: meeting material needs; alleviating the consequences of destitution; correcting injustices; expressing resentment and anger. Only a narrow and purist adherence to positivist principles would insist that all instances of offending by young non-participants need be consistent with a narrow interpretation of the ECC thesis.

Extensive and recurrent evidence of associations between unemployment and crime among young people provided by statistical modelling suggests that unemployment is likely to be a significant factor in their involvement in crime, but only in specific circumstances and under specific conditions. The interpretations of the unemployment-crime relationship among young people in conditions of recession therefore remain tenuous and inconclusive. A defensible summation of the huge accumulation of empirical work in this field over the last half-century would be that remarkably little has been achieved by the endeavour that began with the work of Roscoe Barnes in 1895, and assumed its contemporary guise in Gary Becker's pioneering work in the 1960s. If the balance of evidence is in favour of the claim that there is at least some consistency in the relationship between increased economic strain and crime, echoing the conclusion of Chapter Four, it has not been strong enough to displace the 'consensus of doubt'. More critically, the studies considered in Chapters Four and Five are a small part of an extensive literature, different elements of which have the capacity to support almost any interpretation of the relationship between non-participation and crime. One tenable view of this field of academic endeavour is that it has become a self-perpetuating narrative of quite limited value.

This negative assessment is not a counsel of despair. One of the principal values of further analysis of social unrest as an expression of resentment of unemployment and poverty that Section 3 has begun lies in its power to move attention from an exclusive focus on instrumental motivations, rationality and cognition, to assert the importance of the expressive, the emotional and the affective, and to emphasise the interactions between them, without lapsing into victim-blaming assertions of individual irresponsibility and personal deficiency. In particular, the examples Section 3 provides of extensive social unrest, the questions that arise about when manifestations of unrest constitute criminal activity, and the palpably political nature of the protests described – all confound the simple dominant classifications of crimes and of the causes of crime. In such contexts, confining analysis of the relationship between unemployment and crime to one axis of interpretation to the exclusion of the other is palpably partial in its refusal to acknowledge cross-overs and interactions between categories of crime, motivations for crimes and explanations of crime. It also inhibits recognition of cross-overs and interactions between exogenous and endogenous factors of analysis and nomothetic and idiographic levels of analysis.

Recognitions of this kind open up other possibilities for analysis that delimit reliance on the potentially interminable quest for empirical certainty, they re-centre the importance of interpretative analysis and theorisation, and they invoke consideration of ways of breaking out of the confines of mono-disciplinary, mono-paradigmatic approaches to analysing problems of such complexity. The 'Interlude' that follows elaborates on what this might entail.

**Notes**

[1]    Recessions are defined as two successive quarters of negative economic growth. Those of 1956, 1961, 1973/74 and 1975 were all confined to two (or in one case

three) successive quarter-years of negative economic growth. Only in 1980–81 and 1990–91 did recessions lasting well over a year occur (Jenkins, 2010).

[2] For example, official statistics count only those crimes that are the responsibility of Home Office-controlled police. The overwhelming majority of police-recorded crime depends on public reportage, which is neither consistent nor complete. Perceptions of witnesses to purported crimes vary dramatically in their reliability. Not all reported crimes are acted upon and recorded by the police. Changes in law enforcement also fundamentally affect what crimes are reported, as do changes in police practices and priorities. Increases in crime rates also reflect reportage, rather than the 'actual' extent of crime – if crime can ultimately be conceived in such an objectifiable way at all. For a full exposition, see Muncie (1996/2001 pp 23–43).

[3] Box's (1987) review of 62 studies covering the period between 1960 and 1985, when short recessions became commonplace, found only two focused specifically on recessions (Box and Hale, 1982; Cook and Zarkin, 1985).

[4] See, for example, the Department for Education and Employment evaluation of the effects of JSA which showed that four of 30 respondents had indicated they had seriously contemplated committing property crimes out of desperation when they were sanctioned for non-compliance with JSA rules (Vincent, 1998, p 30).

[5] Levitt and Lochner's (2001) research on this is confirmed by Soothill et al's (2002) findings.

[6] The Office for National Statistics (2014a, para 1.3.1) stated that it lacked sufficient knowledge of: 'the processes involved in the recording of crime by police forces and the checks carried out on the data received from police forces, to be assured that they are accurately recorded. [The data] does not provide enough information to users about the quality of the statistics – most importantly the accuracy and reliability of the statistics'.

[7] For an extended discussion of the statistics of crimes committed by young people, see Fergusson (2013b).

[8] See also Bateman (2012b), which estimates the probable increased scale of recorded youth crime had the reduced first-time entrant policy not been in place.

[9] For the most part, UNICEF, the Organisation for Economic Co-operation and Development (OECD) and the International Monetary Fund (IMF) tend towards hybrid discourses which emphasise supply-side failures of would-be labour market entrants in combination with recognition of the insecurities and legitimate welfare demands that result from failed market entry. For a full exposition, see Fergusson and Yeates (2014).

[10] The inclusion of gangs in the chain of connection between unemployment and criminality draws upon a discourse of idle/troubled/drug-using/aggressive/violent youth which is contested in the literature. Popular media and political efforts to associate the August Riots of 2011 with gang culture are ill-supported in academic studies of this set of episodes (see Newburn, 2012). The wider connections to stigmatised and vilified populations is a focus for discussion in Chapter Seven. For a full analysis of World Bank discourses on youth unemployment, see Fergusson and Yeates (2013).

[11] Claims that the 2011 riots had any coherent political purpose or voice of identifiable social protest are contested. Studies have not evidenced any clear connection (see for example Lewis et al, 2011; National Centre for Social Research, 2011; Briggs, 2012; Newburn, 2012; Nwabuzo, 2012; Treadwell et al, 2012).

[12] The poll surveys 1000 individuals aged 15 and above in 150 countries. The five principal variables for compiling the Social Unrest Index address confidence in government, living standards, employment prospects, personal and democratic freedom, and internet access. The ILO has compared the data in the Gallup index against actual economic indicators (ILO, 2013a, p 15).

[13] Thomson and Stoddard (2015) linked the killing of 17 people in Paris in the 'Charlie Hebdo' attacks in 2015 to the one-in-four unemployment rate among young Muslims in some cities' *banlieus*, and to the high levels of their involvement in Jihadist networks (see also Azinović and Jusić, 2015).

[14] The literature focuses particularly on China (Solinger, 2007; Hassard et al, 2008); North Africa (Hamzawy, 2009; Jawad, 2012); and Egypt (Peeters, 2011; LaGraffe, 2012) among others. See also Institute for International Labour Studies (2011).

[15] For income inequality, see Easterly and Levine (1997); for austerity measures, see Ponticelli and Voth (2011); Walton and Ragin (1990); Woo (2003); for food prices, see Bellemare (2011); and for general social dissatisfaction, see Jenkins (1983); Jenkins and Wallace (1996).

# INTERLUDE

# Interpretive review

The conclusions of the previous chapter indicate a need to pursue one of two divergent paths for refining analysis and advancing thinking in this field of social and criminal justice policy. The first would require a major intensification of empirical work. It would mean taking seriously the critique set out in Chapters Four and Five of the dominant methodologies that have been in use to date. A major shift in methods and research design would be required. Such a shift may be attainable, but would be exceptionally demanding. The risk that it would do no more than add a stratum of understanding to the inconclusive research to date would haunt its advance.

The second path would be to give precedence to a focused, dedicated theorisation of the relationship between non-participation, welfare and crime among young people, of a kind that has not yet been attempted. It would be essential to explore interpretations of the relationship that are largely beyond the reach of existing empirical research. Such an approach would help redress the historical imbalance that has greatly favoured positivistic empirical research over theoretical research in this field. As what follows proposes, such an approach also has important potential to re-steer empirical work in ways that might offer good prospects for reinterpreting it. This approach also has potential to divert policy knowledge and political priorities away from preoccupations with the alleged criminality of non-participants, in favour of developing a broader understanding of the causes and consequences of mass non-participation.

An exploration of what it might mean to theorise non-participation and crime within broader horizons is the subject of the next three chapters. By way of preparation, this interpretive review of Chapters Two to Five draws together their key arguments. Throughout those chapters, the distinctions between exogenous factors of analysis and nomothetic levels of analysis on one side, and endogenous factors of analysis and idiographic levels of analysis on the other have been used to highlight some of the paradigmatically fundamental origins of the conflicted positions and approaches described. This review continues to draw on these distinctions, as a constant reference point that identifies and frames key axes of contestation – many of which also characterise much theorisation in this field.

Each of the three discourses of non-participation in Chapter Two is underpinned by an implicit theorisation of the causes of non-participation. The transitions discourse construes non-participation as a technical failure of matching young people to positions in the labour market. It references demand-side problems in the labour market and supply-side problems in young people's skills and qualifications. In this discourse, a relatively even-handed balance of analysis is maintained between exogenous causes of non-participation (poor provision, poor opportunity, and so on) and endogenous causes (poor choices, poor predisposition, and so on). Both nomothetic and idiographic levels of analysis are deployed.

The social exclusion discourse reconfigured the balance by recognising and responding to disadvantages (predominantly exogenous factors) bearing upon young people which cause the claimed supply-side problems that inhibit labour market entry. The starting position of this discourse was rooted in nomothetic levels of analysis. It advocated making good the deficiencies in young people's educational and training experiences and preparation for work, on condition that those concerned acted responsibly by taking advantage of improved provision and opportunities. Only those who failed to do so became the objects of a range of sanctions and interventions, thus postponing recourse to the deployment of more idiographically influenced analyses and to invoking endogenous explanations of behaviour, as measures of last resort.

The disengagement discourse bypasses the earlier stages of reasoning of the social exclusion discourse, overlooking poor educational preparation and demand-side failures in labour markets, and places the responsibility for non-participation on young people's asserted unwillingness to 'engage' by preparing themselves in suitable ways for employment. In this version, exogenous causes are largely ignored in favour of an emphasis on supposedly endogenous causes of non-participation, drawing on idiographically influenced analyses.

As these three discourses determined successive analyses of non-participation and drove policy outcomes over several decades from the mid-1980s onwards, so the acknowledgement of failures of educational opportunity, training provision and labour market demand has given way to interpretations that place individual deficiencies at the centre of dominant policies. Incrementally, the burden of analysis has shifted from exogenous to endogenous causes of non-participation, and from nomothetic to idiographic levels of analysis. Policy discourse has become reluctant to acknowledge social and economic circumstances as causes of non-participation, and quick to attribute responsibility to individuals, their choices and their predispositions.

This uneven but decisive shift has defined the parameters for conflicted understandings of and responses to non-participation. The discussion of the relationship between skills, wages and welfare entitlement as causes of non-participation in Chapter Three reflects these conflicted interpretations. The key supposed endogenous causes of non-participation are repeatedly reasserted by those who regard non-participants as authors of their own fortunes, resulting from poor skills and qualifications, unrealistic wage expectations, and tendencies to welfare dependency. Chapter Three has argued that these attributions are unfounded, and that many young people's decisions not to participate are economically rational in the face of weak demand for their labour at sustainable rates of remuneration.

The debate about the construction of connections between non-participation and crime in Chapter Four reflects the same conflicted interpretations. The 'economic causes of crime' (ECC) thesis is in principle permissive of both exogenous and endogenous categories of explanation. For those who are convinced that non-participation is principally the product of exogenous socioeconomic and political-economic causes, the thesis provides contingent evidence that the poverty associated with non-participation impels young people towards property crime. Those of the opposite persuasion emphasise that such crimes are impetuous, and that crimes of damage to property or violence against persons have no foundation in material need. Such interpretations variously deploy claims of poor socialisation, debased moral standards and tendencies towards impulsive-reactive behaviour, all of which reference endogenous explanations.

These two positions are paralleled by the criminological distinction between instrumental and expressive motivations for crime. Instrumental crimes are closely aligned with exogenous interpretations of non-participation. These emphasise rational responses to social and economic conditions and typically use nomothetic analyses. Expressive crimes invoke idiographically influenced analyses that reference endogenous factors associated with impetuous and irrational behaviour.

Chapter Five revisited these conflicting interpretations in conditions of recession. Some studies demonstrated a strengthened association between unemployment and property crime, reinforcing the focus on exogenous causes. Others found evidence of increased violence that supports the opposing position. But in all cases, the inherent difficulty of demonstrating causality through statistical association means that the fundamental ambiguities about the relationship between non-participation and crime remain.

The shift to a focus on social unrest in Chapter Five adds a new dimension to the conflicted parameters of analysis. International governmental organisations (IGOs) that express serious concern about the destabilisation effects of mass youth unemployment have been historically aligned with opposing analyses that invoke exogenous or endogenous foci for analysis. But some convergence between the World Bank and the International Labour Organization (ILO) identifies social cohesion and social stability as primary concerns in response to increased risks of social unrest. Nonetheless, two positions grounded in very different understandings of crime and of the significances of social unrest continue. For the World Bank, instability is economically unfavourable, and loss of social cohesion is economically dysfunctional. For the ILO, social injustices in employment deserve redress in their own right. Although some of the historical lines of division have dissolved, their underpinnings survive intact on the terrain of contrasting social values and policy priorities.

These conflicted interpretations of social unrest continue to complicate debate. Insofar as social unrest is realised in civil protests, acts of disobedience, conflicts with police, interpersonal violence and damage to property, it alters the analysis of that relationship. Organised and spontaneous protests are both instrumental in their commitment to drawing attention to perceived injustices, and expressive – of a range of emotions. And yet there is no immediate material gain attached to the instrumental motivation, while deliberate acts of protest that articulate anger challenge assertions that expressive crime is impulsive and irrational.

Table I.1 highlights the ways in which the conflicting explanations and contested analyses that Chapters Two to Five have identified can be interpreted through the distinctions drawn between exogenous and endogenous factors of analysis and nomothetic and idiographic levels of analysis. This is not to claim that these contrasting types of analysis are mutually exclusive or necessarily incompatible in diverse contexts and applications. However, this interpretive frame allows a clear focus on the specific contexts considered in Chapters Two to Five in which these analyses conflict, while also highlighting contexts in which the divisions blur and dissolve.

Refining crude distinctions between exogenous and endogenous accounts of non-participation, between nomothetic and idiographic levels of analysis, between instrumental and expressive crime (and also between the precepts of opposing political-philosophical traditions with which many of these positions are associated) opens up possibilities for promising insights. Such refinements also help establish the key criterion for assessing the value of theories that can offer further insights at the critical and decisive points of conflict and contestation which previous chapters have set out – especially insofar as those theories themselves endeavour to *work across and dissolve* some of the binaries and the disciplinary and paradigmatic divisions in which they are embedded. Theories that maintain these lines of division are to be eschewed in favour of theories that refuse their categorical distinctions and narrow trajectories of analysis, and seek points of entry that are capable of disrupting them. This criterion has strongly influenced the choice of two theorists whose work defines the approach to critical analysis in Part Three.

**Table Interlude.1** Types of analysis used in Chapters Two, Four and Five

| | | | Types of factors/levels of analysis | |
|---|---|---|---|---|
| | | | Exogenous/ nomothetic | Endogenous/ idiographic |
| [Chapter Two] | Influences on discourses of non-participation | Transitions discourse | Broadly equal | Broadly equal |
| | | Social exclusion Discourse | Superordinate/ prior | Subordinate/ subsequent |
| | | Disengagement discourse | Residual/absent | Dominant/ exclusive |
| [Chapter Four] | Causes of motivation for crime | Economic causes of crime thesis | Ambivalent/ irrelevant | Ambivalent/ irrelevant |
| | | Instrumental motivation | Prioritised/ ambiguous | Marginalised/ ambiguous |
| | | Expressive motivation | Marginalised/ ambiguous | Prioritised/ ambiguous |
| | Effects of recession | Effects on claims of ECC thesis | Strengthen ECC thesis but accounts of causality remain fundamentally contested | Strengthen ECC thesis but accounts of causality remain fundamentally contested |
| [Chapter Five] | Primary significance of effects of social unrest | Economically dysfunctional (e.g. World Bank) | Gained in recognition but effect of unrest of greater significance than cause | Reduced in recognition but effect of unrest of greater significance than cause |
| | | Socially unjust (e.g. ILO) | Remain dominant/ exclusive | Remain residual/ absent |

Note: This schematic representation is not intended as definitive in terms of the interpretation that can be placed upon claims made in previous chapters, nor is it intended to capture the conflicts and impasses identified in the foregoing discussions.

# Part Three
# Theorising non-participation

# SIX

# Lines of division, points of entry: two theories

*... systemic disequilibria* become *crises* only when the performances of economy and state remain manifestly below an established level of aspiration and harm the symbolic reproduction of the lifeworld by calling forth conflicts and reactions of resistance there. It is the societal components of the lifeworld that are directly affected by this. Before such conflicts threaten core domains of social integration, they are pushed to the periphery – before anomic conditions arise there are appearances of withdrawal of legitimation or motivation.

*Jürgen Habermas (1981/1987) The theory of communicative action: Lifeworld and system: A critique of functionalist reason, p 385*

One in five young people in Britain between the ages of 16 and 24 are currently defined as NEETs ... This represents about one million young people for whom everyday life is shaped by a crisis of possibility – the idea of a future in which their ability to participate actively in the social life of the state is radically uncertain ... [They] became the abjects they had been told they were.

*Imogen Tyler (2013) Revolting subjects: social abjection and resistance in neoliberal Britain, p 198, p 204*

## Introduction

Theories that are confined in their scope and analysis to either side of the distinctions between the factors and levels of analysis described in Table I.1 in the Interlude are ill-suited to engaging with conflicting interpretations of the relationship between non-participation and crime. In particular, they lack capacity for interrogating the ways in which categorically conflicted analyses are intersected by one another. Theories that are restricted to analyses of structures of political power, economic systems and social institutions are likely to give insufficient recognition to the powers of individual agents and groups, to the predispositions and motivations of individual actors, or to the power and influence of the affective and the emotional. The obverse limitations apply to theories that are restricted by a focus on individual behaviours and predispositions. It is of interest here to find points of entry across these lines of division, in the form of theoretical frameworks that blur and confound them. Encompassing theoretical frameworks (as distinct from specific theories) of this sort are rare. Frameworks that are directly relevant to non-participation, welfare and crime are rarer.

Perhaps surprisingly, one of the few theorists whose work meets these criteria is best known for his analysis of the crises of political and economic legitimation that preceded the shifts to neoliberalism in the US and the UK during the 1970s. More generally he is known for his unusual position as a Marxist social theorist who is highly critical of Marx's social theories.[1] Jürgen Habermas' work is of far greater breadth than these descriptors imply. This chapter and the next draw extensively on *The theory of communicative action: Lifeworld and system: A critique of functionalist reason*, the second volume of his two-volume thesis which is the centrepiece of his social theory (Habermas, 1981/1984, 1981/1987). It is one of five programmes of his research, which also cover theories of meaning and of communicative rationality, discourse ethics and democratic and legal theory. Habermas' erudition is expansive. His social theory draws heavily on the work of Durkheim, Mead, Parsons and Weber, although his intellectual roots were in philosophy, and only subsequently in sociology and cultural theory. Certainly, his definitive works of social theory are heavily influenced by structures and political economy, while its starting points are concerned with meaning, communication and discourse as sources of social integration.

In terms of the breadth of Habermas' theorisation and its capacity to traverse paradigmatic 'lines of division', aspects of his work lead him towards psychology (especially William James) and psychoanalysis (especially Sigmund Freud) in pursuit of his characterisation of failures of social integration and social cohesion as socio-pathologies and psycho-pathologies. Although this focus constitutes only a small fraction of Habermas' work, it is strongly indicative of his recurrent references to the personal, the individual and personality as objects of analysis to be maintained alongside his preoccupation with his grand categories of 'systems' and 'lifeworlds'. In itself, the concept of lifeworld defies categorisation in terms of a focus on the nomothetic, on structures, or on the power of exogenous factors in determining social, economic and political outcomes. In addition, Habermas gives brief but very pertinent attention to the effects on young people of the phenomena he analyses.

The second theorist this chapter focusses on is Imogen Tyler. Her monograph *Revolting subjects: Social abjection and resistance in neoliberal Britain* (Tyler, 2013) is an impassioned work that she variously refers to as 'a polemic [that] also attempts to move us towards revolt' (p 4), an effort to 'induce revulsion' (p 4) and, as 'a backlash against some of the current forms of "post-ideological" scholarship' (p 215). Tyler's work is rooted deep in psychosocial analysis, but her strong interdisciplinary approach tempers this focus with an insistence on the centrality of class to an understanding of social abjection (including by frequent reference to Marx), and with appeals to political-economic analysis, processes of governance and the centrality of neoliberalism to an interpretation of the intensification of the conditions described by the core concept of her text: social abjection. Her work too constantly crosses paradigms.

In many respects Tyler's work stands at some distance from Habermas', and from his epistemology, his quasi-technicist and dispassionate style and the particular but diverse social science disciplines and paradigms that drive his work. In this sense, juxtaposing these theorists may seem incongruous. Yet their approaches share two crucial common features that commend them here: both display a strong and enduring commitment to traversing the lines of binary division. And both are, in different ways, of direct relevance to interpreting young people's non-participation in relation to welfare and crime.

## Section 1: Jürgen Habermas: systems and lifeworlds

### Systems and lifeworlds

Habermas' major theoretical treatise distinguishes and commends itself because of its sustained efforts to bring analysis of systems of power and money together with understandings of the 'lifeworld'. It offers one way of refusing the deterministic tendencies of political-economic accounts while *both* recognising degrees of power and autonomy experienced by individual agents, *and* accepting the fundamental ways in which the minutiae of their daily actions are circumscribed by markets and by states, and governed by aspects of both.

In Habermas' social theory, the effects and consequences of non-participation described in earlier chapters are a facet of the social pathologies that arise when, in his terminology, systems colonise lifeworlds.[2] His concept of system refers to a set of accreted structures and practices that results in established patterns of 'instrumental action' – that is, those purposive actions by agents that are calculated means to the most effective achievement of preconceived ends (Habermas, 1981/1987). The two key subsystems are those of money and power. In capitalist societies, instrumental action within the money system (that is, the economy) is dedicated to the instrumental end of maximising the attainable accumulation of capital that the power system (that is, the polity) will permit and support. The subsystem of power consists of the state, political parties, civil society and other related institutions, which typically function in active support of the instrumental ends of capitalism. Through these two subsystems, organised and managed instrumental action in pursuit of capital accumulation imposes itself substantially upon 'the social' and drives much of the quasi-autonomous action and behaviour of individuals.

Much as these overarching instrumental ends and actions fashion the social world, they do not in and of themselves constitute it. Rather, conceptually separate from the world of systems and its instrumental ends is 'the lifeworld'.[3] It comprises the various multiple structures, forms of organisation and institutions that are essentially informal, distinct and separate from the worlds of government, markets, the state, and so on. Households, families, culture and a range of informal groupings make up these less directly regulated worlds through which people understand one another, meet, act collectively and share meanings. These meanings consist of repositories of common assumptions, knowledge, understandings and ways of communicating which are the central source of social integration and cohesion. They permit 'communicative action' whereby people test out and deploy claims as a valid basis for action and social coordination.

Seen in this light, both systems and lifeworlds have integrative effects on populations. As the actions and instrumental ends of systems integration grow and become more complex, the tasks of social integration conducted through lifeworlds become ever more demanding. The systems and modes of organisation of the market, the state and public administration gradually take increasing hold of the processes of social integration. Systems of power and money drive people toward ends which they have not determined, of which they may have little understanding, and which are not the product of social consensus or communicative action. Instrumental action determined primarily in the systems sphere increasingly takes hold. It begins to *colonise* the lifeworld in ways that distort its balance with systems. This inverts the pre-existing order where individual understandings of the world emanating from fora of communicative action must precede instrumental action if all participants are to be apprised of and guided by the instrumental ends that are the sole purpose of systems of money and power. As instrumental action and the world of systems increasingly shape and drive the lifeworld, significant imbalances between it and systems begin to arise. Eventually, imbalances damage, override or subvert the lifeworlds in which communicative action takes place and shared meanings are achieved. These forces produce 'social pathologies' typified by anomie, alienation, loss of social integration and purpose, declining stability – and ultimately social disorder .

In these circumstances, Habermas argues, individual agents act in irrational ways, in terms of their own self-interest, or respond with passive modes of resistance. This is not because they are victims of false consciousness but because they become inexorably wound into the premises, unfathomable rationalities and instrumental ends of the money and power systems, which are oblivious to the rationalities and priorities of lifeworlds. Individuals lose both their sense of the inherent purposes of what systems require of them, and, as a result, their capacities to function as self-determining and responsible actors.

## Colonisation and uncoupling

For Habermas, the lifeworld is the indispensable locus of social integration, but he also accepts the necessity of systems to secure the essential complex material and organisational needs of modern societies. He acknowledges the irreducibility of money and power as core systems of coordination, exchange and ordering – whatever form they may take, whatever values and priorities they pursue. Since both modes of integration are essential, how they coexist, interpenetrate and act upon one another are critical questions for the maintenance of social and functional integration and cohesion.

In late capitalist societies, in Habermas' analysis, it is always systems that precipitate disequilibrium between the two modes of integration. 'Uncoupling' occurs when the lifeworld becomes reduced to just another subsystem alongside the subsystems of power and money:

> systems mechanisms get further and further detached from the social structures through which social integration takes place. ... modern societies attain a level of system differentiation at which increasingly autonomous organisations are connected with one another ... systemic mechanisms – for example, money – steer a social intercourse that has been largely disconnected from norms

and values, above all in those subsystems of purposive rational economic and administrative action that ... have become independent of their moral-political foundations.

At the same time, the lifeworld remains the subsystem and defines the pattern of the social system as a whole. Thus systemic mechanisms need to be anchored in the lifeworld: they have to be institutionalised ... But in modern societies, economic and bureaucratic spheres emerge in which social relations are regulated only via money and power. Norm-conformative attitudes and identity-forming social memberships are neither necessary nor possible in these spheres; they are made peripheral instead. (Habermas, 1981/1987, p 154)

This isolation of systems from the norms and values around which lifeworld practices and behaviours cohere is a critical facet of uncoupling, as 'the social system definitively bursts out of the horizon of the lifeworld, [and] escapes from the intuitive knowledge of everyday communicative practice' (Habermas, 1981/1987, p 173).

In the capitalist stage of modernisation, this uncoupling seems to have profoundly adverse effects, in the form of 'a deformation, a reification of the symbolic structures of the lifeworld and the imperatives of subsystems differentiated out via money and power and rendered self-sufficient' (Habermas, 1981/1987, p 283).

This manifests itself in various forms as the domination of systems over lifeworlds. Habermas (1981/1987, p 345) argues that under the internal logic of capitalism, the lifeworld is not permitted to place restrictions on the optimum working of the economic system, the functional necessities of which come to dominate technicising norms, so that subsystems 'penetrate ever deeper into the symbolic reproduction of the lifeworld' (p 367). He also emphasises the continuous growth of the monetary-bureaucratic complex, especially 'where socially integrated contexts of life are redefined around the roles of consumer and client and assimilated to systemically integrated domains of action' (p 351).

Habermas (1981/1987, p 356) draws attention to the particular preconditions under which economy and state working in concert, 'intervene with monetary and bureaucratic means in the symbolic reproduction of the lifeworld'. These preconditions are met when the structural components of the lifeworld are themselves becoming dismantled as a result of being increasingly differentiated in ways that inhibit processes of integration. Importantly, the key elements of these components are the *culture* of the lifeworld's societal forms and the *personalities* of its subjects. As the relations of exchange between the subsystem and lifeworld come to be regulated through highly differentiated processes that correspond to differentiated roles in the lifeworld, another axis of integration is eroded.

One example of this is how some forms of labour are rewarded in ways that provide trade-offs against the social rewards of time and money – for example, some state-provided welfare that is intended to offset the detrimental effects of unemployment. This drives those affected *out of participation*, and removes hopes of self-realisation and self-determination. 'Successful' citizens settle for the trade-offs of consumerism as compensations for the fractured elements of their lifeworld, while the 'unsuccessful' are denied access to many of those compensations, and are instead 'canalised into those roles' as clients of the welfare system (Habermas, 1981/1987, p 356).

This aspect of how systems colonise lifeworlds is of central relevance to the analysis that follows, and it builds on three strands of Habermas' theorisation. The first concerns the ill-effects of systems' domination over the lifeworld that result from the erosions and failures of the social reproduction of the lifeworld. The second concerns the centrality of the welfare state to managing these effects. The third concerns the subjection of particular conducts to newly created laws that become an essential feature of the interventions of the welfare state.

## Idiographic effects of the erosions of social reproduction

Habermas is schematically precise and categorically specific about the ways in which the colonisation of the lifeworld by systems creates disturbances that erode the powers of social integration and reproduction of the lifeworld. This occurs across three domains and three structural components that are captured in Figure 6.1. At the point of intersection of these domains and their corresponding components, disturbances in cultural reproduction result in loss of meaning. This is because the organic processes of the construction of shared meaning in the lifeworld are unsettled by the priorities and values of dominant colonising systems. As a result, shared understandings lose legitimacy and reach, interpretive schemes fail, and shared knowledges weaken as they lose contact with their commonly held rationalities. By the same logic, disturbances in the domain of social integration unsettle collective identity and produce anomic effects at the societal level, and alienation at the individual level. Consequently, social solidarity weakens. In parallel, the negative effects of disturbed socialisation also weaken traditions and undermine motivations that constitute the fabric of social integration at the cultural and societal levels. Most importantly for the discussions that follow, these socially degenerative changes result in what Habermas describes in terms of psycho-pathologies in individuals who experience the forces of disturbance and the erosions of inclusive social integration and shared meanings.

It is particularly instructive to read across the 'Socialisation' domain and down the 'Person' component cells of Figure 6.1. Significantly, failures of tradition (which reside in culture), and of motivation (which reside in societal contexts), combine with the 'Crisis in orientation and education' and personal alienation effects of eroded integration and psychopathological effects, *to diminish the social responsibility of individuals so affected.*[4]

**Figure 6.1:** Manifestations of crisis when reproduction processes are disturbed (pathologies)

| Structural components / Disturbances in the domain of | Culture | Society | Person | Dimension of evaluation |
|---|---|---|---|---|
| Cultural reproduction | Loss of meaning | Withdrawal of legitimation | Crisis in orientation and education | Rationality of knowledge |
| Social integration | Unsettling of collective identity | Anomie | Alienation | Solidarity of members |
| Socialisation | Rupture of tradition | Withdrawal of motivation | Psycho-pathologies | Personal responsibility |

Source: Habermas (1981/1987), Figure 22

Throughout his text, Habermas refers to multiple further implications of the erosion of lifeworld domains at the *idiographic level*. The origins of much of Habermas' thinking in phenomenology, in the philosophy of consciousness, and about the centrality of the semantic to communicative action combine to place *individuals, as actors and personalities*, at the centre of some aspects of his analysis. Individual actors are rarely out of sight even when he is most preoccupied with nomothetic aspects of the development of his social theory. As a result, Habermas affords emphasis to the effects of systems colonisation of the lifeworld on *personality and individual actors*. This perspective finds its strongest expression in the concluding section of his treatise:

> We can represent the replacement of steering crises [within systems] with lifeworld pathologies as follows: anomic conditions are avoided, and legitimations and motivations important for maintaining institutional orders are secured at the expense of, and through the ruthless exploitation of, other resources. Culture and personality come under attack for the sake of warding off crises and stabilising society ... The consequences of this substitution can be seen in Figure [6.1]: instead of manifestations of anomie (and instead of the withdrawal of legitimation and motivation in place of anomie), *phenomena of alienation and the unsettling of collective identity emerge.* I have traced such phenomena back to a colonisation of the lifeworld and characterised them as a reification of the communicative practice of everyday life. (Habermas, 1981/1987, p 386, emphasis added)

The lean, crisp brevity of this quote is a powerful assertion that pressures on the lifeworld are routinely applied to accommodate the needs of the subsystems of money and power. Individual actors and their identifying personalities are described as 'other resources' available for 'ruthless exploitation' to ward off crises in the interstices between overriding systems demands, and their ready accommodation within lifeworlds. The implied brutality of imposing burdens and tensions on the personalities of individuals has particular and substantial consequences for the welfare state and the subjection of everyday practices to legal stricture, within and beyond its ambit, as later sections will elaborate.

## Constructing a Habermasian interpretation of non-participation

Some of the developments described in Chapters Two to Five exemplify Habermas' propositions about the consequences of the colonisation of lifeworlds by subsystems very well. It is possible to render an account of non-participation that 'reads off' directly from Habermas' theory of colonisation. Point by point, the experiences of many non-participant young people illustrate the processes of colonisation and destabilisation he describes. First, as the demands of systems begin to dominate the lifeworld, communicative action fails to precede instrumental action, such that inhabitants of the lifeworld are inadequately apprised of the purposes and methods of the operation of the economy. In respect of young people who are unable to obtain paid work, it is exceedingly difficult for them to be interpellated by an economic system in which they have no place in employment, and in which the maximisation of profit takes precedence over the employment of would-be workers. Shared meanings are said to lose legitimacy in these circumstances, in ways that correspond closely to the *'unfathomable rationalities' which result in the detachment of young people from employment*, and hold them partially responsible for their own exclusion.

Second, as a result of the observed loss of meaning and understanding, in response, actors are said to behave in irrational ways in respect of their own self-interest. They may resist passively or actively, or cease to make the expected responses which dominant values regarded as rational. This is a close match with young people's non-participation *and their allegedly non-responsible and disengaged behaviours.*

Third, as structural components of the lifeworld are partially dismantled as a result of monetary and bureaucratic interventions, the key components most directly affected are said to be the culture of the lifeworld and the personalities of its subjects. This is of particular relevance here because it stresses idiographic levels of analysis. Although it is principally structural changes that affect personality, it is at the personal level that these experiences are most clearly manifested. Put differently, recurrent instantiations of non-participation match Habermas' observations that disturbances in the domain of social integration have anomic effects at the societal level while also causing individual alienation. Importantly, *idiographic and nomothetic factors are deeply entwined and intermeshed in producing these effects.* Both collective and personal individual identity are said to be unsettled.

Fourth, and flowing from this, many of the studies referred to earlier report the adverse effects of unemployment and the absence of adequately remunerated work on the morale, motivation and mental wellbeing of non-participants. These are, in effect, what Habermas classifies as psychopathologies and result from the subordination of communicative action (understanding) to instrumental action (adapting to the demands of economy or political power). In the context of non-participation, *such outcomes are likely to encompass the personalisation of failure, in the form of either self-blame or interventions that imply past shortcomings, corresponding with the central precepts of the disengagement discourse.*

Fifth, Habermas' account of the uncompromising imposition of economic and bureaucratic requirements on the lifeworld produces such levels of erosion of social integration and, ultimately, the diminution and loss of social solidarities and cohesion, as to pose significant threats to the social order in ways that might adversely affect systems of money and power. *As the 'ruthless exploitation' of resources of cultural and interpersonal cohesion and identity occurs for the sake of 'warding off crises', the risks to social order become significant.* Applied to contemporary circumstances, there could be no more succinct analysis of the forms of social unrest described in the previous chapter.

So far, then, the cogency of Habermas' analysis for explaining the sources, manifestations and consequences of non-participation is striking. A review of his analysis of the place of the welfare state and the use of law introduces another cogent dimension of the colonisation of lifeworlds by systems.

### The welfare state and juridification

Habermas (1981/1987, pp 347-8) argues that:

> the social-welfare state is supposed to head off immediately negative effects on the lifeworld of the capitalistically organised occupational system, as well as the dysfunctional side-effects thereupon of economic growth that is steered through capital accumulation, and it is supposed to do so without encroaching upon the organisational form, the structure or the drive mechanism of economic production.

In relation to paid employment, the provisions of the welfare state are said to have minimised conflicts over distribution and curtailed their explosive power (Habermas, 1981/1987, pp 349-50). But this also creates dilemmas and contradictions:

while the welfare-state guarantees are intended to serve the goal of social integration, they nevertheless promote the disintegration of life-relations when these are separated, through legalised social intervention, from the consensual mechanisms that coordinate action and are transferred over to media such as power and money. (Habermas, 1981/1987, p 364)

In this sense, the welfare state is itself a source of destabilisation and disempowerment of the pre-existing dispositions and everyday acts of solidarity that once secured and reinforced the socially integrative capacities of the lifeworld.

Habermas deploys the familiar argument that the introduction of state welfare programmes is an unavoidable response to the inability to transfer the essential capacities for social reproduction located in the lifeworld into an environment in which systems considerations dominate. It is therefore to be expected that 'the changeover from social to system integration would take the form of juridification processes' (Habermas, 1981/1987, p 357). In such processes, the reach of law is extended into routine domains of social life to make good the effects of the dwindling forces of social integration. Juridification drives the continuing advance of the boundaries of legitimate intervention of the welfare state. Hence, Habermas (1981/1987, p 362) argues that the juridification of the risks of everyday life 'exacts a noteworthy price in the form of restructuring interventions in the lifeworlds of those who are so entitled'. For him, it is the introduction of *conditionality* into such interventions that is particularly '"foreign" to social relations, and to social causes, dependencies and needs' (p 362).

Habermas' interpretations of the welfare state, the increasing juridification of everyday practices, and the needs of individuals who have been adversely affected by the prioritised demands of economy and polity map onto one another in important ways. State-provided welfare is established as the principal mechanism for the amelioration of a range of damage and losses to social integration caused by the money system, when securing its priorities of continuing accumulation. This form of welfare, with significant elements of redistribution from the productive economy to its casualties, depends on a range of administrative systems to function effectively. In turn, securing the operationalisation of these systems to minimise their financial burden on the productive economy and guard them against fraud and exploitation depends on the juridification of more and more aspects of their activity. Consequently, the interventions of welfare states in people's lives,

Habermas proposes, further disrupt aspects of social integration and sources of solidarity and social cohesion in the lifeworld.

Such interventions have to be achieved using juridificatory extensions of the powers of civil law, where welfare provision is made conditional upon specified actions. In turn, the application of law in support of welfare policy risks producing Habermas' 'pathological' side effects which may themselves establish a need for a range of therapeutic interventions. The defining processes of juridification entail a sometimes continuous extension of the reach of civil law in pursuit of minute interventions of state administration.

## Young people, welfare and disjuncture in Habermas' social theory

During periods of major economic expansion, the almost perpetual advance of the welfare system was contingent on regular extensions to the juridificatory power of the state. In the UK, an increasing number of entitlements were established during that period, and the limits of entitlement were legally defined and actively monitored. But how is this to operate in periods of 'austerity' like those of the global financial crisis (GFC)? If recessions in the money system result in increases in alienation and withdrawal in the lifeworld, then the net demands on the welfare system exacerbate fiscal strain when it is already at critical levels.

The typical response is either to contain or retract entitlement and to increase the vigour with which it is policed, as the changes in welfare provision for young people described in Chapter Three illustrate. The retraction of state benefits from young people during the GFC exemplifies Habermas' theory of the colonisation of the lifeworld by the world of systems.

Policy changes like these match many of Habermas' descriptors of crisis, as represented in Figure 6.1. In the domain of cultural reproduction, a significant element of legitimation was weakened by the retraction of entitlement. In the domain of social integration, a formative moment of young people's development as responsible independent adults was disturbed. In terms of their socialisation, a significant source of motivation was removed. In the dominant discourse, this is the moment when young people as 'social actors' become disengaged. The logic of why they should undertake menial work under the guise of training in return for allowances that are inadequate to sustain them becomes unfathomable. Unable to 'engage with' the rationale (in Habermas' terms, to take instrumental action), or to identify and act on its purpose (that is, to take communicative action), young people's willingness to participate becomes corroded and eroded. They become alienated and unable to locate themselves meaningfully in the lifeworld. The axis of connection and coherence between the world of systems and the lifeworld becomes fragmented and eventually fractured.

Habermas' brief application of his own analytical frame to the lifeworlds of the family, schooling and pedagogy provides another illuminating – but contestable – perspective on non-participation among young people. As forms of social integration in the lifeworld give way to major shifts in systems demands, the temporal disjunctures that follow are, he suggests, likely to be most acutely felt by those who were socialised under one set of relations between systems and lifeworld, but emerge as adolescents in pursuit of adult independence in another.

Ideally, 'the socialisation of the members of the lifeworld ensures that newly arising situations are connected up with existing situations … [through] the acquisition of generalised competencies for action' (Habermas, 1981/1987, p 141). But major changes like those triggered by the GFC mean that the demands of the money system weaken or undermine parents' understanding of what is expected of families, schools and young people as future employees and responsible, self-sufficient citizens. Parental understanding lags behind what their children will experience as pupils, students and trainees.

Also typical of these changes is what Habermas (1981/1987, p 371) terms 'the economic system-imperative to uncouple the school system from the fundamental right to education and to close-circuit it with the employment system'. He argues that juridification has already limited the curricular initiative of the teacher in favour of the 'systemic imperatives of economic and administrative subsystems growing with dynamics of their own' (p 373).

This results in a significant *disjuncture* between what was expected of parents in school, and what will be expected of their children and those who teach them. One facet of this concerns what Habermas terms 'the growing significance of adolescent crises':

> The problem of detaching oneself from the family and forming one's own identity have in any case turned adolescent development … into a critical test for the ability of the coming generation to connect up with the preceding one. When the conditions of socialisation in the family are no longer functionally in tune with the organisational membership conditions that the growing child will one day have to meet, *the problems that young people have to*

*solve in their adolescence become insoluble for more and more of them.* One indication of this is the social and even political significance that *youth protest and withdrawal cultures* have gained since the end of the 1960s. (Habermas, 1981/1987, p 388, emphases added)

These comments on young people's entitlements with regard to welfare, schooling and youth cultures, and on changing expectations of young people, were remarkably prescient of C21st neoliberal societies and political economies. Habermas anticipated the vocationalisation of education and the expectations that young people would be more instrumentally prepared for work, not only in terms of their qualifications, skills and behaviours, but also in terms of their dispositions as compliant and competitive-collaborative workers. The unfolding eventualities of the last three decades and the fallout from the GFC along the lines described in Chapter Five are a close match to Habermas' analysis.

Much of what was described in Chapters Two to Five can be explained in terms of the strident imposition of the structural subsystems' demands on the lifeworld as it affects young people. Habermas' analysis goes some way to providing a coherent analysis of non-participation, in terms of the increasing need for welfare interventions, the claimed public financial constraints on addressing that need, the extension of civil law to manage the consequences, and even the diminishing capacity of many parents to anticipate the demands that will be made of their children, particularly towards the end of their school careers.

## Systems-induced pathologies in the lifeworld

Despite these high claims for Habermas' analysis, there is much that eludes it. His accounts of the underlying causes of adolescent discontent, withdrawal and non-participation at the level of the idiographic rely heavily on the concept of pathology and on psychoanalytic and psychotherapeutic interpretations. Habermas is primarily concerned with social forms of pathology which, drawing on Weber, he glosses as 'symptoms of a distorted everyday practice' (Habermas, 1981/1981, p 327). By this definition, social pathology is shorthand for the most adverse effects on individuals of the imposition of the money and power systems on the lifeworld – and so is primarily exogenous in nature. Pathologies in the lifeworld are said to arise when 'disturbances in the material reproduction of the lifeworld take the form of stubborn systemic disequilibria' (Habermas, 1981/1981, p 385). The mismatch of parental socialisation with the changing priorities of schooling and employment is a tangible example of such disequilibria – as the quotation from Habermas (p 385) with which this chapter began explains.

Habermas (1981/1987, p 385) also argues that in critical instances, disturbances of material reproduction may have to be resolved 'by having recourse to lifeworld resources' – that is by addressing shortfalls in the economy or in state power by making additional demands upon a range of human resources that are normally managed in households. In such cases, social pathologies become manifested in anomic responses, loss of legitimation, and protest and withdrawal, as the opening quotation indicates. The latter is most likely to occur when demands on the resources of the lifeworld take the form of ruthless exploitation, in which social stabilisation is given priority regardless of unsettling and alienating effects.[5] These conditions appear to be nothing more than expressions of intense discontent. They are pathological only in the sense that they are at variance with prevailing priorities. They describe conflict more than damage.

Habermas' use of the concepts of psychopathology is more problematic. Psychopathology normally refers to (quasi-)clinical conditions and describes abnormal mental states, often regarded as hereditary. Although they may be products of abuse or maltreatment, exogenous and environmental causes of psychopathology are notoriously difficult to demonstrate, requiring high standards of proof.[6]

Perhaps surprisingly, it is in relation to state welfare that Habermas is most explicit about the psychopathological needs that arise as a result of systems-induced disturbances in the lifeworld. In a penetrating critique of the contradictions of welfare interventions in response to such disturbances, Habermas observes that the ambivalent nature of the welfare state:

> can be seen with particular clarity in the paradoxical consequences of the social services offered via the therapeutocracy ... [including] the newer psychotherapeutic and group-dynamic forms of support, pastoral care and the building of religious groups, *from youth work, public education and the health system* through *general preventative measures of every type.* (Habermas, 1981/1987, pp 363-4, emphasis added)[7]

Elsewhere, recurrent references to therapeutic interventions bolster the impression of the need to respond to damaged individual lives at the level of the psychopathological, but they do little to elaborate on the connection. Psychoanalytic theories typically assert the existence of a priori individualised psychological causes of social problems. Constructing the psychoanalytic as a critical point of articulation between political-economic effects and individual behaviour risks feeding claims of dysfunctionality and personal failure that deny wider social, economic and political causes of resistance, withdrawal and non-participation. Aspects of this approach have disturbing resonances with oppressive claims and prognoses of the disengagement discourse and its account of non-participation in Chapter Two.

The great core strength of Habermas' social theory is the pioneering approach he adopted by co-analysing systems and lifeworlds. By means of an encompassing integrative analysis of both, he made a major contribution to social analysis uninhibited by distinctions between nomothetic and idiographic levels of analysis. For him, it was only possible to understand the operation and strength of the grand structures of subsystems of money and power in the context of their relationship to the lifeworld. This relationship fundamentally shapes and influences what it is possible to achieve by means of those subsystems, and how they shape the lifeworld.

By adopting this approach, Habermas displayed an exceptional readiness to work across the lines of division between exogenous and endogenous factors as co-determinants of the ways in which human agency in the lifeworld can fashion the capacity of systems and power to achieve alternative objectives, just as much as those subsystems succeed in colonising the lifeworld only by adapting under duress. While the power of structures and systems in this analysis remains superordinate, they constantly adjust their primary objectives.

The great limitation of Habermas' analysis is its construction of the disruptive effects of subsystems on individuals and their behaviour as systems colonise and uncouple the lifeworld. His focus on the concepts of anomie and alienation are appropriate attempts to capture the personal effects of systems disruption of the lifeworld, and their consequences of loss of meaning and debilitation of communicative action. But his analysis risks focusing too much on issues grounded in the idiographic, especially when he classifies acts of passive withdrawal, resistance, refusal and disengagement as pathologies. The essential flaw of this is *its implicit propensity to identify endogenous factors as critical to the inherent conflict between systems and lifeworld, as though they emanated entirely from within (decontextualised) individuals, their personalities, predispositions and conducts.* These, it appears, are to be understood idiographically, as though they were pre-ordained 'givens'.

## Section 2: Imogen Tyler: revolting subjects and social abjection

Considerably more sophisticated interpretations and applications of these idiographic levels of analysis than those adopted by Habermas now interpret the kinds of alienation, withdrawal, resistance, refusal and non-participation that arise from the demands of subsystems on the lifeworld. Imogen Tyler's work is an eminent example. Her analysis includes dedicated attention to the lives of young people at the critical junctures of conflict, disconnection and fracture in which their attempts to adhere to requirements falter or fail. Her analysis turns on the concept of social abjection. The dictionary defines abjection as 'the action or an act of casting down, humbling or degrading; an act of abasement' (OED online, 2012). Tyler defines the social abject, the central focus of her analysis, as 'one who repeatedly finds herself the object of the other's violent objectifying disgust' (Tyler, 2013, p 4). In her analysis, social abjection variously constitutes a conceptual paradigm (p 3), a theory of power, subjugation and resistance (p 4), and a concept forged from imperialist ideologies (p 35). It is an inherently psychosocial and psychoanalytic concept, at the heart of which is the concept of disgust, initially following the anthropological work of Mary Douglas (1966/2003), but then extensively developed in psychoanalysis and psychosocial studies.[8]

Tyler's most relevant chapter in this context, 'The kids are revolting' (2013), takes as its point of departure the English riots of August 2011 and the marginalised and impoverished young people whom she dubs 'revolting subjects'. Characterised in Tyler's powerful description in the quotes with which this chapter began (p 198, p 204), they are the stylised workless young 'NEET' members of a supposed underclass, and the epitome of the 'chav'.[9] In Tyler's interpretation, they exhibit many of the characteristic stigmatised features of other social abjects: 'the social insecurity generated by neoliberal governmentality has given rise to novel modes of (re-)classification – refugees transformed into bogus asylum seekers, unemployed young people into feckless chavs, people with disabilities into welfare cheats' (Tyler, 2013, p 211).

Tyler's central concerns are with the ways in which young people, among others, become socially abject; with the underpinning psychosocial processes of abjection; with the cultural forms that invite abjection; with the forms of (classed) naming associated with abjection; and with the ways in which abjection demonstrates the continuing centrality of social class. Poverty, unemployment, job insecurity and the persistent pressures of workfare programmes are all present throughout

Tyler's account – albeit these features appear more as settings for the psychosocial processes of young people's social abjection than as the driving forces of their oppression.

For Tyler it was in the riots, in Brixton and Toxteth in the UK in 1981, in the Paris *banlieues* of 2005, and in the English riots of August 2011 that the sources and conditions of social abjection affecting a wide range of young people were made transparent. For the 2011 riots, she affords full emphasis to the importance of unemployment as a source of invisibility, alienation, frustration and abandonment (Tyler, 2013, p 197). She draws particular attention to 'a displacement of liberal understandings of citizenship, as a universal status that offers rights and protections, by categories of "active" and "earned" citizenship' (pp 197-8); to evidence of the high proportion of non-participants among the rioters, characterised as those for whom 'everyday life is shaped by a crisis of possibility' (p 198); to loss of services and reduced financial support for participation in post-compulsory education and training; and to 'diminished aspirations and little hope [revealing] not a culture of anti-work, but a lack of expectations born out of experience' (p 200).

She concludes that:

> the representation of the riots entrenches and legitimises the perceptual frame of the underclass and further stigmatises the impoverished communities from which the vast majority of rioters came ... *[They] became the abjects they had been told they were.* (Tyler, 2013, p 204, emphasis added)

Although Tyler's interpretations are rooted in psychosocial analysis, her committedly interdisciplinary approach insists on the centrality of class to an understanding of social abjection, and makes strong reference to processes of governance and the centrality of neoliberalism to an interpretation of the intensification of social abjection. The key point of articulation between the psychosocial nature of social abjection and other aspects of its social, political and cultural contexts is constructed around theories of governmentality. At points, social abjection is described as 'a mode of governmentality' (Tyler, 2013, p 21). The concept of 'hygienic governmentality' extends this to a range of images of cleansing and purging. And this in turn provides the point of intersection with the state, neoliberalism and government, and what Tyler (2013, p 5) describes as her offer to provide a *'thick* social and cultural account of neoliberalism as a form of governance – concentrating in particular on the mechanisms through which public consent is procured for policies and practices that effect inequalities and fundamentally corrode democracy'.

For Tyler, the social stigmatisation and cleansing of the *banlieues* captures this point of intersection between state power and methods of social abjection. In response to the 2005 riots, President Sarkozy described young rioters as *racaille*, which Tyler (2013, p 38) interprets as 'sub-human, inherently evil and criminal'. [10] The state is of central importance in this context, when Tyler (2013, p 46) argues that 'social abjection is an inhabited interpretive frame through which to examine neoliberal practices of state-making because ... *state power is constituted through exclusion*' (emphasis added). For Tyler, understanding the political oppression of the state against its vilified and stigmatised minorities depends upon an understanding of the concept of social abjection. The pertinence of her work to interpreting non-participation and its relationship to crime needs no further elaboration.

## Section 3: Reinterpreting non-participation

This chapter began by drawing attention to the lines of division between studies that place the personal, the psychosocial and the idiographic at the centre of their analysis; and those that prioritise social, political and/or economic structures and the nomothetic. The conflicted paradigms that this separation represents constitute elements of a much wider set of divisions in the social sciences – many of which delegitimise and 'screen out' conflicting lines of enquiry and analysis in ways that impoverish understanding.[11] In different and largely complementary ways Habermas and Tyler resist these lines of division. As a result, their work opens up important points of entry across them.

Habermas' work is celebrated for the encompassing erudition of its approach to developing a framework for theorisation that connects and integrates political–economic phenomena (via his attention to systems) with social processes (via his attention to the lifeworld). In itself, the systems–lifeworld duality blurs divisions between nomothetic and idiographic levels of analysis. It focuses on the ways systems and lifeworld interact, and to what effects. The lifeworld is also fundamentally concerned with individual actors and the ways in which the processes of communicative action connect and bind them, and secure social integration. Habermas' analysis of the manifestations of crisis in the lifeworld identifies systems effects that are one-way impositions of the demands of one element on the other, and the harms they cause. But the processes of colonisation and uncoupling that he describes are interpreted dialectically in at least two respects.

First, the adverse consequences of crisis act back on systems in the form of the welfare needs of its casualties, imposing significant costs on systems. Second, these consequences impact on individuals and limit their capacities to function but they also produce reactions of resistance and protest – notably among young people. Nevertheless, Habermas' core theory gives little attention to powers of individual and collective agency outside of formal processes.

This is one of the limitations of Habermas' analysis, which is in part offset by Tyler's. It concerns the personal and psychic processes of social abjection, whereby those affected 'become abjects'. They are the starting point and the principal objects of her analysis. The distinctive product of her approach has been to strengthen, enrich and diversify the lines of analytical connection between the idiographic and the nomothetic. However, her thesis is weakened by a lack of clarity about the nature of the articulation between the two – itself rooted in the limited attention given to the political-economic drivers of neoliberalism, and the nature and sources of processes of governmentalism.

Tyler and Habermas have traversed important lines of paradigmatic division in their work, and in doing so they have opened up points of entry that endeavour to accommodate analyses from different traditions. In different respects, though, there are shortcomings in their trans-paradigmatic excursions. On the face of it, Habermas' lie in his uncritical use of the notion of pathology, but this is in some measure made good in Tyler's work on social abjection. The shortcomings of Tyler's analysis concern the integration and consolidation of the relevance of neoliberal governmentality to her analysis, although aspects of Habermas' analysis make good on this issue.

In terms of these compensating complementarities, and much more broadly as well, viewed conjointly, the work of Habermas and Tyler opens scope for a reinterpretation of the nature of non-participation among young people and, to some extent, its relevance to crime. The earlier interim assessment of Habermas' coverage summarised its distinctive contribution in relation to loss of meaning and understanding in the lifeworld, to the forms of passive resistance it provokes, to the anomic and alienating effects of eroded social integration, to the personalisation of failure, and to the consequential risks of social unrest. His analysis of the effects of the retraction of welfare provision from young people and the related degradation of connections between systems and lifeworld add an important dimension of reinterpretation. So too does Habermas' analysis of the effects of disjunctures in the intra-familial socialisation of young people.

Tyler's depiction of the ways in which young non-participants are corralled into social abjection, alongside adult welfare dependants and the imagined underclasses of particular racialised and disabled groups and locations is vivid and visceral. The power of these processes to reposition victims as authors of their own oppression, well attuned to being interpellated by derogatory discursive naming, adds a powerful dimension for the reinterpretation of the passivity that apparently characterises much non-participation. Tyler's insights compensate for the limitations of Habermas' attempts to cement the connection between systems and lifeworld. They render fresh accounts and a new analysis of the ways in which young people tolerate and absorb their own denigration as 'disengaged'. And they add new dimensions to understanding of the overwhelming power of systems over lifeworlds.

The combined work of Habermas and Tyler also defines powerful possibilities for reinterpreting the relationship of non-participation to crime. The complementarities of their paradigm-traversing approaches already indicate an important direction for future interpretation and research. In addition to problematising divisions, their analyses define and demand greater attention to the interactions between cognitive and affective (and rational and emotional) elements of young people's responses to non-participation. This in turn opens up reanalyses of claims about young people's rational choices in response to grossly restricted possibilities, and of the problematic separation of instrumental versus expressive interpretations of criminal responses.

Habermas' and Tyler's work also emphasises some critical concepts that are almost entirely absent from the analyses reviewed in Chapters Two to Five. Governance is central to both their theories. Criminalisation is (briefly) explicit in Tyler's work, and heavily implicit in the importance Habermas attaches to juridification. All three concepts should be central to a reinterpretation of non-participation and crime among young people. They are the subjects of the next two chapters.

**Notes**

[1] The work on the legitimation crisis is Habermas (1976). On these wider observations see, for example, Finlayson (2005); Outhwaite (2009).

[2] Habermas' analysis draws on the work of Talcott Parsons (1957) which recognised the ways in which conflicts can 'call into play mechanisms that save the integration of an action system only at the cost of social or individual pathologies' (Habermas, 1981/1987, p 229).

[3] The concept of lifeworld is derived from the founding phenomenological theories of Edmund Husserl (1970), but it has a wide range of uses in Habermas' work that cluster around the common shared worlds of everyday understanding, meaning,

reason and communication that hold social groupings together, underpin their actions and constitute a common basis for shared development.

[4] See Habermas (1981/1987, pp 141-4) and the associated Figures 21-3 for a fuller exposition.

[5] See the indented quote from Habermas (p 386) in the section above (entitled 'Idiographic effects of the erosions of social reproduction'), beginning: 'We can represent the replacement of steering crises...' (p 153).

[6] One paragraph of Habermas' two volumes is devoted to psychoanalysis, regarding intersubjectivity, object relations, ego psychology and defence mechanisms as central to developing understanding of pathogenesis (Habermas, 1981/1987, p 389).

[7] The centrality of preventative measures to policies that seek to address mass non-participation (especially in its relationship to crime) are familiar in the shape of the risk factor analyses and targeting set out in Chapter Four. Their importance to a reinterpretation of non-participation will be evident in Chapters Seven and Eight.

[8] The starting points of Tyler's exposition also draw on the work of Bataille (1934/1993) and Arendt (1958).

[9] An acronym for 'Council-Housed and Violent' or 'Council-House-Associated Vermin' (Tyler, 2013, p 162).

[10] The literal translation of *racaille* is 'rabble, riff-raff' (Knox (ed), 1986, p 308).

[11] This highly schematic division is cross-cut by other binaries that counterpose the material and culture, ideology and discourse, and government and governance. And while there are strong consonances between the material, ideology, government and structuralist analyses, and between culture, discourse, governance and the poststructural, it would be simplistic and reductionist to represent them as simple consolidated binary clusters across the social sciences.

# SEVEN

# Theorising the non-participation–crime relationship

Since crime does not exist as a stable entity, the crime concept is well suited to all sorts of control purposes. It is like a sponge. The term can absorb a lot of acts – and people – when external circumstances make that useful. But it can also be brought to reduce its content, whenever suitable for those with a hand on the sponge. This understanding opens up for new questions. It opens up for a discussion of when enough is enough. It paves the way for a discussion of what is a suitable amount of crime.

*Nils Christie (2002) A suitable amount of crime, pp ix-x*

## Introduction

This chapter explores the complementary possibilities of the work of Habermas and Tyler for reinterpreting non-participation and its relationship to crime among young people. It begins by reflecting on how empirical work on that relationship has clustered around instrumental and expressive motivations for crime, and on how aspects of Habermas' and Tyler's analyses add to understanding it. The possibilities and limitations of these approaches are then tested by two case studies that highlight complexities that both utilise and test the scope of Habermas' and Tyler's analyses. Sections 2 and 3 then consider how theories of governance and theories of 'governing through crime' that utilise and extend Habermas' and Tyler's approaches can provide a reinterpretation of the non-participation–crime relationship.

The majority of explorations of the non-participation–crime relationship have produced findings and analyses influenced by or directly aligned with instrumental or expressive motivations. And, as the Interlude between Parts Two and Three made clear, elements of these motivations are more readily associated either with nomothetic levels of analysis and exogenous factors of analysis, or with idiographic levels of analysis and endogenous factors of analysis.

Table 7.1 builds on these distinctions, and other schematic distinctions employed in earlier chapters. It is primarily intended to provide an overview of the range of distinctions that have been made up to this point, to draw attention to a number of congruences that have been identified in previous chapters, and to highlight some of the possible associations they might imply. Beginning with the 'levels/factors of analysis' distinctions schematised in the Table in the Interlude, it maps them against the two dominant analytical traditions of youth studies, the theoretical approaches of Habermas and Tyler, and the dominant policy responses that emerge from and are associated with both.

It is of course crucial to recognise that typologies of this kind are, as Chapter One stressed, heuristic constructs devised for the purposes of ordering diverse analyses of complex related social phenomena. The

**Table 7.1:** Foci of analysis – motivation for crime – theorists – policy responses

| | Dominant focus of analysis | Structures | Individuals |
|---|---|---|---|
| **Foci of analysis** | Principal level of analysis | Nomothetic | Idiographic |
| | Dominant factors of analysis | Exogenous | Endogenous |
| **Motivation for crime** | Dominant analytical tradition | Youth transitions | Youth cultural studies |
| | Dominant drivers of criminal activity | Instrumental | Expressive |
| | Principal domain of motivation | Cognition and action | Emotion and affect |
| | Principal drivers of action/agency | Objectivity and rational choice | Subjectivity and expression |
| | Sources of motivation | Material gain | Meaning and interaction |
| **Theorists** | Lead academic theorist | Jürgen Habermas | Imogen Tyler |
| | Political-economic context of analysis | Late capitalism | Neoliberalism |
| | Leading focus of theorisation | Systems colonisation of lifeworld | Social abjection and stigmatisation |
| | Trans-binary foci of analysis | Alienation and psycho-pathologies | Neoliberal governmentalisation |
| **Policy responses** | Dominant policy orientation | Institutional/social | Individual/personal |
| | Response to failures of social integration | Welfare intervention Financial compensation | Marginalisation Therapeutic intervention |
| | Response to norm infraction | Juridification Legal sanction | Criminalisation Behaviour modification |

binary nature of these interpretive clusters runs the constant risk of concealing or ignoring nuances, ambivalences and ambiguities within analyses, as well as further distinctions between them. Nonetheless, few of the studies referred to in Chapters Four and Five defy broad categorisation within the binary sets described here. Equally, there is an implicit risk of over-interpreting the alignments of the superordinate categories in this mapping, which appear to co-classify structural foci of analysis with the youth studies tradition, the work of Habermas and institutional/social policy orientations on one side; and individualist foci of analysis, the youth cultural studies tradition, Tyler's theories and individual/personal policy orientations on the other. These associations are at best loose, incomplete and qualified. One of the principal attractions of the theoretical approaches of Habermas and Tyler is their partial refusal of these boundaries. But the defining bases on which their analyses are constructed are unmistakable and irrefutable. These and the many other alignments implied in Table 7.1 are, to repeat, heuristic, not analytic. They offer guidance, highlight possible connections and moot axes of association for critical assessment: they are never either determining or definitive.

## Section 1: Theories of non-participation and crime

Analyses of the relationship between unemployment and crime that focus on the 'economic causes of crime' (ECC) thesis have been dominated by rational choice theories and instrumental interpretations of offending. Many of the studies considered in Chapter Four support the claim that actors' choices are based on cognitive processes of rational calculation of advantage. Meta-studies of the ECC thesis either reaffirmed the dominance of instrumental motivation (Long and Witte, 1981; Box, 1987) or signalled a balanced 'consensus of doubt' (Chiricos, 1987). Some studies that focused on young unemployed people confirmed instrumental motivations for criminal actions.[1] In Chapter Five, Cook and Zarkin (1985) claimed that recessions appeared to cause increases in robbery and burglary, and Bushway at al (2012) argued that recessionary conditions were causal in incentivising instrumental crime. These observations are consistent with the findings of numerous other studies.[2] A large number of studies also found that increased welfare provision during recessions reduced levels of financial hardship with consequential reductions in crime rates.[3]

Pursuing one of the possible alignments suggested in Table 7.1, Habermas' theory of communicative action casts some light on instrumental motivations for crime. His analysis of the effects of systems colonisation of lifeworlds focuses on 'instrumental action' – purposive action that occurs within systems like the money system, in which the most effective means to achieving predetermined ends are repeatedly recalculated. For the most part, this example refers to the pursuit of profit maximisation. Just as this form of instrumental rationality results in imposing money-system priorities on the lifeworld, so those who experience consequences like extended periods of unemployment may imitate the logics of instrumental rationality. Unemployed workers are equally able to calculate actions that will reward self-interest. When money-system priorities result in corporate decisions that show no regard for the social consequences of mass unemployment (that is, in Habermas' terminology, when 'instrumental rationality' not 'communicative rationality' has prevailed), it is difficult to make a case as to why individuals who cannot support themselves should not act with equal disregard.

Persuasive as such logics (and some of the evidence that appears to support them) may seem, it is important to recall the countervailing evidence in Chapter Five of some very low incidences of offending among unemployed young people (Flood-Page et al, 2002; Godfrey et al, 2002). Most of the 'pro-trend' studies that demonstrated an association between crime and unemployment were unable to demonstrate causality. In a number of studies in Chapters Four and Five, the association between unemployment and crime (especially in recessions) appeared to have been realised through violent (expressive) rather than property-related (instrumentally-driven) crime. Buonanno et al's (2014) cross-national study found increased murder rates and overall crime rates that were not reflected in higher robbery and burglary rates; so also the studies by Hannon and DeFronzo (1998) and Lauritsen et al (2012). However, some studies countered these findings. Buonanno et al (2014) judged their own research results to be partially anomalous, and Machin and Marie (2006) found no evidence of increases in violent crime associated with reduced welfare benefit rates.

By far the most significant studies in support of claims that crimes committed by young people are primarily expressive not instrumental are Baron's (2006, 2008). Baron commented on the tendency of studies to ignore subjective aspects of criminality, and stressed feelings of deprivation, resentment and anger emerging from his findings. His questionnaires showed that young people with a strong work ethic displayed increased anger, expressed through violent and drug-related crime – perhaps suggesting refusal of the asymmetrical and inequitable powers of employers and workers.

The limited support for claims that expressive crimes are at least as prevalent as instrumental crimes may be attributable to the dominance of quantitative methods that are unable to capture subjective responses. Tyler's use of secondary research, however, supports an interpretation of youthful revolt that helps to compensate for this possible skew. She represents manifestations of social abjection as both repository and crucible of anger and hatred. The stigmatised legions of the underclass in the shape of racialised groups, welfare dependants, 'chavs' – and NEETs – in Tyler's accounts include young people who are represented as dysfunctional, wasted, ruined and 'lost'. She presents a vivid depiction of the hatred and anger towards these groups, and the reciprocally fomented resentment, anger and hatred on the part of those who experience them. Her description of the English riots in 2011 captures both the visceral release of anger that the disorder allowed, and the ways in which emotion, affect and expression stand as highly plausible representations of how the hopelessness of long-term non-participation is realised in criminal damage and opportunistic theft.[4] Cumulative references in quotations from young people to anger, frustration, violation, alienation, abandonment, disconnection, rage and hatred are significant here in two respects. They indicate important scope for extending Habermas' underdeveloped analyses of crises of adolescence, by transposing them to an alternative paradigm which reconceptualises his problematic notion of pathologies by deploying the concept of social abjection, and understanding crises as psychosocial phenomena. Alternatively, they point to the futile incongruity of trying to juxtapose accounts of youth crime based on rationality, cognition and instrumental motivations with vividly coherent accounts that understand the relationship between social abjection and crime in terms of emotion, affect and expression.

## Beyond binaries: reinterpreting the non-participation–crime relationship

In Chapter Four, Tedeschi and Felson (1994); and Baron (2006, 2008) stressed the inseparability of instrumental and emotional motivations for domestic (and street) violence, respectively. It is not merely the co-presence of material need and anger and resentment that cross these dividing lines: recognition of the interaction between the two in young people's lived experiences of unsupported non-participation may help refine interpretations of causality. Neither study addresses that interaction, but there is much to support the claim that analyses of human behaviour that treat the cognitive and affective domains as separate determinants of action frequently falter. What triggers engagement in property crime, violent crime or other crimes in Baron's analysis remains surprisingly unclear. The precedence to be afforded either to rational action or to emotion in determining 'choices to offend' may remain unclear *because of* their inherently interactive nature.

Understanding intertwined causalities invokes the need for case-specific and context-embedded study that is the antithesis of quantitative analyses *and* of interpretive ethnographies that are devoid of political-economic context.

Shildrick et al's (2012) study, is a rare demonstration of the potential of such an approach. The 'low-pay, no-pay' economy of Teesside after the global financial crisis (GFC) is testimony to the criticality of specificities of time and place. The authors describe the prolific rise and disastrous fall of the socioeconomic profile of Teesside's industries. The experiences of the 60 adults the researchers followed were fundamentally conditioned by the persistence of high levels of unemployment (never below twice the national rate). Fundamental changes in the nature of the work offered switched from male-dominated, full-time, long-duration skilled manual work at good levels of pay to their diametric opposites.

One consequence was the development of a cyclically fast-churning labour market that produced insecurity and working poverty as much as long-term benefit-dependent unemployment. Shildrick and her colleagues' research refutes claims of intergenerational unemployment and cultures of worklessness and refines claims about the relationship between unemployment and crime. A single example epitomises the complex interaction between unemployment, work and crime, and the singular nature of people's choices in the face of all three.

Max was an ex-heroin user with a criminal record and long experience of unemployment. At the time of the study, he had a well-paid docker's job and a strong ethic against heroin and drug dealers. One brief interview extract captures complexity with great lucidity:

> Heroin and crack have done a lot of damage to this area … If I went on the dole and I couldn't handle it, it'd do my fucking head in. I couldn't be on the dole. I have to work, simple as that. So, yes, work is very, very important: an important thing in my life, my job, absolutely. I mean – touch wood – if it did happen [lose his job at the docks] I'd have to work away [from Teesside]. And if I couldn't get a job working away, I'd have to do fucking crime. I'd hate to do it. It would kill me doing it but I really would have

to do it because there is no way I could go on the dole. There's fucking no chance. I'd be suicidal. It'd fucking do me in. I wouldn't be able to do it. I mean I see some lads now and like they can't even afford to just go out and have a couple of pints. (Max, in Shildrick et al, 2012, pp 90-91)

The richness of this brief statement refines many dilemmas that earlier chapters have endeavoured to unravel. The sketchiest history of Max's life gives a clear indication of the dynamic power of the three-way relationship between work, unemployment and crime. First, add the complexities of welfare dependency and drug use, and the richness of the tensions between these elements becomes still clearer. It scarcely matters that Max's account does not establish the cause-effect relationship which led to drug dependency and crime. Of far greater importance is the interlock between the five factors. Second, it is spurious to try to establish whether unemployment caused crime or vice versa, compared with the value of understanding the drivers of Max's impassioned fear of worklessness. Third, Max's powerful expression of fear is made more remarkable by his preference for risking prison. Is his priority an income from crime as an occupation in itself that would ward off anomic tedium, or as a source of funding the social life that would help him avoid a return to heroin use? Both may apply, dialectically.

Max's comments point to rational materialist calculations of best courses of action that are nonetheless deeply intercut by emotion and contention. The rationality is palpable in his awareness of the contradictions of preferring the risks of crime to the risks of impoverished boredom. The emotionality is perfectly emphasised in the strong language, and the reiterations of his worst dilemma: being 'killed' by doing crime or being suicidal on the dole.

The auto-generative circles whereby unemployment causes crime and crime causes unemployment are deeply embedded in Max's story. But it also recognises more 'positive' dynamics by which escape from drug-dependent crime engenders employment that holds both at bay. Any attempt to reduce Max's sophisticated reasoning to classifiable data that affords precedence to rationality or emotionality would be incongruous to the point of absurdity.

This rich example is backed up by another from the same study. It is neatly captured in a brief commentary on the casualised, high turnover, low security hire-and-fire labour market that filled the vacuum left by heavy industry to profit from an apparently undrainable pool of surplus labour with low reservation wage thresholds: 'demonstrated by the fact that a number of interviewees who possessed records of earlier criminal offending and/or problematic drug use were now displaying low-pay, no-pay careers similar to those of the rest of the sample' (Shildrick et al, 2012, p 121).

This strikingly counterintuitive example reframes the logics of discriminatory employment practices. Where much of the claimed criminality associated with worklessness is drug-related, as in this locality, the offences concerned apparently have little direct bearing on employability. Criminal records may be used as easy filters for managing oversubscribed recruitment processes. But once casualised contracts remove employees' job security, the scope for summary dismissal may induce employers to risk quick-and-easy appointments. This describes a speeded-up version of the wage-rate suppression dynamic represented in Figure 3.13. The singular characteristics of locality and time confound established beliefs about at least one aspect the relationship between unemployment and crime, perhaps because they accelerate the cycle.

These examples show the power of rich studies, but they also reveal their limitations. Innumerable parallel examples elsewhere may offer equally informative new understandings. However, just as quantitatively based studies of the relation between non-participation and crime are limited by their inherent opacity for assessing causation, so unpredictable findings like these cannot be generalised. A more practicable approach might anchor the multiple variables in play in a robust theory. A more imaginative approach would create scope for symbiosis between unexpected findings like these and an adaptive approach to theorisation. Frameworks of theorisation that do not funnel investigation towards the conceptual clusters and analytical divisions of Table 7.1 are rare in this field. One of the great merits of Habermas' and Tyler's theories is their inbuilt resilience to being 'channelled' in this way. Despite their *partial* alignment with familiar divisions, their trans-paradigm analyses build capacity to interpret counter-typical examples like those provided by Shildrick and her colleagues.

A more encompassing frame of analysis is needed to review unexpected (even 'aberrant') cases creatively and to leave scope for new interpretations. Habermas' and Tyler's theorisations exhibit important elements of these qualities. Both of their analyses include elements of theories of *governance* and theories of *criminalisation*, neither of which can be decisively located in dominant binary clusters. Governance has strong associations with structures in the form of institutions of government, but it can also be powerfully oriented towards the individual and the personal. This is highlighted by Tyler's interest in neoliberal governmentality, which encompasses the domains of affect and emotion as well as cognition and rationality. Similarly, Habermas' entire theoretical frame is concerned with the acts of governance achieved through systems (those of money and political power), and the ways in which they impact on the social *and emotional* relations of the lifeworld and are capable of degrading those relations towards forms of conduct that are socially anomic and personally alienated.

In turn, the concept of criminalisation has powerful associations with discourse, identification and labelling, on the one hand, and with the constantly extending encroachment of the law into commonplace processes of civil society, on the other. These ambivalences are reflected in Tyler's use of the concept of stigmatisation and Habermas' focus on juridification, respectively.

Habermas' and Tyler's theories of governance and theories of criminalisation have significant potential for theorising non-participation and its connections with crime in ways that seem free of the dichotomous traditions of theorisation and analysis that have dominated this field. Rather than challenge the dichotomies by bridging, blending or dissolving them, the application of both theories to an alternative analysis of non-participation and crime among young people holds out the prospect of reinterpreting the relationship between them. Sections 2 and 3 consider each in turn.

## Section 2: Governing non-participation

In the field of policies for addressing non-participation, the discourse of disengagement emerged at around the same time that governmentality theory was in the ascendant.[5] They hold much in common. As Chapter Two proposed, the defining feature of the disengagement discourse is its assertion that non-participation is to be explained in terms of the personal behaviours, dispositions and choices of young people. It gained considerably in influence in the wake of the discourse of responsibilisation, which drove a sea change in social and criminal justice policy, from the rise of the New Right in the 1980s and throughout the New Labour administrations of the 2000s.[6] And, in turn, the most important intellectual plank of the responsibilisation discourse is to be found in governmentality theory, which emerged in the early 1990s (Rose, 1989/1999; Miller and Rose, 1990; Rose and Miller, 1992).

A central premise of governmentality theory is its claim that states cannot meaningfully be said to 'govern' populations by regulation, assertion of powers and acts of domination, other than when they call on their defining monopolies over the legitimate use of force (Weber, 1919/1965). Rather, the governance of populations is primarily achieved through acts of persuasion and winning consent, recruitment to dominant ideas, and the conditionalisation of rewards and benefits, succinctly expressed in Foucault's (1991, p 100) much-quoted phrase 'Interest at the level of the consciousness of each individual who goes to make up the population ... is the new target and the fundamental instrument of the government of population'.

Rose's (1999) extensive extrapolation from Foucault's brief exploration of governmentality captures this concept succinctly:

> To dominate is to ignore or to attempt to crush the capacity for action of the dominated. But to govern is to recognise the capacity for action and to adjust oneself to it. *To govern is to act upon action.* This entails trying to understand what mobilises the domains or entities to be governed: to govern one must act upon these forces, instrumentalise them in order to shape actions, processes and outcomes in desired directions. Hence, when it comes to governing human beings, *to govern is to presuppose the freedom of the governed. To govern humans is not to crush their capacity to act but to acknowledge it and to utilise it for one's own objectives.* (Rose, 1999, p 4, emphases added)

Government-managed programmes for addressing particular needs or problems constitute a typical medium through which the freedoms and wills of individuals can be utilised in pursuit of the objectives of the state. In this way, workfare programmes epitomise the governmentalisation of target populations that are registered as unemployed. By means of the promise of training, skills development, allowances in lieu of earnings and smooth entry into the labour market, young people are induced to participate in such programmes. Rose (2000, p 334) writes:

> Thus workfare programmes ... micro-manage the behaviour of welfare recipients in order to re-moralise them. ... Within this new politics of conduct, the problems of problematic persons are reformulated as moral or ethical problems, that is to say, problems in the ways in which such persons understand and conduct themselves and their existences.

The premise of such interpretations of programmes is that the subjects to whom they are directed are deficient in their attitudes, beliefs or behaviours and need to be reformed as a precondition of being responsible citizens who provide for themselves, avoid reliance on the state and are accountable for failure to do so. The acts of 'governing the mentalities' of such populations (governance) are the antithesis of forces of regulation, edict and statute (government). This implies the active micromanagement of the lives of targeted populations like young non-participants by agents of state bureaucracies. It also implies multiple structured interventions to secure participation in work programmes in ways that are conducive to deliver improved behaviours, enhanced skills and appropriate attitudes. This is, according to the discourse, the pathway to successful employment.

This raises critical questions about the relative autonomy of such agents, their capacity to adapt their practices to maximise the prospects for success according to the predispositions and predilections of their clientele, and so on. Only by such means can the supposedly ill-adjusted mind-sets of the under-responsibilised and the disengaged be altered in ways that will be conducive to long-term participation in employment.

## 'Governing through unemployment'

An extensive literature on 'technologies of governance' has given rise to the notion of 'governing through unemployment' that makes explicit the ways in which the condition of being unemployed opens up channels for governance (Miller and Rose, 1990; Rose and Miller, 1992; Burchell, 1996; Dean, 1999). Walters' (2000) historical analysis reframes the purposes of means testing as the basis for the administration of unemployment relief. By the end of the depression years of the 1930s, he argues, the powers of investigation that means testing allowed were 'coming to be perceived by senior public officials in new ways. Not just as a means in the pursuit of narrow, fiscal objectives, but, more positively, *as a technology for the promotion of morale and welfare*' (Walters, 2000, p 96).

Walters (2000, p. 138) applies insights from his historical analysis to New Labour's 'New Deal' programme, arguing that the programme 'interpellates a moral subject, an individual who takes responsibility for themselves, but who also acknowledges obligations to society'. He argues that '"Active" programmes stand for a proliferation of countless individualised micro-managements ... the personal strategy has become an instrument of government: official authorities require the individual to govern themselves in terms of a personal strategy' (p 139).

Henman's (2006, p 218) analysis takes this line of interpretation further by drawing attention to a range of contemporary social policies that 'create a grid of categories by which populations are known and acted upon'. 'As a result', he argues, 'the rationality of social insurance is punctured and a rationality of targeting solidifies ... based on data profiling [that] incorporates a greater range of personal and group characteristics that signify riskiness' (p 214).[7] This is epitomised in workfare programmes:

> Governmentality analyses have repeatedly emphasised the neo-liberal character of workfare, and welfare reform, more broadly. Such neo-liberal power is said to operate by governing at a distance, by using choice and actively enrolling the subjectivities of those who are governed. However, such a characterisation of neo-liberalism *must recognise the punitive and coercive elements that lie at the heart of workfare.* ... As a post-structuralist analytic, *governmentality seeks to excavate discourses and rationalities that form and inscribe new domains – subjects, subjectivities, agencies – and make them governable.* (Henman, 2006, pp 33-5, emphases added)

The work of Walters and of Henman envisages modes of realisation of 'governing through unemployment' that adopt a governmentalist perspective which radically reinterprets the ways problematised populations are governed. Understandings based on mechanical forms of coercive control imposed on the wills and actions of targeted populations are substituted with methods to induce and inculcate conduct in which errant individuals adapt their actions and behaviours in response to incentives and firm guidance towards particular conceptions of rational self-interest. At the heart of both accounts is the personalisation and individualisation of acts for the realisation of new policy ambitions. For Walters, the key shift was in the decision to construct a network of policy agents capable of maintaining regular contact with the households of the unemployed. For Henman, with the inception of workfare, the rationality of targeting facilitated by information technologies poses new possibilities that are authoritarian, coercive *or punitive* in intent. For both, the interventions of multiple agents working one-to-one with unemployed people are central to governmentalisation. Crucially, the possibilities of powers for governing populations can then be extended far beyond their initial ostensible legitimising purpose.

## Habermas and Tyler on governance

In very different ways, both Habermas' and Tyler's conceptualisations of governance elaborate on the ways in which it is achieved through the channels opened up by the status 'unemployed', and extended in this way. Habermas' central theme of the colonisation of the lifeworld by systems of money and power (and the consequent uncoupling of systems from the lifeworld) is fundamentally concerned with processes of governance. The express purpose of some forms of juridification, for example, is that state interventions to ameliorate the deleterious effects of economic and political priorities should govern the conduct of the target population.[8]

The administration of systems of unemployment and other welfare benefits constitutes an important example of interventions that result from juridification. Workfare and other instruments of conditionalised unemployment benefit distribution typify the contingent processes of continuously steering target populations. According to Habermas (1981/1987, p 363), because of the administrative need to distribute benefits entitlements by bureaucratic means, the circumstance that occasions the entitlement has to be treated as an *abstraction*, selected from whatever indicators are best suited to centralised, coordinated systems of administration. Support is therefore confined to minimal monetary compensation, which takes no account of needs that cannot be addressed in a market context and that require non-monetary intervention. This erodes the processes of social integration inherent in the social relations of the lifeworld. It separates subjects from activities like productive work that were historically achieved (supposedly, under optimum conditions) through consensual processes of coordination between parties, based on reciprocal relations of trust and mutual dependency. This epitomises the uncoupling of lifeworlds from subsystems, without addressing the personal and social harms inflicted by unemployment – thereby placating but also governing the target population.

Tyler's conception of governance differs significantly from Habermas'. Her interest is in the conditions under which '*stigmatisation operates as a form of governance* which legitimises the reproduction and entrenchment of inequalities and injustices' (Tyler, 2013, p 8, emphasis added). For Tyler, stigmatisation is an important tool for the production of states of social abjection in subjugated populations. The exertions of such harmful and transformative powers are no less acts of governance than are actions taken under the authority of agencies of state. Tyler (2013, p 24) explains a range of ways in which 'revolting subjects' are governed, less by the use of statute designed to prohibit or require, but rather by the ways in which multifarious interactions between agencies and individuals shape the person and their self-perceptions, possibilities and dispositions – including through the operationalisation of a 'disgust consensus'. Of greatest interest to Tyler are the workings and effects of neoliberal governmentalisation.[9] One distinctive feature of governmentalisation is that it has 'reconfigured the relationship between individuals and the body politic *by inducing and capitalising on psychic anxiety* as a mode of (self-) governance' (Tyler, 2013, p 11). In relation to the English Riots of 2011, she posits that citizenship itself is being redesigned as a technology of neoliberal governance (p 197).

Tyler's interpretation of neoliberal governmentalisation by means of social stigmatisation and abjection offers a compelling account of the oppression of young people that results from the political-economic conditions by which they are excluded from labour as a by-product of financial crisis, and suffer the effects of systems imperatives to contain welfare expenditure and drive down the costs of labour, as suggested by the wage rate suppression dynamic represented in Figure 3.13. It is also of interest here to recall the data from Pemberton's (2015) analysis of NEET rates across regime types summarised in Chapter Three. Pemberton's argument, in the context of his wide-ranging analysis of 'harmful societies', is that non-participation classified as 'being NEET' 'may act as a proxy indicator of harm, insofar as it captures the absence of formal opportunities to either engage in productive forms of work, skills acquisition or learning ... as it denies the necessary opportunities for self-actualisation to be realised' (Pemberton, 2015, p 124). He expands on this in relation to the broader psychosocial harms and the widely discussed 'scarring effects' of non-participation, citing Bell and Blanchflower's (2011, p 16) summary of research which draws attention to young people's feelings of shame, rejection, anxiety and insecurity associated with unemployment.[10]

The credibility of governmentality theory rests on analysis of the minutiae of the mechanisms and tiny everyday acts of the kinds described by Tyler (and by Bell and Blanchflower and others), whereby official agents absorb the discourses, values and priorities that prevail in policy, and then strive to ensure their percolation into the consciousness and micro-decisions of those who are the objects of governance. One of the principal strengths of Tyler's analysis is its vivid depiction of such processes. A second is its argument that some manifestations of social abjection call for new class-based analyses, reconceptualising the position of young people as one of several social groupings making up what she terms the 'human waste'(e.g. Tyler, 2013, p 192, 203, 213) of contemporary neoliberalism.

However, these strengths of Tyler's analysis are qualified by some important limitations. Unemployment and other political-economic effects of the crises of neoliberal restructuring tend to appear in her analysis as forces of nature harshly visited upon young people, among many other social groups. Her analysis of the 2011 English riots suggests that young people are credible unprotected victims at whose door damaging outcomes of crisis are easily laid. Beyond this, how, why and at whose behest practices and processes ensure that young people, as distinct from other classed, gendered, racialised and embodied groups, dominate amongst those who are refused access to labour markets for poor dispositions and skills deficiencies remains unexplained. This sits uneasily alongside Tyler's representation of stigmatised abjects as active, resilient 'revolting subjects' who resist interpellation and subjectification. Of course, oppression and resistance coexist in the same subjects in perpetual states of tension which periodically resolve into submission or revolt, according to contingent conditions. But her analysis avoids assessing the net outcomes, and the processes whereby particular socially-differentiated versions of young-ness attract some of the most extreme forms of abjection and inequitable treatment. For all the localised acts of revolt identified by Tyler, the endemic and ubiquitous persistence of young people's exclusion from social and economic participation indicate the depth of their oppression, much more than they describe the sporadic successes of their resistance.

Tyler's account cannot avert the conclusion that 'being governmentalised' determines the lives of most of those it touches, except insofar as the refusal constituted by non-participation is to be interpreted as active resistance, whatever its adverse personal consequences. Her thesis offers too little by way of assurance about the countervailing capacity of refusal to dent the overbearing power of neoliberalism. In the last instance, for all its limited exploration of the ways in which the uncoupling of subsystems of money and power from the lifeworld results in conflicts and reactions of resistance that Tyler's analysis captures so clearly, Habermas' theorisation of the degradation of relations between systems and lifeworld offers a more credible and comprehensive account of the causes of the contemporary condition of non-participant young people – and in some measure an account of why (or at least how) it is their youth that emerges as a critical characteristic that shapes that condition.

## Governmentalisation and social control

This conclusion casts implicit doubt on the distinguishing claims of governmentality theory. Insofar as the processes of governmentalisation succeed in recruiting those who are the objects of intervention to its purposes, and thereby suppress effective resistance, such processes are differentiated from those of social control only by some aspects of their methods. Distinctions between governmentality *theory* and theories of social control become less and less clear as the hard and soft technologies of the monitoring and enforcement of target populations converge. Juxtaposing the work of Loïc Wacquant and Nikolas Rose is instructive for testing the distinction.[11] Wacquant (2004/09) adopts the vocabulary of penal social control without reservation in articulating his views of the state's engagement with the projects of neoliberalism, notably in relation to marginalised populations in the penal complex. For Rose (1999, p 234), in contrast, 'control is not centralised but dispersed; it flows through a network of open circuits that are rhizomatic and not hierarchical'. To Rose, the penal complex is only one element of governing conduct, which occurs throughout a panoply of social settings and contexts that are independent of the state.

When these conflicting positions are applied to the governance of non-participation, governmentalist approaches become exceedingly difficult to sustain in respect of resistant non-participants who become enfolded in the penal net. Addressing this means contemplating an apparent contradiction of governmentality theory. The theory seems at once to celebrate and recruit individual will and freedom as engines of self-management, *and* to identify the successful deployment of tactics that exploit them – thereby legitimising interventions that prevent autonomy and agency. The credibility of Rose's (1999, p 4) epithet, quoted earlier, that 'to govern is to recognise the capacity for action and to adjust oneself to it' is brought into serious question when most of those who are the object of governance either cooperate with being 'remade' (as the denizens of neoliberal workfare) or withdraw in silent protest. Non-participant withdrawal without protest at the moment of extreme pressure might in the short term be an achievement of governmentalisation. However, this holds only for as long as non-participation is survivable by dependence on other means of support. When that is not the case, governmentalisation is at best ephemeral and at worst illusory. Other actions and responses on the part of those who are so-governed inevitably follow.

Seen in this light, the distinction between governmentalisation and social control can only be maintained at the moment in which coercive power is exercised. Certainly, to drive someone into non-participant passivity may not be to coerce them. But to deny them rightful access to the means of basic subsistence is to do so. It may be that, while governmentalisation and social control do not completely converge in this context, the former appears to have become the handmaiden to the latter. In advanced neoliberal states, the exercise of brutal coercive power in response to acts of civil disobedience is, as noted earlier by reference to Weber (1919/1965), reserved as the sanction of last resort. Insofar as the programmes for the would-be enforced participation of young people described in Chapters Two and Three reshape the wills and choices of their subjects, they avert use of coercive power by denying the provision of subsistence. Yet when they fail to do so, they both invoke and legitimise the use of that power, for example in circumstances in which young people have recourse to property crime, whether to express resentment, or to secure their own subsistence. Rare as this may be among 16 to 18-year-olds (and its contemporary incidence is the subject of discussion in the remaining chapters), the minimisation, conditionalisation and retraction of state benefits for young people up to the age of 24 means that the refusal of adequate subsistence is a provocation to petty instrumental crime or more serious forms of expressive crime. The state response to the English riots of 2011 exemplifies its reserved rights to use coercive forces of social control, both to quell rioters and mete out harsh deterrent punishment (Briggs, 2012; Treadwell et al, 2012). Such responses surely constitute failures of governmentalisation, not reinforcements of it – theoretically or materially.

## Section 3: 'Governing through crime'

A clearer theorisation of the gradations of governmentalisation is needed. The continuum of tactics that runs from instrumentalising and incentivising desired behaviours that prompt self-interested 'rational choice', at one pole, to prevailing upon recalcitrant individuals by use of sanctions and punishments, at the other, makes it exceedingly difficult to understand what is distinctive about the precepts of governmentality theory. Only if the continuum explicitly stops short of coercion and the exercise of what Rose (1999, p 5) terms 'force relations' can governmentalisation be differentiated from social control. Otherwise, the distinction becomes one of definitional sophistry more than of substantive difference. Dubious distinctions are drawn between deprivations in the form of the legal suspension of rights to welfare and the punitive enforcement of participation in required activities that are tantamount to deprivations of liberty. Coercive interventions have many guises and devices for their own legitimation.

Nevertheless, specific failures of governmentalisation like those of the English riots do not prevent the continuation of (fallible) processes of governmentalisation. Failures can be addressed in other governmentalising ways. When withholding minimum survivable welfare payments for young people without work triggers petty theft or violent crime, for example, it *criminalises* the young people concerned. It is therefore surprising that theories of governance have paid little attention to the relationship between unemployment and crime. Walters and Henman have proposed that designating people as unemployed opens channels for governing them that extend beyond their status as would-be workers: the conditionalisation of compensation for worklessness (along the lines anticipated by Habermas) emerges as the principal lever by which they are *made governable* 'through' their unemployed status.

Much the same logic underpins the proposition that states also '*govern through crime*', but this axis of governance involves more complex mechanisms of implementation and a diffuse realisation of powers. Jonathon Simon introduced the phrase in 1996.[12] His fullest theoretical exposition traces Foucault's extension of the concept of governance beyond explicitly political structures to: 'modes of action, more or less considered and calculated, that were destined to act upon the possibilities of action of other people. To govern, in this sense, is to *structure the possible field of action of others*' (Foucault, 1982/2000, p 341, quoted in Simon, 2007, p 17).

Simon builds on this conception to argue:

> When we govern through crime, we make crime, and the forms of knowledge historically associated with it – criminal law, popular crime narrative, and criminology – *available outside their limited subject domains as powerful tools with which to interpret and frame all forms of social action as a problem for governance* (Simon, 2007, p 17, emphasis added).

Simon envisages an entire new governmental rationality whereby the techniques of one field-specific form of governance – that of criminal justice – are available to address any other problematised fields of social action. In principle, if poverty, inequality, mass unemployment or non-participation pose 'problems for governance', the tools of the system of criminal justice can act to address them. Indeed, on Simon's interpretation, they are the *best* means available to ameliorate the social dysfunctionality of such conditions *rather than address their political, material or social origins* in ways that might entail 'changes in the status quo of wealth and power' (Simon, 2007, p 25-26).

This reading of the need for major interventions that work between weakened processes of social integration and the domination of political-economic priorities is an (apparently unwitting) exact match with Habermas' analysis, where the processes of juridification become essential to shoring up the damage from systems depredations. However, while Habermas describes a legislative response, Simon describes a response through processes of crime control.

These propositions concerning the capacities of 'governing through crime' in conjunction with theorisations of 'governing through unemployment' need further consideration. A much clearer line of connection between them becomes apparent when they are applied to young unemployed non-participants. Most notably, strong resemblances between technologies for governing workfare regimes (outlined in Chapter Six) and those of preventive pre-emption of juvenile crime (introduced in Chapter Four) are revelatory in their common practices of monitoring, surveillance and actuarial calculus. Similarly, the penal complex that governs criminality shows signs of extending its reach to govern 'the unemployed'. As Walters (2000, pp 155-6) argues:

> one can speak of a 'new punitiveness' which seeks to engage certain 'problem' sections of the population in terms of the logic of the 'crackdown', in terms of a host of disciplinary measures like the boot camp, 'tougher' sentencing regimes, curfews for younger people, and 'zero tolerance' (Wacquant, 1999). It would take detailed empirical work to establish how, and to what extent, a new penal complex is actually *redefining people who would previously have been governed as 'the unemployed', and regulating them as threats to law and public safety.* (Emphasis added)

Although studies like those of Beckett and Western (2001) and Wacquant (2004/09) have drawn attention to the convergence of penal and welfare regimes for the governance of social marginality, most of the detailed empirical work that Walters calls for remains to be done. The actuarial premises of the Risk Factor Prevention Paradigm (RFPP) described in Chapter Four established the principle that the preventative aspects of the governance of crime would, in a fully governmentalised regime, look not only to 'the unemployed' as a target for governing crime, but to the *governmentalisation of unemployment itself* as an active means of governing crime preventatively.

The internal logic of this is self-evident, and difficult to contest seen from within a governmentalist perspective. The contingent and contested nature of *an* association between unemployment and crime among young non-participants that Chapters Four and Five reviewed is supported by ostensibly persuasive evidence, for all its incapacity to identify reliable causal factors of association. However, just as tenuous logics hypothesise causality, so programmes that attempt to manage mass unemployment can profitably transfer the application of the same governmentalist methods and technologies to the governance of *prospective* criminality.

In all spheres where social science knowledge is used for generalised interpretations, there is a significant likelihood of it being over-applied. Suggestiveness, convenience and congruence with dominant discourse fuel this danger.[13] In the conjunctures at which the norms of the actuarial calculus of risk assessment like the RFPP coincide with the pursuit of the managerialist imperatives of economy, efficiency and effectiveness (Clarke et al, 1994; Cutler and Waine, 1994), procedurally driven agencies responsible for workfare and early intervention schemes are urgently induced to rely on the deductive logics that test individual cases against generalised observations to calculate likely outcomes.

Under the influence of such practices, the relationship between the governance of crime and the governance of unemployment becomes consolidated. A direct line of pseudo-scientific connection between the methods and practices of the governance of unemployment and the methods and practices of the governance of crime becomes legitimised and cemented. This connection also paves the way for an important connective axis between governance and *criminalisation*, which is the principal subject of the next chapter.

## Notes

[1] Notably those of Machin and Marie (2006), Petrongolo (2009) and especially Fougère et al (2009).

[2] Most notably, in the US, Britt (1997) found an exaggerated effect of unemployment on property crime among younger age groups, while Levitt and Lochner (2001) found that 18-year-olds are twice as likely to be arrested for property crimes as 35-year-olds; and in the UK, Soothill et al's (2002) definitive study demonstrates that property crime associated with unemployment and economic hardship is concentrated among young people aged 20.

[3] In the US, Hannon and DeFronzo (1998) and Lauritsen et al (2012); in the UK, Feinstein and Sabatés (2005) and Jennings et al (2012). See also Beckett and Savolainen (2000); Western (2001); Worrall (2005).

[4] See quotations from young people in Tyler (2013, pp 197-203).

[5] See the outline of the provenance of disengagement theory in Chapter Two: it was in particular Bandura's (2004) use of the concept in relation to terrorism that established a spillage towards general non-compliance and deviancy during the 1990s, when the discourse of responsibilisation and theories of governmentality gained increasing influence among policy makers.

[6] Among the earliest explorations of the concept of responsibilisation (as a strategy and a discourse) were undertaken by criminologists, notably O'Malley (1992) and Garland (1996, 2001), as well as by Rose (1999).

[7] The resonances between the profiling described by Henman (2006) (in relation to Australia) and the work of the Cambridge Study (Farrington et al, 1986; Farrington, 1994, 1996) in the UK are striking.

[8] For an excellent crystallisation of the distinctive features of governance in such contexts, see Edwards (2013).

[9] Although she never offers her own definition of this concept, her narrative closely follows Rose's.

[10] There is an extensive literature on the economic and lifetime earnings scarring effects of youth unemployment. Studies that include consideration of scarring in relation to psychological and psychosocial effects are scarcer (see for example Chauvel, 2010; Nilsen and Reiso, 2011; McQuaid et al. 2014; Strandh et al, 2014).

[11] It is a symbolic depiction of the mutual dismissal of these two theorists that Wacquant (2004/09) dispatches the views of Rose (along with those of O'Malley and Simon) in a single summary footnote (fn, p xxi), while Rose (1999) pre-empts Wacquant with a similarly dismissive footnote (p 267, note 56).

[12] Simon (1996), in a brief article reviewing punitive sentencing initiatives.

[13] For example, theories about parental role models and juvenile criminality are readily interpreted as normative bases for emphasising deficit in lone-parent households (McCord and McCord, 1958; Brandwein et al, 1974); in classrooms, sophisticated theories about class-differentiated linguistic codes provide an erroneous basis for teachers' determinist rationalisations of the poor performance of working-class children (Bernstein, 1973).

# Part Four
# Criminalising non-participation

# EIGHT

# The advance of criminalisation

> Social science research has not been very effective in providing alternative understandings of youth crime. Neo-positivism, along with administrative criminology, through criminal career research, has dominated the theorising and old explanations of youth crime. Its influence on policy has been enormous, shifting the focus away from exploring how and why the young might engage in crime or how the state might be criminalising the young.
>
> *Alan France (2007) Understanding youth in late modernity, pp 113–14*

## Introduction

The previous chapter argued that Habermas' and Tyler's theories have a distinctive capacity to contribute to a reinterpretation of non-participation and its claimed relationship to crime. It also drew attention to the ways in which the points of intersection between governmentality theories and other theories of the governance of crime offer fruitful ways for understanding how 'governing through unemployment' and 'governing through crime' might be linked. This chapter begins its exploration of the capacity of the work of these two theorists for reinterpreting the non-participation-crime relationship by considering the importance of the concept of juridification to Habermas' theories. Of particular interest are the ways in which the priorities of demands generated by systems of money and power are brought to bear on aspects of the lifeworld; and the relationship between the concepts of juridification and criminalisation. In Section 2, three different modes of criminalisation are identified, and their relationship to modes of governance is considered, referencing Tyler's work. Section 3 extends the discussion through a critical assessment of current manifestations of criminalisation from the perspective of jurisprudence. Sections 4 and 5 consider of the criminalisation of non-participation itself, and the powers for further criminalisation already in place that are available to be deployed as a response to endemic mass non-participation among young people.

## Section 1: Juridification and criminalisation

Habermas (1981/1987, p 357) defines juridification as 'the tendency toward an increase in formal (or positive, written) law that can be observed in modern society'. Of particular significance here, the first recorded use of the term (Kirchheimer, 1928) identified it as a trend towards the increased regulation of political struggle and conflict, particularly in relation to labour law.[1] Habermas identifies four epochal waves of juridification at different stages of state formation. Each wave marks an episode in Habermas' incremental uncoupling of system and lifeworld. His account indicates an ever-growing need for the state to make good the detrimental effects of the superimposition of the needs of the money and power subsystems on people's everyday lives.

In the most recent of these waves in the 20th-century European democratic welfare state, Habermas (1981/1987, p 361) argues, the advance of juridification took the form of 'the institutionalising in legal form of a social power relation anchored in class structure'. This consisted of a rebalancing of power relations between labour and private owners in terms of working hours, pay bargaining, employment rights and social security provision. He characterises this stage as both 'guaranteeing freedom and taking it away' (p 361). This ambivalence arises, he argues, because 'it is now the very means of guaranteeing freedom that endangers the freedom of the beneficiaries' (p 362). This occurs because, while the welfare state guarantees individualised legal entitlements, they are provided under specified legal conditions that take away other freedoms. Juridification therefore means:

> introducing into matters of economic and social distribution an if-then structure of conditional law that is 'foreign' to social relations, to social causes, dependencies and needs. This structure does not, however, allow for appropriate and especially not for preventive, reactions to the causes of the situations requiring compensation. (Habermas, 1981/1987, p 362)

What follows in Habermas' account is particularly telling in the context of young people and non-participation. Taking forward his observations about welfare compensation noted in Chapter Seven, he argues that the centrally administered distribution of entitlements in monetary form takes no account of needs, and has the effect of eroding social integration and weakening reciprocal relations of dependency. He refers to this as 'pacifying the class conflict lodged in the sphere of production'

(Habermas, 1981/1987, p 364), with the implication that the conflict is deferred, not resolved, because the response is disintegrative of social and economic relations.

If it is interpreted in the light of the wage-rate suppression dynamic (see Figure 3.13), Habermas' analysis has resonance for contemporary manifestations of non-participation following the global financial crisis (GFC). As Chapter Three demonstrated, the incremental erosion and retraction of entitlement to monetary compensation for young people at the ages of 18 and 21 that began in the 1980s and continues at present undermines the effects of historical acts of juridification in the form of welfare arrangements that were largely successful in 'pacifying' (class) conflict. As subsequent sections will argue, there is strong support for the claim that these erosions and retractions are now revitalising that conflict in the varied forms of passive refusal, non-participation, hostile resistance and the risks of social unrest among young people.

Towards supporting this claim, processes of juridification first need to be differentiated from processes of criminalisation, while also recognising their connectedness. Juridification occurs when actions or behaviours become subjects of statute law as part of a wider trend towards extending the reach of law into the domains of the lifeworld. It entails a legitimate act of law making that is most likely to take the form of a new civil law for the regulation (or facilitation) of everyday life. In comparison, criminalising an act is unambiguously defined as making it a criminal offence – and refers to multiple disconnected single acts, rather than a 'tendency' in its own right. So *with regard to actions*, what differentiates juridification and criminalisation is that the focus of the former is upon the formal processes whereby proscription (or provision) is enshrined in statute, as part of a wider trend, while the latter refers to the identification of actions deemed to deserve proscription.

An authoritative dictionary definition of the verb 'to criminalise' differentiates two objects of the act of criminalising, as follows:

> To turn (a person) into a criminal, especially by making his or her activities illegal
> To turn (activity) into a criminal offence by making it illegal. (OED, 2014, online version)[2]

As a derivative of this verb, 'criminalisation' (first coined in 1890) means the act or process of turning a person into a criminal, or an activity into a criminal offence. It follows that the criminalisation of a person or act involves the process of construction of meaning; a pre-existing understanding of what constitutes the person or act becomes remade as one in which he, she or it is understood to be criminal. By means of a process of (re)interpretation he, she or it is 'turned into' something different by an act of 'making'. Criminalisation is, therefore, in effect an act of collective redefinition.[3]

Yet, importantly, there are more ambiguous referents of redefinition *when they apply to a person*. At law, only actions are proscribed: persons cannot be proscribed. The use of the word 'especially' in the first definition above makes provision for a wider range of interpretation than applies to criminalising actions. It is an *optional* element of the definition that the person's activity should be illegal. The implication is that a person can be 'turned into a criminal' *without undertaking any specified actions proscribed by laws*.

Consequently, it is possible to criminalise persons without reference to law. The notion of a criminalising process that 'turns a person into a criminal' has at least three meanings. He or she can be turned into a criminal by making his or her action illegal; or by a series of social normative processes in which her or his actions come to deserve the label 'criminal' because they *resemble* a crime; or she or he can be *driven to* already proscribed criminal activity as a result of circumstance (to secure subsistence and survival) or disposition (as an expression of resentment or resistance).

For the first, the perceived recurring behaviours of an identifiable cadre of people might be deemed sufficiently threatening to make them the subject of additional legal sanctions.[4] Neither of the other two meanings have legislatory implications. Rather, they are concerned with new forms of constituting criminality, or more stringent applications of existing law.

Among criminologists, and more generally, the concept of criminalisation has gained currency.[5] It is principally identified with social reaction theory, deviancy theory and labelling theory.[6] Criminologists argue that minor acts are interpreted in the light of projected possibilities for their escalation, on the basis of panic and alarm rather than any substantive evidence. Marginalised groups are inherently susceptible, notably easily identified groups like 'youth', whose activities are already associated with crime in popular discourse. This matches aspects of the first definition above: (categories of) persons are 'turned into' criminals by being (re)interpreted, identified and interpellated as miscreants whose behaviours become formally designated as deviant. This may not be because of the nature of the behaviour itself, but because of the labelling of specific behaviours for which tolerance has decreased, and because of the identification of the behaviour with a readily visibilised and categorised grouping.

Other accounts of criminalisation follow different theoretical premises. Squires (1990, p 51) draws attention to the parallel emergence of discourses of poverty and criminality in the 19th century – the first associated with the maintenance of the material and economic order, the second with the moral and ideological order. By the early 20th century, socio-pathological studies repeatedly explained this residuum by references to handicaps, deficiencies or weaknesses (Squires, 1990, p 120). Chadwick and Scraton's (2013) overview stays close to interpretations that refine political-economic accounts and circumnavigate their shortcomings. It cites Spitzer's (1975) account, which identified criminalisation as both functionally and ideologically driven by the fluctuating needs of the capitalist economy; and Box's (1983), which shows how populations were differentiated to manage the UK unemployment crisis of the 1980s. Here, the focus of criminalisation switches to winning legitimacy for the exercise of harsh authoritarian power in support of the prevailing social and economic order.

## Section 2: Modes of criminalisation and modes of governance

While the conceptualisations of criminalisation identified in Section 1 set critical contextual conditions, they tend to lack specificity about the tangible forms taken by identifiable criminalising actions. Criminalisation is, as has been argued, inextricably bound to governance, and differentiated forms of governance are part of the apparatus whereby different modes of criminalisation occur. Three different modes describe three aspects of the relationship between criminalisation and governance, especially as it applies to non-participation.

The relationship between criminalisation and governance is at its simplest in the *illegalising* mode of criminalisation. The institutions of government themselves are the principal means through which it is secured. New laws are passed and enacted exclusively through the legislature. Self-evidently, the processes of implementation, policing and prosecution are the business of wider forms of governance, primarily those delegated to agencies of state. This is the version in Section 1 in which criminalisation and juridification are overlapping and potentially interdependent. Following Habermas, as part of the juridificatory trend, new laws make legal provision to address needs arising from systems' destabilisation of everyday life, and they criminalise actions antithetical to those priorities. For example, as Chapters Two and Three noted, the 2008 Education and Skills Act made non-participation among 16 to 18-year-olds illegal and subject to criminal prosecution, largely in response to the incapacities of workfare programmes to absorb the surplus inactive population of school-leavers.[7] This mode, then, refers to *criminalising actions by making them illegal using new legislation*.

The *impelling* mode of criminalisation creates conditions whereby people are 'driven to' criminal activity by circumstance and/or disposition – to ensure their material security or as an expression of resentment, for example. When individuals are impelled to commit a crime, their misdemeanours are governed through agencies of law enforcement. The breach of legal requirement is based on pre-existing law, so the emphasis here too is on governance, especially insofar as police and courts maximise use of discretion to respond appropriately if the circumstances warrant it. They use restorative, remedial or preventative elements that might ameliorate the precipitating condition, for example. However, if the outcome on conviction requires participation in programmes of training, workfare or self-management, any therapeutic elements would constitute a *governmentalist* response if they sought to change attitudes, beliefs and reactions. 'Offenders' have been 'made criminal' – that is, impelled to act criminally – as a result of circumstances that lead them to believe that they have no alternative but to commit a criminal act. The findings of the research of Baron (2006, 2008), in Chapter Four, provide clear evidence of such effects.

The impelling mode is often associated with intensified, selective or inconsistent application of existing legislation in response to particular circumstances that trigger political alarm or demands for punitive deterrence. For example, many young people who participated in the English riots of 2011 were angry or frustrated by their poverty, restricted circumstances and lack of prospects (Lewis et al, 2011; Newburn, 2012). As Chapter Six noted, Tyler emphasises the significance of the riots as a response to the penal humiliation of stigmatised populations through harassment and heavy-handed policing. She comments that:

> the underclass is a polluting and racialised category, which is employed to legitimise punitive forms of neoliberal governmentality ... [and] the use of exceptionally vindictive judicial and economic punishments. Notably, the riots were also used to generate greater public consent for the shift from protective liberal forms of welfare to penal workfare regimes. (Tyler, 2013, p 183)

The scale and economic and political consequences of the rioters' actions provoked sufficient alarm to result in an express call for harsh responses (Briggs, 2012; Treadwell et al, 2012). Substantially inflated penalties greatly exceeded the levels that would have been expected had the same offences been committed by individual offenders acting alone. This mode of criminalisation drives people to commit crimes defined by pre-existing legislation, *by creating material need that cannot be met by other means (instrumental crime), or by provocative pressure that inflames emotion (expressive crime)*. This often occurs in combination with an aggravated application of legislation deeming as criminal actions that might in other contexts result in non-criminal disposals, especially for minors. This is typified by hybrid civil-criminal legislation, the distinctive criminalising effects of which are considered in Section 3.

The third mode of criminalisation is of greatest relevance to understanding the proposed connection between criminalisation and non-participation. The *imputing* mode operates by socially normative and regulatory processes whereby people's activities are perceived to be *associated with* criminal acts. In terms of governance, this mode is likely to invoke governmentalist interventions. Distributed powers of governance may bring agents to act upon ostensibly criminally inclined and potentially criminal conducts, however determined. This mode relies primarily on diffuse processes of governmentalisation by means of pre-emptive targeting of putatively high-risk groups, as much as by the close monitoring of vulnerable or dangerous individuals. This is well captured in a particular strand of governmentality theory that is important for understanding the criminalisation of non-participation. Central to its approach is the identification of generalised social problems embedded in policy fields. Recalling aspects of the work of Walters (2000), Henman (2006) and Simon (2007), this field of governance provides a channel *through which* legitimate access to a population that 'needs governing' can be afforded. The identified population can be reached as an *object of governance* by being clients or 'wards'. That is to say, they can be governed *through* their status in that field, in ways that would not otherwise be available. People's status as unemployed, as criminal, *or as being at risk of either, both legitimises and makes practicable the governmentalisation of routine and mundane aspects of their life*, beyond the immediate needs, acts and conditions that have occasioned their status as clients or conscripts.

This warrants further elaboration. One aspect of this mode may result from the cynical introduction of legal powers that address trivial offences as surrogates for classes of activity that are more serious, but difficult to legislate against. For example, the behaviour identified in the 2004 Anti-Social Behaviour Act was justified by perceived concerns about minor non-criminal incivilities and behaviours. Very few of the identified behaviours represented direct threats to the security of any identifiable person, but rather expressed generalised concerns about potential harms or threats.[8] A later attempt to lower the threshold for antisocial behaviour was intended to bring civil sanctions for a much wider range of subjectively defined minor irritations, and substantially thinned and widened the net of activities that could result in criminal sanction.[9]

A second aspect of this imputing mode of criminalisation is based on the use of the proximal concepts *criminality* and *criminalistic*, which refer to actions that (tend to) display the distinguishing characteristics of criminal acts, *or circumstances associated with them*, without being currently designated illegal. Similarly, non-criminal actions may be classified as *incriminating* (susceptible to accusation or formal charge). Many of these supposedly 'sub-criminal', 'proto-criminal' or 'pre-criminal' characteristics and circumstances are the grist of risk factor assessments like those deployed in the Risk Factor Prevention Paradigm (RFPP).

A third aspect entails criminalisation by causing a person to recognise that they are regarded as criminal, or by causing them to regard themselves as criminal, or by bringing about recognition that the conduct in question is viewed by others as criminalistic. This aspect is analogous to the processes identified by deviancy theory in which, as noted earlier, it is the processes of secondary reaction that become the substantive focus of contention. People are 'made criminal' through multiple acts of disapproval, stigmatisation and refusal, and thereby interpellated as deviants displaying proximal qualities of criminality, in much the same ways as they are 'made abject' in Tyler's analysis. For young people identified as non-participants, these processes may occur through governmentalisation, and by being managed, steered and *represented to themselves* as deficient or blameworthy, including, in Tyler's (2013, p 204) resonant phrase, by '[becoming] the abjects they had been told they were'.

The next section extends this discussion through a critical assessment of current legal manifestations of criminalisation, and of emerging indications that, for many young people, the very status of being out of school, out of college and out of work is itself becoming criminalised.

## Section 3: Criminalisation and jurisprudence

The increased currency of the concept of criminalisation has attracted particular attention among academic lawyers, with some studies contributing prospective foundations for a theory of criminalisation, particularly in the broad field of jurisprudence, with an emphasis on 'over-criminalisation'. A number of commentators argue that there is an excessive and rapidly increasing amount of criminal legislation, much of which is at odds with some fundamental principles of justice. Husak (2008, p 3) argues in relation to US law that 'a substantial amount of contemporary punishments are unjust because they are inflicted for conduct that should not have been criminalised at all'. Tadros (2008) relates this trend to issues of security. Tomlin's (2013) analysis centres on the Presumption of Innocence Principal (PIP), which leads him to argue that

> we should be as concerned about punishing [people] for doing things that cannot appropriately be punished as we are about punishing them for what they did not do. Therefore, the same epistemic standards should be applied to decisions concerning criminalisation as to conviction. (Tomlin, 2013, p 65)

From these starting positions, a wide range of objections are brought to bear on the increasing application of criminal law. The proliferation and complexity of new laws is said to militate against the normative process of establishing expected behaviour, such that many inadvertent offenders can claim ignorance of the redesignation of their behaviour as criminal. In the same vein, stigmatising more behaviours by rendering them unlawful diminishes the normative efficacy of the stigmatising function of law (Husak, 2008). In turn, the proportionality of responses is brought into question, and, in Husak's (2008, p 15) view, it is inherent in the tendency to over-criminalise that punishments begin to lose their connection to the seriousness of the crimes committed. Similarly, Tadros (2008) argues that because extensions of criminal law are often the product of hasty, ill-thought-out and poorly designed legislation, legal sanction is often pursued regardless of a range of unintended but anticipatable negative consequences that produce unjust outcomes. For these reasons, it is anomalous and unjust that the stringent tests of the PIP applying at the level of case-specific court judgments are apparently casually and spuriously waived when drawing up generalised legislation to stem specific perceived threats to social order and security. Tomlin's (2013) critique implies that innocent actions and intentions are unjustly prosecuted and punished as a result of ill-conceived criminalising legislation that would constitute a miscarriage of justice (and breach the PIP) were a directly comparable act to result in a guilty verdict at the hands of a jury.

As correctives, Husak, Tadros and Tomlin all propose reference points to constrain over-criminalisation. Husak derives his directly from criminal law by invoking the criteria of non-trivial harm, wrongfulness and desert. He adds further requirements, such that new offences should reduce substantial risk of a consummate harm while also ensuring offenders are demonstrably culpable in relation it. Tadros' (2008, p 940) proposals concern 'the extent to which a theory of criminalisation can be considered in isolation from other questions of justice, such as the distribution of wealth'. He draws attention to citizens' capacities to protect themselves against threats to their own security in ways directly proportional to the material and cultural resources at their disposal. Tomlin focuses on the complexities of arriving at theoretically sustainable criteria for criminalisation. He argues strongly for a cautionary principle whereby 'at the very least a high level of convergence will be required to criminalise conduct in a world where there is reasonable disagreement about the criteria for criminalisation' (Tomlin, 2013, p 63). He captures this in the resonant phrase *'conduct, like persons, must be considered innocent until proven guilty'* (p 61, emphasis added).

Alongside these principled critiques of criminalisation, some more trenchant criticisms of indirect, disguised and covert forms of criminalisation have been made. A number of prominent legal scholars have led the critique of the new hybrid forms of legislation pioneered by New Labour between 1998 and 2008. At the centre of Ashworth and Zender's (2010) objections is what they refer to as 'two-step' criminalisation that results from hybrid preventive orders straddling civil and criminal law, by allowing a breach of the conditions of civil law to be subject to the processes and sanctions of criminal law. As a result, a number of the multiple categories of civil orders do not merely provide a fast-track to criminalisation; in addition to speed and ease of dispensation, in their civil guise they bypass requirements which would apply to the imposition of criminal sanctions, and have a frequently used capacity subsequently to commute offenders to criminal status if the terms of the orders are breached.

Not only is this apparently easy slippage from civil to criminal prosecution a matter for concern, it results in more extreme and adverse outcomes, its legal propriety is highly questionable, and its effects, Ashworth and Zender (2010) argue, are unjust. They identify four specific substantive legal objections. First, hybrid legislation provides insufficient certainty that the legal tests and procedural scrupulousness applied are equivalent to that in criminal cases. Second, the restrictions placed on individuals' liberty are frequently over-extensive because they lack the rigorous application of the tests that would apply in a criminal case. Third, not only are those convicted prevented from contesting restrictions because they are imposed using civil procedures, the level of discretion delegated to courts allows a degree of freedom in the imposition of restrictions that would be unlikely to have been approved by the legislature, had the restrictions been specified in proposals for new legislation. Fourth, remarkably, hybrid preventive orders allow the courts allegedly dealing with lesser offences to circumvent statutory limitations on the imposition of restrictions and the conditions under which custodial sentences may be handed down. Thus, in principle, it was possible for an Anti-Social Behaviour Order (ASBO) to prohibit begging, for example, and for the convicted person to be imprisoned for subsequent breach of this term of the order, even though it is no longer permitted in criminal law for beggars to be imprisoned.[10] Ashworth and Zender (2010, p 87) conclude that 'the existing legal form of civil preventive hybrid measures can be more coercive than many criminal offences, yet they are imposed without protections that adhere to criminalisation, and that is simply unacceptable'.

Simester and Von Hirsch's (2011) interpretation employs many similar points of analysis, but takes the argument further. The critical element of their claim is that the extensive deployment of two-step prohibition orders (TSPOs) constitutes a form of *quasi-criminalisation*. Focusing on the ASBO as a leading example of TSPOs, they argue that civil action can only begin when someone has been shown to do something antisocial. However, to the extent that the person's conduct when the qualifying behaviour occurs is relied upon to justify the imposition of, say, exclusion orders:

> *the specification of the qualifying conduct itself counts as a form of quasi-criminalisation … [thus] proving that conduct at trial should be governed by criminal rules.* Suppose that [a particular act] is prescribed as a qualifying conduct, proof of which makes it legitimate to issue a TSPO. In effect, while persons who [commit that act] will not immediately receive a criminal conviction, the state announces *ex ante* [before the event] that such persons will be directly subject to sanctions, … and will therefore become liable to criminal dispositions.
>
> As such the specifications of [the particular act] itself should be constrained by principles such as the Offence Principle. But the criteria under which a TSPO is available

> *tend to include [qualifying behaviour] that is not by itself either wrong or offensive or harmful, and which need not be a criminal offence.* ... Indeed, in England the ASBO criteria go further ... in that the behaviour complained of need not in fact cause any distress; it is sufficient that it be 'likely' so to do. (Simester and Von Hirsch, 2011, pp 222-3, emphases added)

Simester and Von Hirsch deduce from this analysis that the imposition of deprivations on the accused person 'ought as a minimum to be predicated on a wrong' (p 224). Legislation that allows the imposition of ASBOs also allows courts to restrict or prohibit behaviour that is 'not otherwise criminally proscribed, and which may be harmless ... Neither the triggering conduct, nor the prohibitory response, need satisfy the Harm Principle or Offence Principle' (p 230). As a result, TSPOs known to be capable of resulting in criminal prosecution *contravene the fundamental principles of jurisprudence regarding what constitutes criminal behaviour.* The authors' conclusion is damning:

> TSPOs are an inappropriate means of delegating and personalising the legislative powers to prohibit behaviour by citizens. In our view, *the TSP order poses foundational challenges to the preservation of rights and freedoms within a free society.* ... Two-step schemes cannot be sustainable as proper forms of criminal prohibition – because the order issued is not made by a representative body *and is targeted to particular persons.* ... As a device, the TSP order is capable of exploiting the poorly understood distinction, between ex-ante [before the event] and ex-post [after the event] dimensions of the criminal law, to evade some of the standard constitutional limitations on criminalisation. (Simester and Von Hirsch, 2011, p 232, emphases added)

## Section 4: Modes and manifestations of criminalisation

The concept of criminalisation emerges from this exploration as multifaceted, polyvalent and in some respects elusive and ambiguous. The word itself signifies anything from a general tendency to drive more actions and people towards the criminal justice system, to the highly specific practices of making breaches of civil orders criminal in ways that do not meet the accepted epistemic and ethical standards of jurisprudence. Criminalisation manifests itself in at least three modes as illegalising, impelling or imputing. It can apply equally to a person, an act or a form of conduct. It is not necessarily connected with illegal behaviour, or even with regulatory breaches of civil law. Its definitional existence and effective force are highly context-specific. It embraces normative and associational aspects. It may draw newly problematised behaviours into the ambit of law. It may take the form of ratcheting pressures forcing a simple bifurcation between those who adapt to imposed conditions and those who refuse them. It invents new offences for normative and stigmatising purposes in response to new social and economic circumstances. It is distinct from juridification, while being difficult to separate from it in some contexts. In its formal modes it is a product of acts of government, and one of many instruments of the more diffuse and distributed processes of governance. In all, it is, in some circumstances, a highly specific tool of the corrective inducements and levered pressures of governmentalisation.

In these senses, criminalisation assumes a range of guises, from specific measures to secure particular forms of social order, to providing pressures to modify behaviour, and onwards to the discursive processes of portraying individuals and groups to themselves and to others for the purposes of enforcing compliance and, ultimately, legitimising coercion. Some manifestations of criminalisation have high risks of triggering unintended consequences and punitive responses incommensurate with the conduct that prompted them. When they blur the line between civil and criminal offences, some manifestations run high risks of inconsistency by establishing unjust epistemic bases for determining culpability; by bypassing due processes of scrutiny; by making criminal conducts which are elsewhere expressly exempted from prosecution; and by using statutes as proxies for the de facto prosecution of people or behaviours that cannot legitimately be identified as targets for legal and regulatory intervention. Ultimately, some manifestations of criminalisation are capable of taking coercive forms, of circumventing due processes of justice, of transcending foundational precepts of jurisprudence, *and ultimately of subverting rights, removing freedoms and imposing unjust punishments.*

Such a broad palette of characteristics, manifestations and powers associated with a single concept is rare. Delineating its breadth in this way is not to suggest that all of these guises of criminalisation are prominent or continuously advancing, nor that they are regularly deployed in relation to young people who are unable to participate in approved forms of economic activity, or who refuse to do so. Rather, the point is to identify the availability of criminalisation as a tool of governance and governmentalisation, and to draw attention to the multiple guises and complex and sometimes deceptive forms it takes.

## Conditions conducive to the criminalisation of non-participation

Whether the criminalisation of non-participation remains a relative rarity or the product of an advancing tide of juridification, the purpose of this discussion is to demonstrate the number of ways in which conducive conditions for the criminalisation of non-participation are already partially in place, as well as being readily adaptable to speedy and pre-legitimated roll-out as the perceived need arises.

In at least one welfare-related sphere, a highly significant precedent has been set by the construction of a bridge between two modes of governance. At present, governance of and through welfare provision can be roughly divided between those policy spheres that are focused on behaviour, and rely heavily on civil pre-emptive and preventive interventions (pertaining to curfews, child safety, parenting.[11] Also antisocial behaviour, and eleven other orders[12]; and those controlled by use of financial sanctions, most notably welfare benefits, including unemployment allowances. Watts et al's (2014, pp 2–3) overview of the extent and impact of welfare conditionality observes that:

> Behavioural conditions tend to be enforced through the use of penalties that reduce, suspend or end access to benefits, housing or other welfare 'goods', though conditional welfare arrangements may also combine sanctions with support and/or incentives to enable and encourage welfare recipients to behave in particular ways. *Relevant interventions range from overt 'punishments'* – such as the withdrawal of benefits, eviction from social housing, or the imposition of Anti-Social Behaviour Orders (ASBOs) – *to broader forms of 'social control' that seek to change behaviour through a more subtle mix of 'nudging', 'persuasion' and/or 'social pressure'.* (Emphases added)

One example clarifies the pertinence of these observations. Housing benefit can be sanctioned 'where a person has been evicted for anti-social behaviour and refuses to address their behaviour using the support and help offered to them' (Department for Work and Pensions, 2006, p 1).[13] The significance of this for the case being made here is that, if preventive orders become a vehicle for legitimising benefit sanctions, it is in principle both possible and potentially effective to impose them where sanctions are either unsuccessful or inappropriate because of their impact on other 'innocent' members of the household of the person who defaults. One of the principal difficulties of applying sanctions within separated spheres of welfare policy activity (housing, (un)employment, disability, family policy, and so on) concerns the uncoordinated and legislatively unintended effects of sanctions in one sphere of provision, and the consequential need for emergency interventions in another. In this way, the application of civil orders to prevent particular actions on pain of criminal proceedings opens up a new channel of response to benefit claimants whose actions cannot safely be countered by financial sanctions, and vice versa.

Although there is no official record or monitoring of the numbers of people who rely on multiple benefits, who experience multiple sanctions, and who are also the subject of civil preventive orders, the compounding effect of controls that cross these two categories of governance necessarily increases the risk of successive breaches and defaults. Strains of loss of benefits will inevitably manifest themselves in a greater propensity to breach conditions of orders, and vice versa. As a result, in specific cases, the effects of preventive orders, conditions of benefits, and sanctions for failure to meet conditions become profoundly intertwined in ways that magnify and proliferate the crossover effects of difficulties from one regulatory sphere into another.

Freedland and King (2003) offer an unusually broad-based analysis of the forms of contractualist governance that such intertwining entails, combining legal, economic and political elements. Their focus is on the increasing trend towards illiberal aspects of contractualism in the governance of the conduct of problematised populations. They draw on the work of Vincent-Jones (2000, p 473), which directs attention to concerns about 'the frequent lack of "responsiveness" of contracts as an instrument of governance of social relations between the state and citizens [which are] really concerns with the process of making and implementing contracts such as jobseeker's agreements or youth offender contracts'. Vincent-Jones pays particular attention to the adverse effects of sanctions and their disproportionate application for breaches of contract.[14] Freedland and King apply this critique to the New Deal workfare programme, and draw attention to the effects of sanctions for failure to follow contractual requirements of participation. They argue that:

> These illiberal effects can perhaps best be identified by concentrating on *the tendency of the workfare regime to function*

*as a quasi-criminal one, in which the failure of the jobseeker to comply with the terms and conditions of his or her 'agreement' with the benefit authorities assumes the character of an offence,* and by which the job-seeker who is not in compliance with the requirements of the agreement is therefore identified as an offender against a publicly maintained code of behaviour, albeit one which is couched in contractual form. ... The concerns one may feel about this kind of quasi-criminalisation may be linked up with some wider concerns about the excessive use of the criminal law in modern times in such a way as to dilute or over-extend societal notions of criminality in pursuit of regulatory objectives. (*That control rarely, if ever, involves the enforcement of these agreements as legal contracts – so rarely that it is normally unclear and untested whether these agreements have the force of legally binding contracts in any ordinary sense*). (Freedland and King, 2003, p 476, emphases added)

This closing parenthetical comment draws revelatory attention to the links between the quasi-criminalisation of those people who fail to comply with contractualist methods for governing the conduct of jobseekers, and the earlier observations about two-step criminalisation, hybrid civil-criminal orders, and the opacity, ambiguity and potential illegality of strictures and procedures for the governance of antisocial and other behaviours. These two tendencies are connected by their propensity to operate in twilight zones, mostly fractionally below the threshold of criminal legislation, but constantly able to invoke the spectre of criminal prosecution as a governmentalising gambit to secure compliance with specific contestable conditions. This closely parallels the intrinsically liminal quality of hybrid civil-criminal instruments of governance noted earlier, which bestow extraordinary powers to breach normal criminal codes and tests of criminality, out of the view of normal criminal procedure.

The insidious effects of these half-hidden powers and ambiguous rights and obligations render these shadowlands of the management and coercion of non-participants as informative examples of how problematised populations become 'governed through crime'. The injustices to which this form of governance gives rise are compounded by the opacity of their processes – and by the obscurity of their justifications to those towards whom they are directed (recalling Husak's earlier observations about lack of public knowledge of newly criminalised acts). The disproportionate nature and unintended consequences of the compound effects of civil orders, benefit conditions and financial sanctions become acutely evident.

Set in context, it is exceedingly unlikely that Freedland and King's (2003) exemplifications of the criminalising pursuit of regulatory objectives would satisfy the 'Presumption of Innocence Principle' or meet Tomlin's (2013, p 61) adage that 'conducts, like persons, must be presumed innocent until proven guilty'. In such instances, there can be no basis for confidence that the actions and motivations of those who are incrementally reeled into the widening and thinning criminal net are predicated on a wrong or a harm in the sense of these concepts in jurisprudence. More specifically, scenarios like those depicted by Freedland and King (2003) and Vincent-Jones (2000) appear to fall foul of a clear understanding of the distinction between 'before the event' and 'after the event' dimensions of criminal law emphasised by Simester and Von Hirsch (2011).

The sustainability of any claim that non-participation is being incrementally criminalised rests less on the precise legal terms of sanctions, preventive orders and criminal breach, and more on a range of powers brought to bear on the populations affected, the places they live in, and the responses they make to their plight. As Kadish (1987) points out, vagrancy laws have a lengthy and powerful provenance as a catch-all category for criminalising particular actions and categories of people whose deeds cannot be associated with any demonstrable harm or wrongful behaviour:

> The usual components of the offence include living in idleness without employment and having no visible means of support; roaming, wandering or loitering; begging; being a common prostitute, drunkard or gambler; and sleeping outdoors or in a residential building without permission. Beginning in feudal days, when these laws had their beginnings, they have been pressed into a great variety of services. Today, they are widely and regularly used by police as a basis for arresting, searching, questioning or detaining persons (who otherwise could not legally be subjected to such interventions) because of suspicion that they have committed or may commit a crime or for other police purposes. (Kadish, 1987, p 31)

Seen in this light, the foregoing discussion provides a strong basis for arguing that non-participation is emerging as the new face of vagrancy.

## Section 5: Reserve powers for the criminalisation of non-participation

A number of aspects of young people's non-participation have long been juridified, and non-participation is already criminalised by statute in particular circumstances. As Chapter Two explained, since 1870, there has been a legal obligation for children to attend school, but parents held the legal responsibility for securing attendance. In various ways, young people detained within the juvenile secure estate or subjected to supervision orders have also been compelled to certain forms of participation in educational activity, or required to participate in approved activities on threat of prosecution.[15] This responsibility was strengthened by the Criminal Justice and Police Act 2001, which created a new offence of aggravated truancy. As a result, parents judged to have colluded with or condoned their children's truancy were subject to a custodial sentence.[16]

The most tangible form of criminalisation of non-participation may also be its least significant, but the symbolic significance of New Labour's Education and Skills Act 2008 is without precedent, because it transfers the legal responsibility for participation in education or training from parents alone to the young people who are the focus of the legislation (in conjunction with their parents). Following Leitch (2006), the government's proposals placed a duty upon all young people in England to engage in education or training until the age of 18. The Act extends pre-existing obligations upon local authorities to make provision for all 16 to 18-year-olds, including those in employment.[17] It includes provision to identify young people who are not participating, involving a range of public bodies to enforce participation. Local authorities were empowered to issue attendance notices to young people (breach of which could in certain circumstances eventually result in a non-criminal custodial sentence), as well as parenting contracts or orders to their parents, and to set up independent attendance panels to monitor enforcement. In addition, employers had a duty to take all reasonable steps to ascertain that any young person that they contracted made appropriate arrangements for part-time education or training, and to monitor compliance. Contravention by employers could result in penalty notices, enforcement notices and financial penalties.

A number of the terms of the Act were suspended by the coalition government in the 2011 Education Act, pending review by the Secretary of State in 2016. The explanatory notes to the amendment read:

the Secretary of State will keep under review the appropriateness of commencing Chapter 5 of Part 1, which provides for an enforcement mechanism involving local authority enforcement notices, panels, penalty notices, and ultimately a criminal offence for failure to comply with an attendance notice. The commencement of other duties may be affected, including those on employers, parents, and the requirement on local authorities to identify those young people not meeting the central duty (House of Commons, 2011, para 354).

This removal of legal obligations was reinforced by clarification that non-participation will not result in legal sanction, and that the legal obligation to participate falls upon the young person themselves.[18] In practice, the absence of monitoring left 16 and 17-year-olds free to work without training, or to be 'non-participant', as they were previously.

This juridificatory reach of law into an aspect of civil life that has previously been dealt with by informal or welfare measures is without precedent. In its original 'unsuspended' form, it marked the intensification of the personal responsibilisation of young people below the age of majority, and a symbolic shift that enshrines in law a requirement of economic or educational participation, both despite and because of their unfavourable employment prospects. It constitutes the first potential criminalisation of non-participation within the 'illegalising' mode, as defined in Section 4.

Chapter Three noted that implementation of the amended 2008 legislation in 2013 coincided with withdrawal of the Education Maintenance Allowance (EMA). This was combined with an obligation placed upon 16 and 17-year-olds who continued in full-time education to pursue a course of study in GCSE English and mathematics if they had not already achieved a pass. Both measures were significant deterrents to those categories of low-achieving young people who are consistently among those least likely 'stay on' beyond the statutory age requirement. So far as can be ascertained from aggregate statistical data, the impact on increased participation among those aged 16+ between the autumn intakes of 2012 and 2013 was indistinguishable from the normal profile of variable annual changes, leaving almost a million 16 to 24-year-olds still outside education and training.[19]

If the 2008 legislation is ever implemented in its original form, on the face of it, the numbers of young people who receive civil orders for non-participation is likely to be considerably smaller than the numbers of 16 and 17 year olds who commit crimes. The administrative and bureaucratic costs of monitoring non-participation and of prosecuting offenders (especially among employers) may be regarded to be prohibitive. However, the evidence of Table 3.1 clearly indicates that the capacity of young non-participants to render themselves invisible to record-keepers is extensive, and may well continue to rise unmonitored. Reduced rates of offending associated with the youngest age groups in Chapter Five (see Figures 5.1-5.3) also complicate this claim. Certainly, the complexities of interpreting the data in Chapters Four and Five concerning the relationship between unemployment and crime among young people make clear the difficulty (if not futility) of attempting to estimate such outcomes. Moreover, there is ample evidence of the extent of discontent, hopelessness, low expectations, depression and resentment among young people who experienced long periods of inactivity in the years following the GFC. The extent and strains of sanctioning for non-compliance with Jobseeker's Allowance (JSA) claims among 16 to 24-year-olds alone establish preconditions that substantially increase the risks of responses involving property-related crimes. Sanctions have consistently been disproportionately high since the GFC, with some instances in which young people were twice as likely to be sanctioned as adults.[20] The impact of sanctions on security of supplies of food alone speaks to these risks.[21] Before the crisis, data from 2005 showed that about half of homeless 16 to 18-year-olds were non-participants (more than five times the national rate) (Pleace et al, 2008; see also Quilgars et al, 2008). During the early stages of the crisis in the supply of low-cost and public housing, in the immediate wake of the GFC, Centrepoint reported that the proportion of non-participants had escalated to a dramatic 76% among 20 to 25-year-olds.[22]

Whether such experiences have driven some young people to property crime for reasons of survival, or for its cathartic effects, and in what numbers, remains largely opaque. But it is crucial to recognise that connecting hardship and anger to criminal acts of acquisition of and damage to property concerns only one specific facet of criminalisation. It may also be the least significant facet, the least insidious – and the least informative about a deeper social malaise. In some profoundly important ways, these distinctions are a diversion and distraction of analytical and political energies away from other crucial meanings and manifestations of the multifaceted concept of criminalisation. Of far greater importance are the progressive governmentalisation, control, marginalisation and, ultimately, illegalisation of more avenues by means of which non-participants negotiate their plight – both to find tolerable, survivable modes of existence not premised on prolonged adolescent dependency on parents or carers, and to circumnavigate resentful capitulation to economic and other forms of exploitation.

An extended closing case study of a recent change in policy aptly illustrates the pertinence of this claim, and of the arguments made throughout this chapter. Until recently, looked-after young people were legally obliged to leave their foster homes at the age of 18, regardless of their circumstances as students, employees or non-participants. In 2014 the Children and Young People Act raised the age threshold to 21. The so-called 'staying put' arrangements oblige local authorities to enable 18 year-olds to remain with their foster parents until the age of 21, under specified conditions, if both parties agree. In exceptional circumstances a local authority may decline to allow a young person to remain in his or her foster home, but only on the grounds that it is not in the young person's best interests.

This enlightened change in policy followed a pilot project in 11 local authorities between 2008 and 2011. One of its key objectives was to enable looked-after young people to achieve in education, training or employment, in order to ease their 'transition' to adult life in the same way as other young people are able to. It was therefore a particular and telling irony that most of the pilot local authorities made existing or imminent participation in employment, education or training a criterion of eligibility for 'staying put' (although some authorities made exceptions on the basis of very restrictive and limiting conditions). The evaluation report of the pilots (Munro et al, 2012) found that some authorities appeared to have made participation in employment, education or training '*a 'condition' rather than an objective* or longer term outcome' (p 28, emphasis added). Epitomising the thinking behind this approach (and the extensive reach of the disengagement discourse), one care manager said '"if young people are not engaged, just staying in bed all day... [you're spending a lot of money for nothing]"' ( p 28).

Munro et al (2012) comment that 'expecting young people to be in [employment, education or training] potentially excludes the most vulnerable young people from ongoing placements with foster carers' (p 29). Certainly, the records of educational achievement of looked-after young people are consistently much lower than those of their peers, thus reducing their prospects for meeting this condition.[23] The researchers point out that this epitomises the 'inverse care law' (Hart, 1971), whereby it is those with the greatest needs who are excluded from care. In the UK over 60% of all 20 to 24-year-olds were living in their parental home at the peak of the effects of the GFC in 2011 (Stephens and Blenkinsopp, 2015, Figure 6). Even those young people leaving care who elect to remain looked-after until they are aged 21 therefore remain at a substantial disadvantage, by comparison. When this comparison is compounded by their poorer aggregate levels of educational attainment their relative disadvantage increases further. In all, looked-after young people leaving care who are already non-participants are least likely to meet the objectives of the 2014 Act of being securely in work or appropriately employable – even by the time they are required to leave their foster home at the age of 21.

In the light of this major limitation of many of the pilots, it is on the face of it reassuring to note that the 2014 Act and the supporting government guidance makes no provision for local authorities to impose participation in employment, education or training as an eligibility criterion for 'staying put'. However, they are not prohibited from doing so by the primary legislation, and a number of considerations leave room for significant doubt as to how the legislation may be working in practice.[24] Under the Act, the local authority is required to set out a 'pathway plan' which 'should cover arrangements such as ….education, training and employment activities' (HM Government, 2013, p 25). Some local authority guidance has a strongly normative push towards some form of recognised participation during extended residence with foster parents. Funding allocated in support of the scheme is not ring fenced, and is in some cases ostensibly diminutive and probably inadequate.[25] This will almost inevitably drive many local authorities with depleted budgets to prioritise by minimising the risks of low success rates, and concentrate resources on young people already in employment or on courses. The likely 'success' of 18 to 21-year-olds with the poorest educational and/or employment records will inevitably be assessed with particular care. Were future funding allocations to become performance related on the basis of each local authority's past records of participation amongst looked-after 21 year-olds leaving care, the risk-minimising approach would be very likely to produce outcomes that match the predictions of Hart's (1971) inverse care law.

All these factors exert additional pressure on looked-after young people leaving care to accept almost any form of work or training to improve their chances of remaining with their foster parents. It is in one sense encouraging that the exacting eligibility conditions of many of the 'staying put' pilots were not enshrined in the 2014 Act (even if they are not expressly precluded). It remains revealing that the majority of pilot authorities elected to exclude non-participants, and that the same thinking as that displayed by the care manager who regarded supporting non-participants as pointless expenditure seems very likely to continue where protected budgets prove inadequate to support all who want to 'stay put'.

One interpretation of the way in which the 2014 Act responded to the findings of the pilot is that it is pragmatic. A second is that it is deliberately designed to bring pressure to bear on the most prospectively high-risk care-leavers. For them, it is a harsh governmentalising measure that acts to place looked-after young people leaving care in precarious circumstances. It is in one sense irrelevant that there is no positive legislative provision for local authorities to make participation a condition of 'staying put' with foster parents. That several of the pilot authorities were both permitted to and chose to impose such a condition, and that the 2014 Act did not expressly prohibit this practice strongly implies that its principal objective embodies a strongly governmentalising intent. That is to say, the emphasis is on incentivising the desired behaviour (participating in order to remain looked after) irrespective of the costs to the wellbeing and future prospects of those young people who are, as a consequence, shut out of three additional years of foster care.

Care-leavers are disproportionately over-represented among convicted young offenders. At the time of writing, the levels of over-representation have become sufficiently extreme to prompt a major Prison Reform Trust review, chaired by Lord Laming.[26] If the 2014 Act succeeds in its own terms, it will funnel the most vulnerable into work (or training) under whatever conditions of poor pay, supervision and prospects prevail in their locality. For those who refuse these conditions (or are not offered the opportunity to try them) the alternatives are substantially increased risks of poverty, vulnerability or destitution, having nominally reached adulthood and ceased to be the responsibility of the state. The very existence of the Laming Review is a public recognition of the inherently criminogenic nature of the conditions under which some of the most vulnerable young people must survive at the threshold of the legal age of adulthood.

Such trajectories of looked-after young people leaving care at the age of 18 add new dimensions of meaning to the concept of 'governing through crime', and to the proposition that non-participation is itself becoming criminalised. The circumstances of many such young people undoubtedly match both the impelling and the imputing modes of criminalisation proposed in Section 2. By extending foster care to the age of 21, the statuses of some of these young people are those of de facto 'wards of state' in adulthood. Although their status is neither obligatory nor formally legally conditional, as Section 2 proposed, it both legitimises and makes practicable the governmentalisation of defining aspects of their lives. This is especially so if local authorities concentrate resources on those who are most likely to leave care three years later as financially independent young workers, at the expense of those who have the poorest prospects of doing so. By leaving the latter group without extended foster care, the state thereby exposes to yet higher risks of poverty and instrumental (or expressive) crime the sub-set of care-leavers who are already known to be the highest risk group. In this sense the state impels some of the most vulnerable towards crime.

The circumstances of looked-after young care leavers could easily be dismissed as exceptional – a 'special case'. But they are a special case only in the sense that they are a distinctive category whose profile of vulnerability to such harms is most easily monitored, best known and most readily made generalisable. The defining circumstances of large numbers of other young people expose them to comparable risks and harms if deprived of the protection of parents or other carers.

As 18 year-olds with poor or absent records of employment and educational qualifications, many other young people are equally vulnerable to being impelled towards crime or imputed as proto-criminal.

## Notes

[1] The adjective 'juridical' from which juridification is derived, meaning 'of or pertaining to the law' (*Oxford English Dictionary* (OED), 2014, online version) strongly implies a definition of 'the process of subjecting identified acts to law and legal sanction'. It nonetheless remains important to remember that Habermas' use of the term refers less to individual acts of legislation, and more to an underlying trend of the increasing application of law to (commonplace or routine) actions.

[2] Etymologically, the verb 'to criminalise' derives from the Middle French verb '*criminalisé*', meaning 'to accuse', with the earliest recorded usage in English being in the late 17th century, where it meant 'to pass a case from the civil to the criminal jurisdiction'. As later sections show, this act of 'passing' is highly pertinent in the context of contemporary hybrid civil-criminal legislation.

[3] The semantics of this definition are not, of course, in themselves, an authoritative source for understanding what it means to criminalise a person or act. But the OED's differentiation of the criminalisation of an act and the criminalisation of a person draws attention to the ways in which the processes of criminalisation might operate.

[4] This manifestation of criminalisation is generally criticised as an exceptional and new dimension of juridification in the form of intrusions into the private sphere of household, family and civil life. A significant proportion of the new social policy legislation introduced by the New Labour governments after 1997 was directed to forms of behaviour management, particularly in relation to parents, children and young people, that made many forms of conduct the subject of civil law, breaches of which could result in criminal proceedings - see below.

5    Among the earliest usages were those of Blagg et al (1988); Crawford 1997, 1999), Muncie (1999), Wacquant (1999), Presdee (2000).

6    Following Lemert (1951), the common thread of deviancy is not the forms it takes, but the social reaction it provokes. As this line of theorisation developed into labelling theory, Becker (1963, p 9) argued that 'deviance is not a quality of the act a person commits, but rather *a consequence of the application by others of rules and sanctions* to an "offender"'(emphasis added). In this interpretation, the focus of analysis shifts from the allegedly deviant act to the social reaction to it. Through such processes, undesirable activity results in labelling and stigmatisation. These processes prompt disproportionate social reactions that invoke pathologised forms of behaviour. Following Wilkins' (1964) concept of 'deviation amplification', intolerant responses to deviant behaviours produce self-perpetuating spirals of reaction and response. Subsequent theorists, notably Young (1971) and Cohen (1972, 2002), demonstrated how mass media, police reporting and methods of estimating such behaviours intensified the speed of the cycle and amplified its impact.

7    These provisions were subsequently temporarily suspended by the 2011 Education Act – see Section 5.

8    See, for example, the tabular representation of the Home Office typology of antisocial behaviour in Harradine et al (2004, Table 2.1).

9    Clauses in the Bill that resulted in the Antisocial Behaviour, Crime and Policing Act of 2014 sought to lower the threshold of indicted behaviour from harassment, alarm or fear to 'nuisance and annoyance'. They were later removed, on the grounds that the categories of nuisance and annoyance were not susceptible to clear legal definition, and were highly subjective, and more criminalising than the outgoing legislation (for a fuller discussion see Fergusson, 2014b).

10   As specified by in the Criminal Justice Act, 1982. Simester and Von Hirsch (2011, p 231) add to this example by reference to specific cases of ASBOs that have been issued against individuals attempting suicide, against autistic young people and against sex workers, all of which expose the defendant to a criminal record and a custodial sentence, despite the fact that all these actions on the part of these specified categories of people have also long since been decriminalised. ASBOs were replaced by Criminal Behaviour Orders in the 2014 Antisocial Behaviour, Crime and Policing Act.

11   For a full account see Pitts (2003, pp 52-3).

12   For a full listing see Ashworth and Zender (2010, p 65).

13   The sanction can apply for up to five years, which Grover (2010, para 4.4) describes as 'a particularly harsh penalty'. As a consequence, Flint (2009, pp 249-50) points out, this raises the serious prospect of households that have been evicted from their first home for antisocial behaviour being at high risk of eviction from their second home for rent arrears. In the UK, and also in the Republic of Ireland (see Wright, 2011), there appears to have been no evaluation of the extent and effects of this – so far unique – bridge between preventive civil orders and sanctions facilitated by welfare conditionalisation.

14   Vincent-Jones looks particularly at the damage to relationality as arrangements that can be expected to be responsive to client needs are revealed to be more harshly and punitively contractual. He argues that 'Such reciprocity might be argued to exist in Jobseekers Agreements in the payment to the claimant of welfare benefits. However, there is little evidence here of genuine consent. "There seems little leeway for a meeting of minds but rather more the concept of take it or leave it"

(Fulbrook, 1995)' (Vincent-Jones, 2000, n 155, p 348). This analysis once again powerfully exemplifies Habermas' notions of damage within the lifeworld when the priorities of economy and state power are imposed upon it with relative disregard for their impact.

15    The 1988 Criminal Justice Act, for example, attached conditions of compliance with Local Education Authority requirements to supervision orders which 'in effect criminalised non-school attendance' (Brown, 1998, p 66).

16    The first implementation of this legislation in 2002 infamously subjected an Oxfordshire mother to a 60-day sentence, following her daughter's persistent truancy (BBC (2002) 'Mother jailed for girls' truancy' http://news.bbc.co.uk/1/hi/england/1984502.stm (see also: BBC (2004) 'Truancy mother sent to jail again' http://news.bbc.co.uk/1/hi/england/oxfordshire/3561655.stm)).

17    This can take a number of forms. The part-time education or training constitutes 280 guided learning hours per year, which must lead to a qualification offered by any accredited provider. The Act places a duty upon local authorities to 'promote the effective participation of all 16 and 17-year-olds'.

18    In 2013, as the amended 2008 legislation was about to come into force, employers were reminded that there were no duties on them and that therefore no action could be taken if an employee failed to undertake part-time education or training. Subsequent website advice left ambiguities for young people regarding their obligation to participate in training when employed, but reinforced employers' exoneration from responsibility. If their employer refuses to allow them to attend, he or she is exempt from sanction, but the young person is, technically, in breach of the terms of the 2008 Act (see Department for Education, 2013/14).

19    The proportion of 16-year-olds recorded as 'not in education or training' (NEET) in England fell by 1.5 percentage points between the end of 2012 and the end of 2013. Recent data shows that while NEET rates amongst 16 and 17 year olds have been declining steadily since 2006 (some time before the implementation of the 2008 Education and Skills Act in 2013) and are currently below 5%, there was a sharp compensating rise in the rate amongst 18-24 year olds between 2008 and 2012 that has only begun to decline as the 2008 Act was implemented. Since the Act does not apply to the older age group, it suggests that this may be more a function of slowly-declining unemployment nationally (and of the continuing withdrawal of 16-17 year olds from the labour market). For 18-24 year olds the rate remains above 15%, affecting almost 900,00 young people. In both age groups the UK NEET rate continues to be above the OECD average (Mizra-Davies, 2015).

20    Around 42% of sanctions of JSA claimants resulting in some or all of benefits entitlement being stopped were of 16 to 25-year-olds, who accounted for 27% of claimants (TUC, 2015, p 16). In Scotland, between 23,000 and 35,000 16 to 24-year-olds, who made up less than a quarter of JSA claimants, had been sanctioned every year since 2009, representing between 41% and 50% of those sanctioned (Scottish Government, 2014). Almost every English region observed a substantial increase in the number of vulnerable young people who had been sanctioned between 2011 and 2013 (YMCA, 2014).

21    Interviews with 59 vulnerable 16 to 24-year-olds in English YMCAs found that between 75% and 86% of them had been forced to forgo food, housing costs or the purchase of toiletries as a result of the sanctions they experienced (YMCA, 2014). In Scotland, JSA claimants who had been sanctioned accounted for a quarter of users of Food Banks (Citizens Advice Scotland, 2012).

[22] Memorandum to House of Commons, Children, Schools and Families Committee (session 2009-10) (2009).

[23] The gap between the attainment levels of looked-after children and those of the remainder of the population was consistently greater than 40 percentage points between 2009/10 and 2011/12 in England (Department for Education, 2012 – see for example Chart 2).

[24] The Children's Partnership, which is a 'strategic partner' of the Department for Education, asserts that '[t]he legislation does not permit local authorities to introduce their own eligibility rules' (National Children's Bureau, 2014, p 13). However, it is not clear in the Act or the accompanying guidance that this is legally precluded.

[25] In the 2015-16 allocations in England more than 30 local authorities were each allocated less than £50,000 to support the scheme (www.gov.uk/government/uploads/system/uploads/attachment_data/file/413094/STAYING_PUT_GRANT_LETTER_2015-16.pdf).

[26] In 2015 the Prison Reform Trust set up the 'Keeping children in care out of trouble' review to establish why almost two thirds of young people below the age of 18 who were or had been in custody had also spent part of their life in the care system (www.prisonreformtrust.org.uk/ProjectsResearch/CareReview).

# NINE

# Review and concluding comments

## Introduction

Chapter One set out the aims of this book:

- to provide a wide-ranging critical assessment of existing evidence about the causes of non-participation, its interpretation and its impact on policy;

- to locate the relationship between non-participation, welfare and crime in its historical, political-economic and policy contexts in the UK;

- to consider the effects of the global financial crisis on the relationship, set in UK and international contexts;

- to review competing theorisations of key elements of the relationship;

- and to establish the non-participation-welfare-crime relationship at the centre of critical policy analysis in the fields of social and criminal justice policies.

Parts Two and Three have pursued these aims by working beyond the two dominant traditions of youth studies summarised in Table 2.1 and across policy fields, social science disciplines and theoretical and analytical approaches (Tables Interlude.1 and 7.1). Parts Three and Four have focused on theories of governance and of criminalisation, towards developing a dedicated theorisation of the non-participation-welfare-crime relationship (Table 7.1).

This final chapter has two purposes. The first, in the next section, is to review and assess the ways in which the analyses of the preceding chapters have met these aims, and the approaches by which they have done so. The second, in the final section, is to consider what the analysis might imply for future research in this field, and the need for a programme of political action.

## Section 1: Review

The book is organised in four parts. Part One provides an introduction, an overview of the book's scope and coverage, and a selective literature review. Part Two, comprising Chapters Two to Five, is focused on a critical review of research and policy concerning work, welfare and crime and their relationships to non-participation among young people. Following an Interlude which reviews Part Two, Part Three (Chapters Six and Seven) is concerned with ways in which the non-participation-welfare-crime relationship could be theorised differently. Part Four (Chapters Eight and Nine) considers the extent to which non-participation is becoming criminalised, and concludes with this review.

Chapter One begins by highlighting evidence of a crisis of non-participation among young people in the UK and internationally, and by identifying a parallel crisis in academic analysis of non-participation and its relationship to crime. Emblematic of the international crisis of non-participation is the grossly disproportionate burden of global unemployment borne by 15 to 24-year-olds, and the massive rises in youth unemployment to more than 50% in parts of Western Europe, and more than 80% in parts of Eastern Europe. In the UK, almost half of the million young people who were recorded as NEET in 2014 were in effect out of sight of and support from recognised forms of economic and educational activity. Rising suicide rates in this age range in the UK from the onset of the GFC onwards, in close correlation to regional patterns of unemployment, provide further evidence of crisis. So do the associations between unemployment and social unrest among young people in the UK and beyond.

In parallel, Chapter One argues that the academic study of young people has had little to contribute to a convincing account of how and why mass unemployment and non-participation has become associated with crime, and identifies this as a crisis in academic analyses. Divisions between analytical approaches are proposed as a contributory factor. The chapter queries claims of a rapprochement between the divided traditions of youth studies. Subsequent chapters propose that the divisions remain in place in part because the decline of one tradition (youth cultural studies) is partly attributable to the dominance of the other (especially the most positivistic quantitative branch of the youth transitions tradition). A range of significant insights into the relationship between non-participants' criminal conduct that take full account of the effects of changing education and welfare policies and labour market circumstances have been underplayed in the few analyses developed since the onset of the GFC. The tendency for researchers to work in disciplinary and paradigmatic silos has exacerbated this limitation. One outcome has been that the youth cultural studies tradition has not given full attention to the ways in which youthful transgression and deviant behaviour may have been related to political-economic conditions since the GFC. And at the same time, the risk-factor analysis approach to youth transitions has continued largely oblivious to the conflicting interpretations of young people's criminal conducts proposed by the youth cultural studies tradition.

## Review of Part Two

In response, Part Two redresses the marginalisation of political-economic factors in analyses within the youth transitions tradition and the youth cultural studies tradition alike. It also disrupts interpretations of criminal motivation narrowly focused on psychosocial, moral or financial causes without regard to political-economic, social and welfare policy contexts. Moreover, it shows the limitations of analyses that confine themselves within paradigmatic clusters.

Chapter Two reviews three overlapping post-war discourses that have dominated accounts of the shifting relationship between employment, schooling and non-participation. It begins with critiques of the transitions discourse which manifested fundamental divisions that continue to characterise interpretations of non-participation, and focuses on the analyses put forward within the two youth studies traditions. The social exclusion discourse marked a major shift to an emphasis on interventionist policy, the responsibilisation of young people and the conditionalisation of entitlement, leading with a focus on exogenous factors of analysis and nomothetic levels of analysis that took account of social and labour market contexts. In turn, the disengagement discourse moves interpretation towards individual choices, endogenous factors and idiographic levels of analysis that place strong reliance on psychosocial and moral referents.

Chapter Three traces the post-war profile of youth unemployment, the deepening divergence between rates of youth and adult unemployment, and some global trends which contextualise the exceptional levels of youth unemployment and non-participation in the UK. It develops a critique of the claims that high levels of unemployment and non-participation could be attributed to poor skills and qualifications, focusing instead on the chronically low mean wage rates of young people since the GFC, and providing an analysis of the incremental withdrawal of sustainable state welfare for young people without jobs, courses or training places that began in the 1980s. Finally, it identifies the 'wage rate suppression dynamic', and examines its consequences, arguing that many young people make rational choices to refuse labour market participation under prevailing conditions.

Chapter Four considers the extent and nature of the mooted relationship between non-participation and criminal offending among young people, most notably as reflected in the social exclusion discourse and the Risk Factor Prevention Paradigm (RFPP). It argues that a purely empirical approach to understanding these connections is unsustainable, that such an approach requires an explicit theorisation of the connections between non-participation and crime, and that claims of a causal connection have not been consistently demonstrated. It reviews the influence of actuarial studies on interventionist policies intended to pre-empt crime, aspects of which display strong congruencies with the 'economic causes of crime' (ECC) thesis in stressing rational action and instrumental motivation as causal factors linking unemployment to property crime. A critical assessment of several studies offers no clear support for the ECC thesis, despite some evidence that welfare provision that ameliorates economic duress may also reduce crime. This tentative finding demonstrates the importance of understanding the unemployment-crime relationship in the context of welfare provision, workfare conditionality and income. Continuing uncertainties about causality reinforce the need for a major refinement of or retreat from the ECC thesis, which should include enhanced capacity for taking into account the crucial distinction between instrumental and expressive motivations for crime, and the relationship between them.

Chapter Five develops an analysis of the impact of economic recession on the relationship between unemployment and crime. A detailed review of recent studies reveals conflicting findings that demonstrate the limitations of aggregate historical statistical analyses for understanding claims about the mooted causal relationship between them, including in recessionary conditions that might be expected to intensify evidence of causation. This underscores the conclusion that conjuncture and contextual specificity are critical to understanding any such relationship. A review of youth offending rates during the GFC recessions reinforces this conclusion. It demonstrates that, while official statistics indicate a counter-trend decrease, major weaknesses in the reliability and validity of the data undermine this claim, and further demonstrate the perils of 'reading off' connections between unemployment and crime, and the hazards of the methodologies that underpin the ECC thesis.

Recognition of the faltering claims of causal connections between unemployment and crime, even in recessions, raise questions about other ways in which unemployment and non-participation might be associated with crime – or rather with particular conceptions and discourses of criminality. The chapter provides extensive international evidence of social unrest among young people that coincided with the GFC. This in turn reinforces the earlier recognition that understandings of the non-participation–crime relationship must move beyond a narrow focus on acquisitive crimes, instrumental motivations, rational choices and cognition, not only by affording recognition to expressive motivations and their underlying emotions of anger and resentment, but by understanding interactions between categories of motivation, and by taking into account the allegedly criminalising effects of recession.

## Interlude: interpretive review

The Interlude between Parts Two and Three makes the case for a dedicated theorisation of the relationship between non-participation, welfare and crime that explores interpretations beyond the scope of mainstream empirical research. The express purpose has been to divert analysis from a focus on the alleged criminality of non-participant young people, towards an understanding of the causes and consequences of endemic mass non-participation by means of a more broadly based analysis, fully cognisant of diverse political-economic and policy contexts.

This case is in part a direct response to the recognition that emerges from Part Two, that successive changes in policy-led research over several decades have incrementally shifted the burden of analysis from exogenous to endogenous causes of non-participation, and from nomothetic to idiographic levels of analysis. In effect, policy analysis and response has become less predisposed to acknowledge the role of social and economic circumstances as causes of non-participation, and increasingly inclined towards attributing responsibility to personal shortcomings. In place of this approach, promising insights come from analyses that reject some of the crude distinctions that are embedded in competing accounts of non-participation, opposing levels of analysis and conflicted accounts of motivations for crime. These prospects are enhanced if the prevailing focus on theories that accept and embed longstanding lines of division is suspended in favour of theories that disrupt them.

## Review of Part Three

In pursuit of this approach, Parts Three and Four are built on the insights and complementarities offered by the theories of Jürgen Habermas and Imogen Tyler. Both parts incorporate an unfolding assessment of the ways in which these theories have provided an alternative analysis that illuminates and exceeds understandings of the relationship between non-participation, welfare and crime that are considered in Part Two.

In Chapter Six, Habermas' approach is shown to work across paradigms by virtue of his attention to the individual, the idiographic and the endogenous, alongside his emphasis on structures, nomothetic levels of analysis and the influence of exogenous factors on human conduct and action. Exemplifying this are his analyses of the alienating, anomic and pathological effects of systems colonisation of lifeworlds, of the centrality of the welfare state to the 'pacification' of these effects, and of how both bear upon young people. For Habermas, as the demands of money and power systems begin to dominate the lifeworld, communicative action fails to precede instrumental action, such that inhabitants of the lifeworld are less well apprised of the purposes and methods of the operation of the economy. Disturbances of social integration have anomic social effects while also causing individual alienation. Full exploitation of resources of cultural and interpersonal cohesion and identity is necessary to avoid crises of power and money, and social disorder. It is then difficult for young people who are unable to obtain employment to be interpellated by and give credence to an economic system in which they have no place. In the dominant discourse this is the moment at which young people become 'disengaged'. The logic of why they should undertake menial workfare in return for allowances that are inadequate to sustain basic needs becomes opaque. The strident imposition of the demands of the systems of money and political power on the lifeworld profoundly affects young people at the critical protracted tipping point between diminishing adolescent dependence and growing adult independence.

Importantly, throughout Habermas' analysis, idiographic and nomothetic dimensions of analysis are intermixed with endogenous and exogenous factors in ways that are rare, as well as being significant for identifying tangible connections between two domains of analysis that are typically separated. This analysis nevertheless courts serious risks when Habermas classifies acts of passive withdrawal, resistance, refusal and disengagement as pathologies. Its essential flaw, the chapter argues, is its implicit propensity to identify endogenous factors as critical to the inherent conflict between systems and lifeworld, as though they emanated entirely from within (decontextualised) individuals, as if predetermined.

These limitations of Habermas' approach highlight the value of Tyler's equally paradigm-traversing analysis of social abjection and oppression under rising powers of neoliberal governmentalisation, while maintaining her overarching emphasis on the personal and psychosocial focus of both concepts. Tyler maintains the centrality of class to her analysis of social abjection, and highlights processes of governance to interpret it. Her analysis of the ways in which young non-participants are made abject vividly portrays the power of these processes to reposition victims as authors of their own oppression. In doing so, it makes good some limitations of Habermas' analysis by demonstrating ways in which many young people accept and adopt their categorisation as 'disengaged', thereby opening the door to the impositions they encounter and may subsequently refuse.

The remainder of Chapter Six seeks out further complementarities and intersectionalities of Tyler's and Habermas' work. This opens up possibilities for examining the interactions between cognitive and affective (and rational and emotional) elements of young people's responses to non-participation, in ways that have been overlooked as foci of previous analyses.

Chapter Seven draws on Habermas' theories to develop an interpretation of the relationship between non-participation and crime founded in rational, cognitive and instrumentalist paradigms for understanding the non-participation–welfare–crime relation, and on Tyler's theories to interpret those founded in the opposing paradigms. Using recent evidence of the textured complexity of young lives at the margins of poverty, insecurity and criminalisation, the complementary insights of Habermas' and Tyler's theories are shown to highlight the ways in which their respective understandings of the governance of problematised populations add to the analysis of unemployment and its relationship with crime. Habermas' theorisations primarily support interpretations of the non-participation–crime relationship that are constructed around the rationality–cognition–instrumentality cluster, and Tyler's are more inclined to support those founded in emotion, affect and expression. However, crucially, both their approaches are seen to draw on the other paradigm.

Chapter Seven invokes the need for research that moves beyond the premises of the quantitative analyses that dominate attempts to understand 'failed' transitions, and the correlates of the onset of crime. In addition to these complementarities of Tyler's and

Habermas' analyses, Chapter Seven identifies others. Both authors incorporate theories of governance and theories of criminalisation, albeit with differing foci and orientations. Tyler's interest in neoliberal governmentality encompasses the domains of affect and emotion as well as cognition and rationality, while Habermas' entire theoretical frame is concerned with acts of governance achieved through systems of money and political power, and with the ways in which they impact on the social and emotional relations of the lifeworld. Alongside these potential complementarities, Tyler's use of the concept of stigmatisation and Habermas' focus on juridification identify powerful connections for understanding criminalisation. All of these alignments, it is suggested, offer rare possibilities for reassessing the non-participation-crime relationship in innovative ways.

The introduction of theories of governance – particularly governmentality theory – into the debate opens a further dimension of the non-participation-crime relationship. Other theorists' work on the ways in which problematised populations can be 'governed through unemployment' draws attention to close congruencies between Habermas' explorations of welfare conditionalisation and juridification, and Jonathan Simon's conceptualisation of 'governing through crime'. On this view, the state finds ever more sophisticated ways of resolving structural problems by requiring specified forms of participation and by using the powers of civil and criminal law to bear down upon those who refuse them. In this way, it is argued, the governmentalisation of unemployment can be seen as an active means of governing crime preventatively.

## Review of Part Four

The closing analysis of Chapter Seven establishes a connecting axis between processes of governance and of criminalisation that are the subject of Part Four. As Chapter Eight shows, Habermas' work demonstrates how juridification processes provide a channel to address the deleterious effects of allowing political-economic priorities to dominate the social sphere of the lifeworld. The chapter proposes that juridification and criminalisation are closely connected in practice as well as conceptually. Criminalisation is described as multifaceted and ambiguous, signifying a wide range of actions, from increased use of the criminal justice system, to blurring the boundaries between civil and criminal proceedings, circumventing due processes, breaching precepts of jurisprudence, subverting rights and imposing unjust punishments. This analysis stresses the primary significance of increased juridification (as predicted by Habermas) and more intensive criminalisation (as described by Tyler) as indicating the availability of both as tools of governance and tools for governmentalisation in relation to young people's non-participation.

The chapter sets out a number of ways in which conditions conducive to criminalising non-participation are already in place, as 'reserve powers' for more coercive forms of 'governing non-participation' on the part of the state. It argues that there is no basis for confidence that the alleged offences which are prosecuted because of the (in)actions of those who commit them are predicated on a wrong or a harm, in the senses intended in jurisprudence. The test of their status as criminalising acts, it is argued, will reside in the particularities of context and circumstance that allow grounded assessments as to whether they are consistent with the precepts of social as well as criminal justice – and whether criminalised non-participants are becoming the 'new vagrants' of early 21st century neoliberal states, whose very status provides a pretext for prosecution.

## Section 2: Concluding comments

Non-participation among 16 and 17-year-olds has already been legislatively proscribed in the UK. The means by which young people can elude unsuitable, exploitative and oppressive forms of enforced participation are being incrementally closed off. Despite the pressures this imposes on those born into socially and economically disadvantaged regions, localities and households, and despite the increasing number of instruments of regulation, governance and civil law by which their options can be channelled, the UK continues to be among the OECD countries with the highest levels of non-participation. In addition to the million 16 to 24-year-olds who were recorded as being without a job or a course of education or training at the height of the GFC, in some of the most populous English regions, the 'activity statuses' of at least one in five 18 year-olds were not know (and more than twice that proportion in some local authorities). A substantial proportion of them were undoubtedly hidden non-participants. As such, they occupy an ambiguous and risky hinterland between self-invisibilisation and self-identification as targets for monitoring and intervention. Protracted dependency on partners, parents and others sets the limiting parameters of their future prospects. Those young people who do not have these forms of refuge, and those who refuse the limitations they may imply, are also those who are most likely to become criminalised through civil action, by imputation or by being impelled to secure their own material survival through crime.

The persistent search for better quantitative data for identifying solutions to historically enduring socioeconomic and political-economic problems like mass non-participation now seems misconceived as well as futile. By the same token, it is of only the most limited relevance to refine official counts of those young non-participants who are incrementally drawn into the thinning net between workfare sanctions, breaches of civil orders and survival crime.

Most young people whose post-school trajectory falls within the purview of the agencies of governmentalisation and control know, however implicitly, that they are on the wrong side of a regulatory regime. For those who feel interpellated in this way, crossing the line to being stereotyped, channelled or suspect may be a small step. Tyler's (2013) anatomies of social abjection capture these insidious inductive pathways to criminalisation with powerful lucidity. Persistent stigmatisation can induce young non-participants to believe in their standing as 'failed citizens', and open up further interpellative episodes of self-recognition.

Tyler's (2013, p 193) depiction highlights 'the revolting figure of the profligate, criminalised welfare recipient', and the general abuse and stigmatisation of those who are made socially abject: hapless subjects encounter, accept and absorb the legitimising discourses of their own oppression. This recalls the debate about the cultural sources of 'failed transitions' and social exclusion discussed in Chapters Two and Three, in which the denial of the possibilities to work, to earn, to consume (and so to engage in contingent forms of social belonging) foster the formation of alternative modalities of existence constructed on the ambiguous terrain of state abandonment and state surveillance. There, young people can find sources of recognition and intra-group respect that counteract what Tyler (2013, pp 198, 200) describes as diminished aspirations, low expectations and 'a crisis of possibility'. At the same time, the risks of their stigmatisation – and ultimately of their coercive and potentially criminalising governmentalisation – increase exponentially in self-fulfilling predictions that fuel the self-proving power of actuarial calculus like that used by the RFPP and the more determinist versions of the ECC thesis. If states pursue those young people whom their flawed models predict to be likely offenders, they automatically reinforce the credibility of the instruments of governance they deploy, however ill-founded they may be.

In this respect, the sophistication and power of Tyler's analysis exceeds and largely displaces the purchase of Habermas' specific endeavours to recognise the importance of endogenous factors and idiographic levels of analysis. Nevertheless, the power of his highly developed analysis of the economic drivers and uncoupling effects of systems priorities that are imposed on social worlds prevails, and complements Tyler's analysis. There can be no starker version of such imposed powers than those of states that secure arrangements that are economically advantageous to employers, and combine them with the power of those who govern and secure enforced participation.

An extensive apparatus for criminalising non-participation has begun to accumulate. By making illegal some forms of survival behaviour that proliferate in the environments of Tyler's stigmatised communities, contingent behaviours associated with boredom, poverty and unoccupied non-participation can be relatively easily criminalised using the two-step tactics typified by antisocial behaviour legislation. At the same time, the punitive proto-criminalisation of non-compliance used in the management of workfare schemes funnels those most determined to resist them towards extended periods of non-participation. Whether they are trawled into the criminal net using hybrid civil-criminal orders, or impelled to petty theft or forced entry into vacant properties for want of food or shelter, the reserve powers of criminalisation stand ready to target young people who explore the diminishing range of escape routes from enforced participation. Here, the 'soft' powers of governmentalisation that Tyler's analysis emphasises blend easily with the exercise of the raw juridificatory powers of state that dominate Habermas'. The processes of criminalisation in their latent forms have already begun to take control of the meeting ground on which the soft powers of governance bring more resistant non-participants face to face with harder powers, first those of civil law, and eventually those of criminal law.

The full potential of Tyler's and Habermas' unexpectedly complementary paradigm-traversing analyses for understanding these processes has yet to be realised and assessed. Understanding the insidious drift of creeping criminalisation that their analyses allow should now be a priority for the purposes of programmes of research and political action alike.

## Implications for a programme of research

The key task for research and analysis in this field is to gauge the unfolding new modalities of criminalisation, map their advance and assess their 'reserve powers'. Such research should neither begin from nor confine itself to case-study evidence and counts, or instances of criminal prosecution that result from the enforcement of existing legislation. The multifaceted character of the concept of criminalisation demands a broader vista of investigation. Researchers should search wherever extended unemployment and persistent refusal of alternative activities are responded to as breaches of regulation or civil law. They should focus on settings in which welfare provision falls short of the pacifying and compensatory purposes envisaged in Habermas' theory. They should investigate settings in which young people's resistance to enforced participation occasions labelling associated with deviancy, as part of the characteristic processes of stigmatisation Tyler identifies.

Research should therefore also be alert to policy interventions that close off the few remaining avenues that allow would-be non-participants to render themselves invisible, and focus on those who use them. It should systematically monitor programmes of intervention that open up new channels for tracking the everyday behaviours of non-participants, or set increasingly stringent prescriptions for programmes of activity that substitute for paid work. It should interrogate legislation that seeks to control places, behaviours and activities with which extended non-participation and refusal are associated. It should challenge the ever-evolving refinement of actuarial methodologies that purport to identify criminalistic conducts in common behavioural traits. Perhaps most of all, it should maintain ongoing critical observation of activities that enable, induce or pressure young people to recognise themselves and their behaviours as proto-criminal.

In support of the crucial task of challenging the erosion of the Presumption of Innocence Principle, research should also afford urgent attention to the pursuit of quasi-criminalising policies and practices and hybrid forms of legislation that circumnavigate the standard tests of jurisprudence. In doing so it should monitor adherence to Tomlin's (2013, p 61) principle that 'conduct, like persons, must be considered innocent until proven guilty', against the threat of governmentalising and criminalising policies designed to mandate participation and punish non-participation.

Some of these injunctions to researchers are now more likely to be met in partnership with the best of investigative journalism or the politically committed work of campaigning organisations, think tanks and programmes of civil action. Most of them require assiduous monitoring of the marginal incremental erosion of the liberal rights of 'free labour' in notionally free markets to refuse unsafe, exploitative and intolerable conditions of work, at rates of sub-poverty pay designed to undercut competitors, in pursuit of price advantage. Some of this monitoring may still be best suited to academic study based on expert analytical understanding of social and criminal justice policy and law, protected by expectations of scholarly impartiality and the advancement of knowledge though the imaginative boundary-traversing application of the disciplines of the social sciences. However, much of the work of managing, monitoring and governing young people at and beyond the margins of mainstream employment is contracted to private providers, who work competitively with other for-profit providers. Here the historical traditions of managed access for researchers (whose work is seen to deliver on statutory obligations of transparency in public sector administration) do not reliably open the requisite doors. Skilled investigative journalists, campaigners and think-tank researchers are better placed to gain access, monitor and then interrogate what they find. As the closing paragraphs propose, the case for collaboration between academic researchers and others may offer a way forward.

## The need for a programme of political action

Policies that shape the fate of young people who leave school with poor qualifications in weak labour markets, in times of recession or in economically depressed localities are part of a Leviathan programme of welfare reform in the UK. Programmes like Universal Credit in the hands of governments determined to reduce the costs of state welfare and incentivise the lowest-paid forms of (often-unregulated) work (in often-unregulated work-places) represent a starkly zealous revival of the less-eligibility principle embodied in the Poor Law. Nowhere has this zeal been more energetically applied over the last three decades than to young people. Their marginal propensities to accept or reject diminutive workfare allowances have long been a test-bed for driving down wages. One of the critical moments in the neoliberalisation of state welfare provision is the one in which the tendency for welfare benefit rates to track wage-driven inflation is being put into reverse gear. As Pemberton's (2015) analysis shows, high levels of non-participation among young people are distinctive markers of neoliberal (and some liberal) regimes. The GFC and the legitimising austerity discourse to which it has given rise have provided propitious conditions for initiating the reversal that may assist the UK's transition to unbridled neoliberalism. By driving down benefit rates, reservation wage expectations can be lowered, so long as labour is in surplus. Youth labour markets, reliably in perpetual surplus, are ideal testing grounds.

A programme of political action to challenge this reversed dynamic and address the neglectful disregard for the most economically vulnerable young people is unlikely to arise from a grassroots movement. Their fate requires transnational social and political attention. In the UK and far beyond it, a generation of adults who experienced the best of the post-war welfare settlements is witnessing (and in many cases presiding over) a profound erosion of the benefits they have enjoyed. In the aftermath of the GFC, this realisation has fuelled ill-directed, misconceived polemics about intergenerational inequality. Unknowledgeable assertions have substituted age for class as the engine of social injustice. This promotes a dangerous discourse, as much for the political project that it masks as for the false claims that it makes.

A programme of political action to challenge the reversed dynamics of benefits and wages is therefore of vital political importance if mistaken interpretations of young people's plight are not to fuel the current rise of xenophobic, exclusionary nationalism in Europe and elsewhere – in which the advantaged first post-second-world-war generation risks becoming another vilified social category. The political programme capable of reawakening a popular sense of social injustice is likely to be the one that is most successful at depicting the consequences, over several generations, of the massive resurgence in extremes of socioeconomic inequality that are already becoming socially normalised and politically destabilising, especially in the poorest societies.

A clearer vision of the consequences of social and economic polarisation has the power to raise awareness of the values of social solidarity and social cohesion. A programme that raises that awareness will also be capable of re-envisioning the injustices of endemic, ubiquitous, transnational youth unemployment and non-participation. Constructing a vividly evidenced profile of the medium-term social and economic consequences of 'standing by' while the most impoverished, prospect-less 16 to 24-year-olds reach their middle years, as parents who cannot support their own non-participant sons and daughters (or their own 'retirements'), has the power to counter the current indifference to burgeoning inequality – among voters, policy makers and many governments.

Academic researchers are less likely to construct this vision and communicate it effectively if they work alone. Invaluable complementarities and mutual protections can be achieved by academics working in partnerships with investigative journalists, campaigners, think-tank researchers and political organisations, as suggested. Programmes of political or policy-driven research that are resilient to the pressures towards policy-determined evidence have powerful potential to investigate alternative models and inform new policy thinking.

A world away from this, the powers of post-academic research based on partnership have been shown to be invaluable in the often-treacherous politics of international trade policy negotiations. As one participant author has shown, collaborative work that builds beyond academic research has distinctive qualities (Tussie, 2009). It eschews the detachment of academics. It validates the policy process. It is accountable to stakeholders. And perhaps most importantly, it embeds the research agenda politically, and produces 'problem-driven knowledge that is required and used because it is not only technically sound but also socially robust, i.e. it is perceived as legitimate and fair' (Tussie, 2009, p. 16).

Translated to the context of endemic, ubiquitous, transnational mass non-participation among young people, such partnerships are surely capable of creating politically purposeful programmes that cannot be imagined separately. In such historically unlikely pairings as the World Bank and the International Labour Organization, partnerships run major programmes of experimental non-exploitive job creation for young people in the world's poorest countries.

If such advances are possible in the high politics of international trade and between historically opposed organisations of global governance, their methods deserve attention. Publicly engaged academic researchers and politically informed activists have the power to propose and promote potentially radical alternatives. Using the principles of bounded post-academic research, they can work with others in and beyond epistemic communities to map new programmes and reimagine policy. They have the power to stall *and perhaps to turn* the rising tide of young people who suffer the immiserating and impoverishing conditions of worklessness and semi-forced labour – and whose plight is becoming a distinctive and consistent transnational hallmark of the advance of neoliberalism.

# References

Adams, E. and Smart, D. (2005) *Mapping employability and support services for disengaged young people*, Glasgow: Scottish Executive Social Research.

Ainley, P. and Allen, M. (2010) *Lost generation? New strategies for youth and education*, London: Continuum.

Alcock, P. (2003) *Work to welfare: How men become detached from the labour market*, Cambridge: Cambridge University Press.

Arendt, H. (1958) *The human condition*, Chicago, IL: Chicago University Press.

Arezki, R. and Bruckner, M. (2011) 'Food prices and political instability', Washington DC: International Monetary Fund.

Arvanites, T. M. and Defina, R. H. (2006) 'Business cycles and street crime', *Criminology*, 44: 139-64.

Ashton, D. N. (1973) 'The transition from school to work: Notes on the development of different frames of reference among young male workers', *The Sociological Review*, 21(1): 101-25.

Ashton, D. N. and Field, D. (1976). *Young workers: The transition from school to work*, London: Hutchinson.

Ashton, D. N. and Maguire, M. J. (1986) *Young adults in the labour market* (no 55), London: Department of Employment.

Ashton, D. N., Maguire, M. J. and Garland, V. (1982) *Youth in the labour-market* (no 34), London: Department of Employment.

Ashton, D. N., Maguire, M. and Spilsbury, M. (1990) *Restructuring the labour market: The implications for youth*, London: Macmillan.

Ashworth, A. and Zender, L. (2010) 'Punitive orders: A problem of under criminalisation?', in R. A. Duff, L. Farmer, S. E. Marshall, M. Renzo and V. Tadros (eds), *The boundaries of the criminal law*, Oxford: Oxford University Press.

Atkinson, R. and Davoudi, S. (2000) 'The concept of social exclusion in the European Union: Context, development and possibilities', *JCMS: Journal of Common Market Studies*, 38(3): 427-48.

Atkinson, P. and Rees, T. (1982) 'Youth unemployment and state intervention', in T. Rees and P. Atkinson (eds) *Youth unemployment and state intervention*, London: Routledge and Kegan Paul.

Auer, P. and Cazes, S. (eds) (2003) 'Employment stability in an age of flexibility: Evidence from industrialized countries', Geneva: International Labour Organization.

Avis, J., Bloomer, M., Esland, G., Gleeson, D. and Hodgkinson, P. (eds) (1996) *Knowledge and nationhood: Education, politics and work*, London: Cassell.

Azinović, V. and Jusić, M. (2015) *The lure of the Syrian war*, Sarajevo: The Atlantic Initiative.

Back, L. (1996) *New ethnicities and urban culture: Racism and multi culture*, Abingdon: Routledge.

Ball, L. (1993) *Youth Aid's guide to training and benefits for young people*, London: Youthaid.

Bandura, A. (1991) 'Social cognitive theory of moral thought and action', *Handbook of Moral Behavior and Development*, 1: 45-103.

Bandura, A. (2004) 'The role of selective moral disengagement in terrorism and counterterrorism', in F. M. Mogahaddam and A. J. Marsella (eds), *Understanding terrorism: Psychological roots, consequences and interventions*, Washington, DC: American Psychological Association, pp 121-50.

Bandura, A., Barbaranelli, C., Caprara, G. V. and Pastorelli, C. (1996) 'Mechanisms of moral disengagement in the exercise of moral agency', *Journal of Personality and Social Psychology*, 71(2): 364-74.

Banks, M., Bates, I., Breakwell, G. M., Bynner, J., Emler, N., Jamieson, L. and Roberts, K. (1992) *Careers and identities*, Buckingham: Open University Press.

Barham, C. / Office for National Statistics (2002) 'Economic inactivity and the labour market', *Labour Market Trends*, February

Barker, R. (1972) *Education and politics, 1900-1951: a study of the Labour Party*, Oxford: Clarendon Press

Barnes, G. M., Welte, J. W., Hoffman, J. H. and Dintcheff, B. A. (1999) 'Gambling and alcohol use among youth: Influences of demographic, socialization, and individual factors', *Addictive Behaviors*, 24(6): 749-67.

Barnes, R. A. (1895) *Economic causes of crime*, Madison, WI: University of Wisconsin-Madison.

Baron, S. W. (2006) 'Street youth, strain theory, and crime', *Journal of Criminal Justice*, 34(2): 209-23.

Baron, S. W. (2008) 'Street youth, unemployment, and crime: Is it that simple? Using general strain theory to untangle the relationship', *Canadian Journal of Criminology and Criminal Justice*, 50(4): 399-434.

Baron, S. and Hartnagel, T. (1998) 'Street youth and criminal violence', *Journal of Research in Crime and Delinquency*, 35(2): 166-92.

Barr, D., Taylor-Robinson, A., McKee, M. and Stuckler, D. (2012) 'Suicides associated with the 2008-10 economic recession in England: Time trend analysis', *British Medical Journal*, 345: 13.

Bartley M., Sacker A. and Clarke P. (2004) 'Employment status, employment conditions, and limiting illness: Prospective evidence from the British household panel survey 1991–2001', *Journal of Epidemiology and Community Health*, 58: 501-6.

Bataille, G. (1934/1993) 'Abjection and miserable forms', *More and Less*, 2: 87-101.

Bateman, T. (2012a) *Children in conflict with the law: an overview of trends and developments 2010/11*, London, National Association of Youth Justice.

Bateman, T. (2012b) 'Who pulled the plug? Towards an explanation of the fall in child imprisonment in England and Wales', *Youth justice*, 12(1), 36-52.

Bateman, T. (2015) 'Trends in contemporary youth crime and state responses', in B. Goldson and J. Muncie (eds), *Youth crime and justice* (2nd edn), London: Sage.

Bates, I., Clarke, J., Cohen, P., Finn, D. and Moore, R. (Eds.) (1984) *Schooling for the dole? The new vocationalism*, Basingstoke: Macmillan.

Beck, U. (1992) *Risk society: Towards a new modernity*, London: Sage.

Beck, U., Giddens, A. and Lash, S. (1994) *Reflexive modernisation,* Cambridge: Polity Press

Becker, H. S. (1963) *Outsiders: Studies in the sociology of deviance*, New York: Free Press.

Becker, G. S. (1968) 'Crime and punishment: An economic approach', *Journal of Political Economy*, 76(2): 169-217.

Beckett, K. and Western, B. (2001) 'Governing social marginality welfare, incarceration, and the transformation of state policy', *Punishment and Society*, 3(1): 43-59.

Behrens, M. and Brown, A. (1991) 'Routes to skilled work' in J. Bynner and K. Roberts (eds) (1991) *Youth and work: Transition to employment in England and Germany*, London: Anglo-German Foundation.

Béland, D. (2007) 'The social exclusion discourse: ideas and policy change', *Policy and Politics*, 35(1): 123-39.

Béland, D. and Hansen, R. (2000) 'Reforming the French welfare state: Solidarity, social exclusion and the three crises of citizenship', *West European Politics*, 23(1): 47-64.

Bell, D. and Blanchflower, D. (2011) 'Young people and the Great Recession', *Oxford Review of Economic Policy*, 2(2): 241-67.

Bellemare, M. F. (2015) 'Rising food prices, food price volatility, and political unrest', *American Journal of Agricultural Economics*, 97(1): 1-21.

Berman, G. (2014) *The August 2011 riots: A statistical summary,* London: House of Commons Library, http://researchbriefings.parliament. uk/ResearchBriefing/Summary/SN06099 www.parliament.uk/ briefingpapers/SN06099

Bernstein, B. (1973) *Class, codes and control: Applied studies towards a sociology of language, Vol. 2,* London: Routledge and Kegan Paul

Bhavnani, K. K. (1991) *Talking politics: A psychological framing of views from youth in Britain,* Cambridge: Cambridge University Press.

Birdwell, J., Grist, M. and Margo, J. (2011) *The forgotten half,* London: Demos/Private Equity Foundation.

Bivand, P., Gardiner, L., Whitehurst, D. and Wilson T. (2011) *Youth unemployment: A million reasons to act?,* London: Centre for Economic and Social Inclusion.

Blagg, H., Pearson, G., Sampson, A., Smith, D. and Stubbs, P. (1988) 'Inter-agency Co-operation; Rhetoric and Reality', in Hope, T. and Shaw, M. (eds.) *Communities and Crime Reduction,* London: HMSO

Bonger, W. (1916) *Criminality and economic conditions,* Chicago, IL: Little, Brown and Company.

Bottoms, A. (2007) 'Place, space, crime, and disorder', in *The Oxford Handbook of Criminology* (4th edn), Oxford: Oxford University Press, pp 528-74.

Box, S. (1983) *Crime, power and mystification,* London: Tavistock.

Box, S. (1987) *Recession, crime and punishment,* Basingstoke: Macmillan Education.

Box, S. and Hale, C. (1982), 'Economic crisis and the rising prisoner population in England and Wales', *Crime and Social Justice,* 17: 20-35.

Bradshaw, J., Kemp, P., Baldwin, S. and Rowe, A. (2004) *The drivers of social exclusion: A review of the literature for the Social Exclusion Unit,* London: Social Exclusion Unit.

Brand, R. (2013) 'We no longer have the luxury of tradition', *The New Statesman,* 24 October.

Brandwein, R. A., Brown, C. A., and Fox, E. M. (1974). 'Women and children last: The social situation of divorced mothers and their families', *Journal of Marriage and the Family,* 36 (3) 498-514.

Briggs, D. (2012) *The English riots of 2011: A summer of discontent,* Hook, UK: Waterside Press.

Brinton, M. C. (2010) *Lost in transition: Youth, work, and instability in post-industrial Japan,* Cambridge: Cambridge University Press.

Britt, C. L. (1997) 'Reconsidering the unemployment and crime relationship: variation by age group and historical period', *Journal of Quantitative Criminology,* 13(4): 405-28.

Brown, P. (1987) *Schooling ordinary kids: Inequality, unemployment, and the new vocationalism*, London: Routledge.

Brown, S. (1998) *Understanding youth and crime: Listening to youth?*, Buckingham: Open University Press.

Buchmann, M. (1989) *The script of life in modern society: Entry into adulthood*, Chicago: University of Chicago Press.

Buonanno, P. (2006) 'Crime and labour market opportunities in Italy (1993–2002)', *Labour*, 20 (4), 601-624.

Buonanno, P., Drago, F. and Galbiati, R. (2014) 'Response of crime to unemployment: An international comparison', *Journal of Contemporary Criminal Justice*, 30 (February): 29-40.

Burchell, G. (1996) 'Liberal government and techniques of the self', in A. Barry, T. Osborne and N. Rose (eds), *Foucault and political reason*, London: UCL Press.

Bushway, S., Cook, P. and Phillips, M. (2012) 'The overall effect of the business cycle on crime', *German Economic Review,* 13(4): 436-46.

Bushway, S., Cook, P. J. and Phillips, M. (2013) 'The net effect of the business cycle on crime and violence', in R. Rosenfeld, M. Edberg, X. Fang and C. S. Florence (eds), *Economics and youth violence: Crime, disadvantage, and community*, New York: New York University Press.

Bynner, J. (2004) *Participation and progression: Use of birth cohort study data in illuminating the role of basic skills and other factors*, Nuffield Review of 14-19 Education and Training, Working paper 9, London: Nuffield Foundation.

Bynner, J. (2009) *Lifelong learning and crime*, Leicester: National Institute for Adult and Continuing Education.

Bynner, J. and Ashford, S. (1990) *Youth politics and lifestyles,* London: Social Statistics Research Unit, City University.

Bynner, J. and Parsons, S. (2002) 'Social exclusion and the transition from school to work: The case of young people not in education, employment, or training (NEET)', *Journal of Vocational Behavior*, 60(2): 289-309.

Bynner, J. and Roberts, K. (eds) (1991) *Youth and work: Transition to employment in England and Germany*, London: Anglo-German Foundation.

Byrne, D. (2005) *Social exclusion* (2nd edn), Maidenhead: Open University Press.

Bynner, J., Londra, M. and Jones, G. (2004) *the impact of government policy on social exclusion among young people*, London: Social Exclusion Unit.

Cam, S., Purcell, J. and Tailby, S. (2003) 'Contingent employment in the UK', in O. Bergstrom and D. Storrie (eds). *Contingent Employment in Europe and the United States*, Cheltenham, Edward Elgar.

Carlen, P. (1988) 'Out of care and into custody', in P. Carlen and A. Worrall (eds) *Gender, crime and justice*, Milton Keynes: Open University Press.

Carmichael, F. and Ward, R. (2000) 'Youth unemployment and crime in the English regions and Wales', *Applied Economics*, 32: 559-71.

Centre for Economic and Social Inclusion and Bateman, N. (2009) *The young person's handbook: Learning, work and financial support for 14-19 year olds*, London: Centre for Economic and Social Inclusion.

Chadwick, K. and Scraton, P. (2013) 'Criminalisation', in E. McLaughlin and J. Muncie (eds) *The Sage dictionary of criminology* (3rd edn), London: Sage Publications.

Chadwick, S. (1997) 'Resource dependence in the further education marketplace: Considerations for the managers of college mergers', *Journal of Further and Higher Education*, 21(3): 305-16.

Chambliss, W. J. (1975) 'Toward a political economy of crime', *Theory and Society*, 2(1): 149-70.

Chang, S., Stuckler, D., Yip, P. and Gunnell, D. (2013) 'Impact of 2008 global economic crisis on suicide: Time trend study in 54 countries', *British Medical Journal*, 347: 5239.

Chatrick, B. (1999) *Guide to training and benefits for young people*, London: Unemployment Unit/Youthaid.

Chauvel, L. (2010) 'The long-term destabilization of youth, scarring effects, and the future of the welfare regime in post-trente glorieuses France', *French Politics, Culture & Society*, 28(3), 74-96.

Child Poverty Action Group (2013) *Welfare benefits and tax credits handbook*, 2013-14, London: CPAG.

Chiricos, T. G. (1987) 'Rates of crime and unemployment: an analysis of aggregate research evidence', *Social Problems*, 34(2): 187-212.

Christie, N. (2004) *A suitable amount of crime*, New York: Routledge.

Cinalli M. and Giugni, M. (2013) 'New challenges for the welfare state: The emergence of youth unemployment regimes in Europe?', *International Journal of Social Welfare*, 22(3): 290-99.

Citizens Advice Scotland (2012) *Voices from the frontline ... The rising demand for food parcels*, www.cas.org.uk/publications/voices-frontline-rising-demand-food-parcels

Clark, T. (2014) *Hard times: The divisive toll of the economic slump* (with Heath, A.), London: Yale University Press.

Clarke, J. (2004) *Changing welfare, changing states*, London: Sage Publications.

Clarke, J. and Critcher, C. (1985) *The devil makes work: Leisure in capitalist Britain*, Basingstoke: Macmillan.

Clarke, J. and Jefferson, T. (1973) *Working class youth cultures* (no 18), Birmingham: Centre for Contemporary Cultural Studies, University of Birmingham.

Clarke, J., Cochrane, A. and McLaughlin, E. (eds) (1994) *Managing social policy*, London: Sage Publications.

Clarke, L. (1980) *The transition from school to work: A critical review of research in the United Kingdom*, London: HMSO.

Clarke, R. (1992) *Situational crime prevention*, New York: Harrow and Heston.

Cockburn, C. (1987) *Two-track training: Sex inequalities and the YTS*, Basingstoke: Macmillan Education.

Cohen, P. (2003) 'Mods and shockers: Youth cultural studies in Britain', *Researching Youth*, Basingstoke: Palgrave Macmillan, pp 13-28.

Cohen, P. and Ainley, P. (2000) 'In the country of the blind? Youth studies and cultural studies in Britain', *Journal of Youth Studies*, 3(1): 79-95.

Cohen, S. (1972) *Folk devils and moral panics*, London: McGibbon and Kee.

Cohen, S. (2002) *Folk devils and moral panics: The creation of the Mods and Rockers* (3rd edn), London: Routledge.

Cohn, E. and Rotton, J. (2003) 'Even criminals take a holiday: Instrumental and expressive crimes on major and minor holidays', *Journal of Criminal Justice*, 31(4): 351-60.

Coleman, S. (2007) 'How democracies have disengaged from young people', in *Young citizens in the digital age: Political engagement, young people and new media*, London: Routledge, pp 166-85.

Coles, B. (1995) *Youth and social policy: Youth citizenship and young careers*, London: UCL Press.

Coles, B., Hutton, S., Bradshaw, J., Craig, G., Godfrey, C. and Johnson, J. (2002) *Literature review of the costs of being 'not in education, employment or training' at age 16–18*, Department for Education and Skills, Research Report 347, Norwich: HMSO.

Colley, H. and Hodkinson, P. (2001) 'Problems with bridging the gap: The reversal of structure and agency in addressing social exclusion', *Critical Social Policy*, 21(3): 335-59.

Cook, P. J. and Zarkin, G. (1985) 'Crime and the business cycle', *Journal of Legal Studies*, 14: 115-28.

Courtenay, G. and Britain, G. (1988) *England and Wales youth cohort study: Report on cohort 1, sweep 1,* London: Manpower Services Commission.

Courtenay, G. and McAleese, I. (1986) *England and Wales youth cohort study: First summary report*, London: Social and Community Planning and Research.

Craig, G. (1988) *Young people at the crossroads: Education, jobs, social security and training*, London: Family Policy Studies Centre.

Craig, G. (2008) 'Social exclusion', in B. Goldson (ed), *Dictionary of youth justice*, Cullompton: Willan.

Craine, S. (1988) *The hoisters: Survival crime and informal community networks*, unpublished paper.

Crawford, A. (1997) *The Local Governance of Crime: Appeals to Community and Partnerships*, Oxford: Clarendon.

Crawford, A. (1999), 'Questioning appeals to community within crime prevention and control', *European Journal on Criminal Policy and Research*, 7(4), 509-530.

Cribb, J. and Joyce, R. (2015) 'Earnings since the recession', in C. Emmerson, P. Johnson and R. Joyce (eds), *The 2015 IFS Green Budget*, London: Institute for Fiscal Studies.

Crawford, A. (1999) *The local governments of crime: Appeals to community and partnerships*, Oxford: Oxford University Press.

Cullen, J. and Levitt, S. (1999) 'Crime, Urban Flight, and the Consequences for Cities', *Review of Economics and Statistics*, 81(2): 159–69.

Cumming, E. and Henry, W. (1961) *Growing old*, New York: Basic Books.

Cunningham, H. (1990) 'The employment and unemployment of children in England c.1680-1851', *Past and Present*, 126: 115-50.

Cutler, T. and Waine, B. (1994), *Managing the welfare state: The politics of public sector management,* Oxford: Berg.

Deacon, A. (1981) 'Unemployment and politics in Britain since 1945', in B. Showler and A. Sinfield (eds), *The workless state*, Oxford: Martin Roberton.

Dean, M. (1999) 'Governmentality: Power and rule', in *Modern society*, London: Sage Publications.

DeLuca, C., Hutchinson, N. L., deLugt, J. S., Beyer, W., Thornton, A., Versnel, J., Chin, P. and Munby, H. (2010) 'Learning in the workplace: Fostering resilience in disengaged youth', *Work: A Journal of Prevention, Assessment and Rehabilitation*, 36(3): 305-19.

Department for Education (2011) *NEET statistics – quarterly brief, quarter 4*, London: HMSO.

Department for Education (2012) 'Outcomes for Children Looked After by Local Authorities in England, as at 31 March 2012', 12 December, SFR 32/2012, www.gov.uk/government/uploads/system/uploads/attachment_data/file/191969/SFR32_2012Text.pdf

Department for Education (2013/14) *Participation of young people in education, employment or training, (Statutory Guidance) Published March 2013, Updated September 2014* (Ref. DFE-00561-2014 ) London: Department for Education, www.gov.uk/government/uploads/system/uploads/attachment_data/file/349300/Participation_of_Young_People_Statutory_Guidance.pdf

Department for Education (2015) *NEET data by local authority: 2014 local authority NEET figures*, London: Department for Education, www.gov.uk/government/publications/neet-data-by-local-authority-2012-16-to-18-year-olds-not-in-education-employment-or-training

Department for Education and Skills (2005) *Youth matters,* Cm 6629, London: HMSO.

Department of Employment (1981) *The New Training Initiative: a programme for action,* London: HMSO

Department of Work and Pensions (DWP) (2006) *Welfare Reform Bill 2006 –Regulatory impact assessment*, London: DWP.

Department for Work and Pensions (2010) *Households Below Average Income: An analysis of the income distribution*, London: Department for Work and Pensions.

Department for Work and Pensions (DWP) (2013) *Jobseeker's Allowance and employment and support allowance sanctions – Decisions made to June 2013*, London: DWP, www.gov.uk/government/uploads/system/uploads/attachment_data/file/255176/sanctions-nov-2013.pdf

Dillabough, J. A. and Kennelly, J. (2010) *Lost youth in the global city: Class, culture, and the urban imaginary*, Abingdon: Routledge.

Dorling, D. (2013) 'The defrauding of young Britain', *New Statesman*, 1 November: 23-7.

Douglas, M. (1966/2003) *Purity and danger: An analysis of concepts of pollution and taboo*, London: Routledge.

Downes, D. and Hansen, K. (2006) *Welfare and punishment in comparative perspective*, Oxford: Oxford University Press.

Drew, D., Gray, J. and Sime, N. (1992) *Against the odds: The education and labour market experiences of black young people*, London: Research Strategy Branch, Employment Department.

Dwyer, P. and Wyn, K. (1998) 'Post-compulsory education policy in Australia and its impact on participant pathways and outcomes in the 1990s', *Journal of Education Policy*, 13(3): 285-300.

Easterly, W. and Levine, R. (1997) 'Africa's growth tragedy: Policies and ethnic divisions', *Quarterly Journal of Economics*, 112(4): 1203–50.

Edwards, A. (2013) 'Governance', in E. McLaughlin and J. Muncie (eds), *The Sage dictionary of criminology* (3rd edn), London: Sage Publications.

Ellison, M. (2014) 'No future to risk? The impact of economic crises and austerity on young people at the margins of European employment and welfare settings', in K. Farnsworth, Z. Irving and M. Fenger (eds) *Social policy review 26: Analysis and debate in social policy, 2014*, Bristol: Policy Press.

European Committee on Crime Problems (1994) *Crime and economy, eleventh criminological colloquium*, Strasbourg: Council of Europe.

Evans, K. and Furlong, A. (1997) 'Metaphors of youth transitions: Niches, pathways, trajectories or navigations', in J. Bynner, K. Evans and A. Furlong (eds), *Youth, citizenship and social change in a European context*, Aldershot: Ashgate.

Fairclough, N. (2000) *New Labour, new language*, London: Routledge.

Farmer, E. (1993) 'Externalising behaviour in the life-course', *Journal of Emotional and Behavioral Disorders*, 1(3): 179–88.

Farrington, D. (1994) 'Early developmental prevention of juvenile delinquency', *RSA Journal*: 22–34.

Farrington, D. P. (1996) 'Understanding and preventing youth crime' (vol 93), York: York Publishing Services Limited.

Farrington, D. P., Gallagher, B., Morley, L., Ledger, R. J. S. and West, D. J. (1986) 'Unemployment, school leaving, and crime', *British Journal of Criminology*, 26(4): 335–56.

Feinstein, L. and Sabatés, R. (2005) *Education and youth crime: Effects of introducing the Education Maintenance Allowance programme*, London: London School of Economics and Political Science.

Fend, H. (1994) 'The historical context of transition to work and youth unemployment', in A. C. Petersen and J. T. Mortimer (eds), *Youth, unemployment and society*, New York: Cambridge University Press.

Fergusson, R. (2002) 'Rethinking youth transitions: policy transfer and new exclusions in New Labour's New Deal', *Policy Studies*, 23(3/4): 173–90.

Fergusson, R. (2004) 'Discourses of exclusion: reconceptualising participation amongst young people', *Journal of Social Policy*, 33(2): 289–320.

Fergusson, R. (2013a) 'Against disengagement: nonparticipation as an object of governance', *Research in Post-Compulsory Education*, 18 (1), 12–18.

Fergusson, R. (2013b) 'Risk, responsibilities and rights: reassessing the 'economic causes of crime' thesis in a recession', *Youth Justice*, 13 (1), 31-56.

Fergusson, R. (2014a) 'Warehouse, marketise, shelter, juridify: On the political economy and government extending school participation in England', in K. Farnworth, Z. Irving and M. Fenger (eds), *Social policy review 26: Analysis and debate in social policy, 2014*, Bristol: Policy Press.

Fergusson, R. (2014b) 'Regulate or abandon: Two-speed tracks to criminalising precarious youth', *Criminal Justice Matters*, 96(1): 18-19.

Fergusson, R. and Unwin, L. (1996) 'Making better sense of post-16 destinations: A case study of an English shire county', *Research Papers in Education*, 11(1): 53-80.

Fergusson, R. and Yeates, N. (2013) 'Business, as usual: The policy priorities of the World Bank's discourses on youth unemployment, and the global financial crisis', *Journal of International and Comparative Social Policy*, 29(1): 64-78.

Fergusson, R. and Yeates, N. (2014) 'International governmental organisations and global youth unemployment: The normative and ideational foundations of policy discourses', *Policy and Politics*, 42(3): 439-58.

Fergusson, R., Pye, D., Esland, G., McLaughlin, E. and Muncie, J. (2000) 'Normalised dislocation and new subjectivities in post-16 markets for education and work', *Critical Social Policy*, 20(3): 283-304.

Ferrell, J., Hayward, K., Morrison, W. and Presdee, M. (eds) (2004) *Cultural criminology unleashed*, London: Routledge.

Finlayson, J. G. (2005) *Habermas: A very short introduction*, Oxford: Oxford University Press.

Finn, D. (1987) *Training without jobs: New deals and broken promises: From raising the school leaving age to the Youth Training Scheme*, London: Macmillan.

Flint, J. (2009) 'Governing marginalised populations: the role of coercion, support and agency', *European Journal of Homelessness*, 3: 247–60.

Flood-Page, C., Campbell, S., Harrington, V. and Miller, J. (2002) 'Youth crime: Findings from the 1998/99 youth lifestyles survey', *Home Office Research Study 209*, London: Home Office.

Ford, G. (1998) *Career Guidance Mentoring for Disengaged Young People*, Cambridge: National Institute for Careers Education and Counselling.

Fornas, J. and Bolin, G. (eds) (1995) *Youth culture in late modernity*, London: Sage Publications.

Foskett, N. and Hesketh, A. (1997) 'Constructing choice in contiguous and parallel markets: institutional and school leavers' responses to the new post-16 marketplace', *Oxford Review of Education*, 23(3): 299-319.

Foucault, M. (1982/2000) 'The subject and power', in J. D. Faubion (ed), *Power. Essential works of Foucault* (vol 3), New York: New York Press.

Foucault, M. (1991) 'Governmentality', in C. Gordon, G. Burchell and P. Miller (eds), *The Foucault effect: Studies in governmentality*, Hemel Hempstead: Harvester Wheatsheaf.

Fougère, D., Kramarz, F. and Pouget, J. (2009) 'Youth unemployment and crime in France', *Journal of the European Economic Association*, 7(5): 909-38.

France, A. (2007) *Understanding youth in late modernity*, Maidenhead: Open University Press/McGraw Hill Education.

Freedland, M. and King, D. (2003) 'Contractual governance and illiberal contracts: Some problems of contractualism as an instrument of behaviour management by agencies of government', *Cambridge Journal of Economics*, 27: 465-77.

Freeman, R. and Sturdy, S. (eds) (2014) *Knowledge in policy: Embodied, inscribed, enacted*, Bristol: Policy Press.

Fulbrook, J. (1995) 'The Jobseekers Act 1995: Consolidation with a sting of contractual compliance', *Industrial Law Journal*, 24: 395-401.

Furlong, A. (1992) *Growing up in a classless society? School to work transitions*, Edinburgh: Edinburgh University Press.

Furlong, A. and Cartmel, F. (1997/2007) *Young people and social change: Individualisation and risk*, Maidenhead: Open University Press.

Furlong, A., Woodman, D. and Wyn, J. (2011) 'Changing times, changing perspectives: Reconciling "transition" and "cultural" perspectives on youth and young adulthood', *Journal of Sociology*, 47: 355-70.

Gardiner, L. (2014) *Totalling the hidden talent: Youth unemployment and underemployment in England and Wales*, London, Local Government Association/Centre for Economic and Social Exclusion.

Garland, D. (1996) 'The limits of the sovereign state strategies of crime control in contemporary society', *British Journal of Criminology*, 36(4): 445-71.

Garland, D. (2001) *The culture of control: Crime and social order in contemporary society*, Oxford: Oxford University Press.

General Synod, Church of England (2012) *'Testing the bridges': Understanding the role of the church amidst riots, disturbances and disorder*, London: Church House.

Ghosh, S. (2011) 'Youth disengagement: The biggest issue of our time?', *Working Brief*, London: Centre for Social and Economic Inclusion, Winter: 6-8.

Gleeson, D. (1986) ' Life skills training and the politics of personal effectiveness', *The Sociological Review*, *34*(2): 381-395.

Gleeson, D. (1993) 'Legislating for change: Missed opportunities in the Further and Higher Education Act', *Journal of Education and Work*, 6(2): 29-40.

Godfrey, C., Hutton, S., Bradshaw, J., Coles, B., Craig, G. and Johnson, J. (2002) 'Estimating the cost of being "not in education, employment or training" at age 16-18', *Research Report RR346*, London: Department for Education and Skills.

Goffman, E. (1961) *Encounters: Two studies in the sociology of interaction*, Indianapolis: Bobbs-Merrill Co.

Gordon, A. (1980) 'Leaving school: A question of money?', *Educational Studies*, 6(1): 43-54.

Gordon, C., Burchell, G. and Miller, P. (eds) (1991) *The Foucault effect: Studies in governmentality*, Hemel Hempstead: Harvester Wheatsheaf.

Gough, I. (2011) 'From financial crisis to fiscal crisis', in K. Farnsworth and Z. Irving (eds), *Social policy in challenging times: Economic crisis and welfare systems*, Bristol: Policy Press.

Gould, E. D., Weinberg, B. A. and Mustard, D. B. (2002) 'Crime rates and local labor market opportunities in the United States: 1979-1997', *Review of Economics and Statistics*, 84: 45-61.

Gray, J. and Sime, N. (1990) 'Extended routes and delayed transitions amongst 16–19 year olds: National trends and local contexts', *Journal of Education and Work*, 3(2): 13-40.

Gray, J., Jesson, D. and Tranmer, M. (1993) *English and Wales Youth Cohort Study: Boosting post-16 participation in full-time education: A study of some key factors*, Youth Cohort Report, no 20, Sheffield: Employment Department.

Great Britain, Department of Employment (1971) *British labour statistics: Historical abstract 1886-1968*, London: HMSO.

Gregg, P. (2014) *Youth unemployment – Still waiting for the upturn*, Bath: Institute for Policy Research, University of Bath.

Gregg, P. and Machin, S. (2012) *What a drag: The chilling impact of unemployment on real wages*, London: Resolution Foundation.

Gregg, P. and MacMillan, L. (2010) 'Evidence and the EMA', *Public Finance,* 10 December, London: Chartered Institute of Public Finance and Accountancy.

Green, A., Preston, J., and Sabates, R. (2003) *Education, equity and social cohesion: A distributional model,* Centre for Research on the Wider Benefits of Learning, London: Institute of Education.

Griffin, C. (1993) *Representations of youth: The study of youth and adolescence in Britain and America,* Cambridge: Polity Press.

Grogger, J. (1992), 'Arrests, persistent youth joblessness, and black-white employment differentials', *Review of Economics and Statistics,* 74: 100-106.

Grogger, J. (1998) 'Market wages and youth crime', *Journal of Labor Economics,* 16(4): 756-91.

Grönqvist, H. (2011) *Youth unemployment and crime: New lessons exploring longitudinal register data,* Stockholm University, The Swedish Institute for Social Research, Stockholm: Sweden, www.diva-portal.org/smash/get/diva2:408248/FULLTEXT01.pdf

Grover, C. (2008) *Crime and inequality,* London: Routledge.

Grover, C. (2010) 'Social security policy and vindictiveness', *Sociological Research Online,* 15(2): 8.

Grover, C. (2016) *Social security and wage poverty: Historical and policy aspects of supplementing wages in Britain and beyond,* Basingstoke: Palgrave Macmillan.

Giuliano, P., and Spilimbergo, A. (2009) 'Growing up in a recession: Beliefs and the macroeconomy', National Bureau of Economic Research, working paper no 15321.

Habermas, J. (1976) *Legitimation crisis,* London: Heinemann

Habermas, J. (1981/1984) *The theory of communicative action* (vol 1). *Reason and the rationalisation of society,* Cambridge: Polity Press/Oxford: Basil Blackwell.

Habermas, J. (1981/1987) *The theory of communicative action* (vol 2). *Lifeworld and system: A critique of functionalist reason,* Cambridge: Polity Press/Oxford: Basil Blackwell.

Hackman, J. R., and Oldham, G. R. (1980) *Work redesign.* Reading, Mass.: Addison-Wesley.

Hagan, J. and McCarthy, B. (1997) *Mean street: Youth crime and homelessness,* Cambridge: Cambridge University Press.

Hamilton, S. F. and Crouter A. C. (1980) 'Work and growth: A review of research on the impact of work experience on adolescents', *Journal of Youth and Adolescence,* 9(4): 323-38.

Hamzawy, A. (2009) 'Rising social distress: The case of Morocco, Egypt, and Jordan', *International Economic Bulletin,* Carnegie Endowment for International Peace, June.

Hannon, L. and DeFronzo, J. (1998) 'Welfare and property crime', *Justice Quarterly,* 15(2): 273-88.

Harradine, S., Kodz, J., Lemetti, F. and Jones, B. (2004) *Defining and measuring anti-social behaviour*, Development and Practice Report 26, London: Home Office.

Harris, N. (1988) 'Raising the minimum age of entitlement to income support: Social Security Act 1988', *Journal of Law and Society*, 15 (2): 201-15.

Harris, N. (1989) *Social security for young people*, Aldershot: Avebury.

Harris, N. (2008) 'From unemployment to active jobseeking: Changes and continuities in social security law in the United Kingdom', in S. Stendahl, T. Erhag and S. Devetzi (eds) *A European work-first welfare state*, Gothenburg: Centre for European Research, University of Gothenburg, https://gupea.ub.gu.se/bitstream/2077/20227/1/gupea_2077_20227_1.pdf

Hart, J. T. (1971) 'The inverse care law', *The Lancet*, 297(7696): 405-12.

Hassard, J., Sheehan, J. and Yuxin, X. (2008) 'Chinese state-enterprise reform: Economic transition, labour unrest and worker representation', *Capital and Class*, 32(3): 31-52.

Hayes, D. (2013) 'Young people take brunt of tougher jobseeker sanctions', *Children and Young People Now*, 7 November.

Hayward, K. (2002) 'The vilification and pleasures of youthful transgression', in J.Muncie, G.Hughes and E. McLaughlin (eds) *Youth justice: Critical readings*, London: Sage Publications, pp 80-93.

Hayward, K. J. (2004) *City limits: Crime, consumer culture and the urban experience*, London: GlassHouse.

Hebdidge, D. (1979) *Subculture, the meaning of style*, London: Methuen.

Hendrick, H. (1997) 'Constructions and reconstructions of British childhood: an interpretative survey, 1800 to the present', in A. Prout and A. James (eds) *Constructing and reconstructing childhood: Contemporary issues in the sociological study of childhood*, Barcombe: Falmer Press

Henman, P. (2006) 'Welfare reform as governance reform: The prospects of a governmentality perspective', in P. Henman and M. Fenger (eds), *Administering welfare reform: International transformations in welfare governance*, Bristol: Policy Press.

Henn, M., Weinstein, M. and Forrest, S. (2005) 'Uninterested youth? Young people's attitudes towards party politics in Britain', *Political Studies*, 53(3): 556-78.

Hill, J. M. M. (1969). *The transition from school to work; a study of the child's changing perception of work from the age of seven*, London: Tavistock Institute of Human Relations (Centre for Applied Social Research).

Hills, J., Le Grand, J. and Piachaud, D. (2002) *Understanding social exclusion*, London: London School of Economics and Political Science.

Hirsch, D. (1983) *Youth unemployment: A background paper*, London: Youthaid.

HM Government (2013) '*Staying put': Arrangements for care leavers aged 18 and above to stay on with their former foster carers*: DfE, DWP and HMRC Guidance, (DfE-00061-2013), London: The Stationery Office

Hollands, R. G. (1990) *The long transition: Class, culture and youth training*, London: Macmillan Education.

Hochschild, A. R. (1983) *The managed heart: Commercialization of human feeling*. Berkeley: University of California Press.

Hoogvelt, A. and France, A. (2000) 'New Deal: the experience and views of clients in one pathfinder city (Sheffield)', *Local Economy*, 15, 2: 112-127.

House of Commons (2011) *Education Act 2011: Explanatory Notes* (Commentary on Sections, Part 7, Section 74), London: House of Commons, www.legislation.gov.uk/ukpga/2011/21/notes/division/6/7/4/1

House of Commons, Children, Schools and Families Committee (session 2009-10) (2009) Young People not in Education, Employment or Training, *Memorandum submitted by Centrepoint*, December, London: House of Commons, www.publications.parliament.uk/pa/cm200910/cmselect/cmchilsch/memo/youngpeo/me50.htm

House of Commons, Library (2014) 'What do young people do?', *Second Reading: The House of Commons Library Blog*, 3 March, http://commonslibraryblog.com/2014/03/03/what–do–young–people–do/

House of Commons, Public Accounts Committee (2015) *16-18 year old participation in education and training*, 31st Report of Session 2014-15, 22nd January, HC707, London: The Stationery Office, www.parliament.uk/business/committees/committees-a-z/commons-select/public-accounts-committee/news/16-18-participation-education-training/

House of Commons, Work and Pensions Committee (2012) *Youth unemployment and the youth contract*, Second Report of Session 2012-13, London: The Stationery Office

House of Commons, Work and Pensions Committee (2013) *Inquiry into the role of Jobcentre Plus in the reformed welfare system*, London: The Stationery Office, www.publications.parliament.uk/pa/cm201314/cmselect/cmworpen/479/479vw.pdf

Howe, P. (2010) *Citizens adrift: The democratic disengagement of young Canadians*, Vancouver: UBC Press.

Howker, E. and Malik, S. (2010) *The jilted generation: How Britain has bankrupted its youth*, London: Icon Books.

Hui, W. (1991) 'Reservation wage analysis of unemployed youths in Australia', *Applied Economics*, 23(8): 1341-50.

Husak, D. (2008) *Overcriminalization: The limits of the criminal law*, Oxford: Oxford University Press, pp 65-72.

Husserl, E. (1970) *The crisis of European sciences and transcendental phenomenology: an introduction to phenomenological philosophy*, Evanston: Northwestern University Press

Hutton, W. (2005) *Where are the gaps? An analysis of UK skills and education strategy in the light of the Kok Group and European Commission midterm review of the Lisbon goals*, Lancaster: The Work Foundation, University of Lancaster. www.theworkfoundation.com/assets/docs/publications/150_where%20are%20the%20gaps.pdf

Hyland, T. and Johnson, S. (1998) 'Of cabbages and key skills: Exploding the mythology of core transferable skills in post-school education', *Journal of Further and Higher Education*, 22(2): 163-72.

Hymel, S., Rocke-Henderson, N. and Buonanno, R. A. (2005) 'Moral disengagement: A framework for understanding bullying among adolescents', *Journal of Social Sciences*, 8(1): 1-11.

Institute of Welsh Affairs (2010) *Engaging Wales' Disengaged Youth*, Cardiff: IWA. www.iwa.org.uk/en/publications/view/202

Institute for Fiscal Studies (2005) *Evaluation of education maintenance allowance pilots: Young people aged 16–19 years final report of the quantitative evaluation*, London: Department for Education and Skills.

Institute for International Labour Studies (2011) *World of work report 2011: Making markets work for jobs*, Geneva: ILO.

International Bank for Reconstruction and Development (The World Bank) (2012) *World Development Report, 2013: Jobs*, Washington DC: International Bank for Reconstruction and Development.

International Labour Organization (ILO) (2010) *World social security report, 2010/11*, Geneva: ILO.

International Labour Organization (ILO) (2011) *World of work report 2011: Making markets work for jobs*, Geneva: ILO.

International Labour Organization (ILO) (2013a) *Global trends for youth 2013: A generation at risk*, Geneva: ILO.

International Labour Organization (ILO) (2013b) *World of work report 2013: Repairing the economic and social fabric*, Geneva: ILO.

International Labour Organization (ILO) (2014) *World of work report 2014: Developing with jobs*, Geneva: ILO.

International Labour Organization (ILO) (2015) *Global employment trends for youth 2015: scaling up investments in decent jobs for youth*, Geneva: ILO

International Monetary Fund/International Labour Organization (2010) *The Challenges of Growth, Employment and Social Cohesion*, Joint International Monetary Fund/International Labour Organization Conference, Oslo: IMF/ILO, http://osloconference2010.org/index.htm.

Jawad, R. (2012) 'From black hole to spring: The coming of age of social policy in the Arab Countries?', in M. Kilkey, G. Ramia and K. Farnsworth (eds), *Social policy review, 24: Analysis and debate in social policy*, Bristol: Policy Press.

Jeffs, T. and Smith, M. (1998) 'The problem of "youth" for youth work', *Youth and Policy*, 62: 45-66.

Jenkins, J. C. (1983) 'Resource mobilization theory and the study of social movements', *Annual Review of Sociology*: 527-53.

Jenkins, J. (2010) 'The labour market in the 1980s, 1990s and 2008/09 recessions', *Economic & Labour Market Review*, 4(9): 29-36 (Office for National Statistics).

Jenkins, J. and Wallace, M. (1996) 'The generalised action potential of protest movements: The new class, social trends, and political exclusion explanations', *Sociological Forum*, 11(2): 183-207.

Jennings, W., Farrall, S. and Bevan, S. (2012) 'The economy, crime and time: An analysis of recorded property crime in England and Wales, 1961-2006', *International Journal of Law, Crime and Justice*, 40(3): 192-210.

Johnson, R. (1976) 'Notes on the schooling of the English working class 1780–1850', in R. Dale, G. Esland and M. Macdonald (eds), *Schooling and capitalism: A sociological reader*, London: Routledge and Kegan Paul.

Jones, C. and Novak, T. (2012) *Poverty, welfare and the disciplinary state*, London: Routledge.

Jones, G. (2009) *Youth*, Cambridge: Policy Press

Jones, G. and Wallace, C. (1992) *Youth, family, and citizenship*, Buckingham: Open University Press.

Jones, O. (2012) *Chavs: The demonization of the working class*, London: Verso Books.

Jordan, B. (1982) *Mass unemployment and the future of Britain*, Oxford: Basil Blackwell.

Jordan, B. and Drakeford, M. (2012) *Social work and social policy under austerity*, Basingstoke: Palgrave Macmillan.

Kadish, S.H. (1987) *Blame and punishment: Essays on the criminal law*, New York: Macmillan.

Kahn, W. (1990) 'Psychological conditions of personal engagement and disengagement at work', *The Academy of Management Journal*, 33(4): 692-724.

Katikireddi, V., Niedzwiedz, C. L. and Popham, F. (2012) 'Trends in population mental health before and after the 2008 recession: A repeat cross-sectional analysis of the 1991-2010 Health Surveys of England', *British Medical Journal Open*, 2(5): 1790.

Katz, J. (1988) *Seductions of crime*, New York: Basic Books.

Keep, E. and K. Mayhew (2010) 'Moving beyond skills as a social and economic panacea', *Work, Employment and Society*, 24(3): 565-77.

Kelly, E., McGuinness, S. and O'Connell, P. (2012) 'Transitions to long-term unemployment risk among young people: Evidence from Ireland', *Journal of Youth Studies*, 15(6): 780-801.

Kemp, P. A. and Rugg, J. (2001) 'Young people, housing benefit and the risk society', *Social Policy and Administration*, 35(6): 688-700.

Kendall, S., Cullen, M. A., White, R. and Kinder, K. (2001) 'The delivery of the curriculum to disengaged young people in Scotland', *National Foundation for Educational Research* (August).

Kirchheimer, O. (1928) 'Zur staatslehre das socializmus and bolschewismus', *Zeithschrift fur Politik*, 17: 592-611.

Kiriakidis, S. P. (2008) 'Moral disengagement: relation to delinquency and independence from indices of social dysfunction', *International Journal of Offender Therapy and Comparative Criminology*, 52(5): 571-83.

Kling, J. (2006) 'Incarceration Length, Employment and Earnings', *American Economic Review*, 96(3): 863–76.

Knox, H. (ed) (1986) *Harrap's Dictionaire Anglais-Francais*, London: Harrap Ltd.

Labour Party (1997) *Because Britain deserves better*, (General Election Manifesto), London: Labour Party.

LaGraffe, D. (2012) 'The youth bulge in Egypt: An intersection of demographics, security, and the Arab Spring', *Journal of Strategic Security*, 5(2): 65-80.

Lauritsen, J., Rezey, M. and Heimer, K. (2014) 'Violence and economic conditions in the United States, 1973-2011: Gender, race, and ethnicity patterns in the National Crime Victimization Survey', *Journal of Contemporary Criminal Justice*, 30(1): 7-28.

Lawton, K. (2009) *Nice work if you can get it*, London: Institute for Public Policy Research.

Lea, J. and Hallsworth, S. (2013) 'Bringing the state back in: Understanding neoliberal security', in P. Squires and J. Lea (eds), *Criminalisation and advanced marginality: Critically exploring the work of Loïc Wacquant*, Bristol: Policy Press.

Leach, J. and Hanton, A. (2015) *Intergenerational fairness index, 2015,* London: Intergenerational Foundation.

Leitch, S. (2006) *Prosperity for all in the global economy: World-class skills: Final report,* London: HMSO.

Lemert, E. M. (1951) *Social pathology,* New York: McGraw Hill.

Levitas, R. (1996) 'The concept of social exclusion and the new Durkheimian hegemony', *Critical Social Policy,* 16(1): 5-20.

Levitas, R. (1998) *The inclusive society? Social exclusion and New Labour,* London: Macmillan.

Levitas, R. (2006) 'The concept and measurement of social exclusion', in C. Pantazis, D. Gordon and R. Levitas (eds), *Poverty and social exclusion in Britain.* Bristol: Policy Press.

Levitt, S. and Lochner, L. (2001) 'The determinants of juvenile crime', in J. Gruber (ed), *Risky behavior among youths: An economic analysis,* Chicago, IL: University of Chicago Press, pp 327-73.

Lewis, P., Newburn, T., Taylor, M., Mcgillivray, C., Greenhill, A., Frayman, H. and Proctor, R. (2011) *Reading the riots: Investigating England's summer of disorder,* London: The Guardian/LSE.

Loader, I. (2006) 'Fall of the "platonic guardians". Liberalism, criminology and political responses to crime in England and Wales', *British Journal of Criminology,* 46(4): 561-86.

Lombroso, C. and Ferrero, W. (1895) *The female offender,* London: Fisher and Unwin.

London Research Centre (1999) *Housing benefit and the private rented sector,* London: Department of the Environment, Transport and the Regions.

Loney, M. (1983) 'The Youth Opportunities Programme: Requiem and rebirth', in R. Fiddy (ed), *In place of work: Policy and provision for the young unemployed,* Lewes: Falmer.

Long, S. K. and Witte, A. D. (1981) 'Current economic trends – implications for crime and criminal justice', in K. N. Wright (ed), *Crime and criminal justice in a declining economy,* Oelgeschlager, Gunn and Hain.

Low Pay Commission (2014) *The national minimum wage report, 2014,* Low Pay Commission Report, London: HMSO, Cm 8816.

Low Pay Commission (2015) *The national minimum wage report, 2015,* Low Pay Commission Report, London: HMSO, Cm 8816.

Low Pay Commission and Department for Business, Innovation and Skills (2014) *National minimum wage,* London: Low Pay Commission, www.gov.uk/government/publications/national-minimum-wage-low-pay-commission-report-2014

Lynch, L. (1985) 'State dependency in youth unemployment: A lost generation?', *Journal of Econometrics*, 28(1): 71-84.

MacDonald, R. (ed) (1997) *Youth, the underclass and social exclusion*, London: Routledge.

MacDonald, R. (2011) 'Youth transitions, unemployment and underemployment: Plus ça change, plus c'est la meme chose?', *Journal of Sociology*, 47: 427-44.

MacDonald, R. and Marsh, J. (2005) *Disconnected youth? Growing up in Britain's poor neighbourhoods*, Houndmills: Palgrave Macmillan.

MacDonald, R., Mason, P., Shildrick, T., Webster, C., Johnston, L. and Ridley, L. (2001) 'Snakes and ladders: In defence of studies of youth transition', *Sociological Research Online*, 5(4).

MacLeod, D. and Clarke, N. (2009) *Engaging for success: Enhancing performance through employee engagement*, London: Department for Business, Innovation and Skills.

Maclure, J. S. (ed) (1986) *Educational documents: England and Wales, 1816 to the present day* (5th edn), London: Methuen.

McCord, J. and McCord, W. (1958) 'The effects of parental role model on criminality', *Journal of Social Issues*, 14(3): 66-75.

McDowell, L., Rootham, E. and Hardgrove, A. (2014) 'Precarious work, protest masculinity and communal regulation: South Asian young men in Luton, UK', *Work, Employment and Society*, 28(6): 847-64

McQuaid, R., Raeside, R., Egdell, V. and Graham, H. (2014) *Multiple scarring effects of youth unemployment in the UK*, http://unissalzburg.at/fileadmin/multimedia/SOWI/documents/VWL/FOSEM/FOSEM_SS_2014/mcquaid_paper.pdf

Macey, W. H. and Schneider, B. (2008) 'The meaning of employee engagement', *Industrial and Organizational Psychology*, 1(1): 3-30.

Machin, S. and Marie, O. (2006) 'Crime and benefit sanctions', *Portuguese Economic Journal*, 5(2): 149-65.

Magarey, S. (1978) 'The invention of juvenile delinquency in early nineteenth-century England', *Labour History Review, 34*, 11-27.

Maguire, S. (2015) 'NEET, unemployed, inactive or unknown – why does it matter?', *Educational Research, 57*(2): 121-32

Manchester Citizens Advisory Bureau (2013) *Punishing poverty: A review of benefit sanctions and their impact*, Manchester: Manchester CAB, https://onedrive.live.com/view.aspx?resid=CB5ED957FE0B849F!350andapp=WordPdfandauthkey=!AJTbB-gzwsSCayQ

Maslach, C. (1982) *The cost of caring*, Englewood Cliffs, N.J.: Prentice-Hall.

May, M. (2002) 'Innocence and experience: The evolution of the concept of juvenile delinquency in the mid-nineteenth century', in Muncie, J. Hughes, G. and McLaughlin, E. (eds). *Youth justice: critical readings*, London: Sage / Open University

Miles, S. (2000) *Youth lifestyles in a changing world*, Buckingham: Open University Press.

Miller, P. and Rose, N. (1990) 'Governing economic life', *Economy and Society*, 19(1): 1–31.

Miscampbell, G. (2014) *Smarter sanctions: Sorting out the system*, London: Policy Exchange.

Mizen, P. (2004) *The changing state of youth*, Houndmills: Palgrave Macmillan.

Mizra-Davies, J. (2014) *NEET: Young people not in education, employment or training* (briefing paper 06705), London: House of Commons library, www.parliament.uk/briefing–papers/sn06705

Mizra-Davies, J. (2015) *NEET: Young people not in education, employment or training* (briefing paper 06705), London: House of Commons library, http://researchbriefings.files.parliament.uk/documents/SN06705/SN06705.pdf

Moore, R. (1988)'Education, employment and recruitment', in R. Dale, R. Fergusson and A. Robinson (eds) *Frameworks for Teaching*, London, Hodder and Stoughton

Morris, L. (1998) 'Legitimate membership of the welfare community', in Langan, M. (ed) *Welfare: needs, rights and risks*, London: Routledge / Open University

Muncie, J. (1984) *'The trouble with kids today': Youth and crime in post-war Britain*, London: Hutchinson.

Muncie, J. (1996/2001) 'The construction and deconstruction of crime', in J. Muncie and E. McLaughlin (eds), *The problem of crime*, London: Sage Publications.

Muncie, J. (1999) *Youth and crime: A critical introduction* (1st edn), London: Sage Publications.

Muncie, J. (2009) *Youth and crime* (3rd edn), London: Sage Publications.

Muncie, J. (2015) *Youth and crime* (4th edn), London: Sage Publications.

Munro, E., Lushey, C., National Care Advisory Service, Maskell-Graham, D. and Ward, H. with Holmes, L. / Centre for Child and Family Research, Loughborough University (2012) *Evaluation of the Staying Put: 18 Plus Family Placement Programme: Final report*, Research Report DFE-RR191, London: Department for Education

Mustard, D. (2010) 'How do labor markets affect crime? New evidence on an old puzzle', IZA Discussion Paper 4856.

Narayan, P. K. and Smyth, R. (2004) 'Crime rates, male youth unemployment and real income in Australia: Evidence from Granger causality tests', *Applied Economics*, 36(18): 2079-95.

National Centre for Social Research (2011) *The August riots in England: Understanding the involvement of young people*, London: National Centre for Social Research.

National Children's Bureau (2014)/*The Children's Partnership Staying put: Good practice guide*, London: NCB, www.ncb.org.uk/media/1154341/staying_put.pdf

Newburn, T. (2012) 'Counterblast: Young people and the August 2011 riots', *The Howard Journal of Criminal Justice*, 51(3): 331-5.

Nilsen, Ø. A., and Reiso, K. H. (2011), 'Scarring effects of early-career unemployment', Bonn, IZA, (http://www.iza.org/conference_files/YULMI2012/reiso_k7487.pdf)

Nilsson, A. and Agell, J. (2003) 'Crime, unemployment and labor market programs in turbulent times' (no 2003: 14), Working Paper, Uppsala: IFAU-Institute for Labour Market Policy Evaluation.

Nwabuzo, O. (2012) *The riot roundtables: Race and all the riots of August 2011*, London: Runnymede Trust.

Office for National Statistics (ONS) (2013) *Suicides in the United Kingdom, 2011*, London: ONS, www.ons.gov.uk/ons/rel/subnational-health4/suicides-in-the-united-kingdom/2011/stb-suicide-bulletin.html

Office for National Statistics (ONS) (2014a) *Assessment of compliance with the Code of Practice for Official Statistics: Statistics on crime in England and Wales*, London: ONS, www.statisticsauthority.gov.uk/assessment/assessment/assessment-reports/index.html

Office for National Statistics (ONS) (2014b) *Young people in the labour market, 2014*, Coverage: UK, 5 March, London: ONS.

O'Malley, P. (1992) 'Risk, power and crime prevention', *Economy and Society*, 21(3): 252-75.

Organisation for Economic Co-operation and Development (OECD) (2008) *Jobs for youth: United Kingdom*, Paris: OECD.

Organisation for Economic Co-operation and Development (OECD) (2011) *Employment Outlook, 2011*, Paris: OECD, www.oecd-ilibrary.org/employment/oecd-employment-outlook-2011_empl_outlook-2011-en

Organisation for Economic Co-operation and Development (2015) *Labour market statistics, Main Economic Indicators*, Paris: Organisation for Economic Co-operation and Development, DOI: http://dx.doi.org/10.1787/data-00046-en (Accessed on 29 September 2015).

Outhwaite, W. (2009) *Habermas: A critical introduction*, Cambridge: Polity Press.

Oxford English Dictionary Online (2014) www.oxforddictionaries. com/

Palmer, G. (2010) *The poverty site: Children with a criminal record*, www. poverty.org.uk/28/index.shtml?2

Papadopoulos, T. and Roumpakis, A. (2012) 'The Greek welfare state in the age of austerity: Anti-social policy and the politico-economic crisis', in M.Kilkey, K. Farnsworth and Z. Irving (eds) *Social policy review 24: Analysis and debate in social policy, 2012*, Bristol: Policy Press

Papps, K. and Winkelmann, R. (2000) 'Unemployment and crime: New evidence for an old question', *New Zealand Economic Papers*, 34(1): 53-71.

Parsons, T. (1951) (ed) *Towards a general theory of action*, Cambridge, Mass: Harvard University Press

Payne, J. (2000) 'The unbearable lightness of skill: The changing meaning of skill in UK policy discourses and some implications for education and training', *Journal of Education Policy*, 15(3): 353-69.

Payne, J. and Keep, E. (2011) 'One step forward, two steps back? Skills policy in England under the coalition government', *SKOPE research paper*, 102, Cardiff: University of Cardiff.

Pearce, N. and Hillman, J. (1998) *Wasted youth: Raising achievement and tackling social exclusion*, London: Institute for Public Policy Research.

Pearson, G. (1983) *Hooligan: A history of respectable fears*, London: Macmillan.

Pech, R. and Slade, B. (2006) 'Employee disengagement: Is there evidence of a growing problem?', *Handbook of Business Strategy*: www. emeraldinsight.com/doi/abs/10.1108/10775730610618585

Peeters, M. (2011) 'Modelling unemployment in the presence of excess labour supply: An application to Egypt', *Journal of Economics and Econometrics*, 54: 58-92.

Pemberton, S. (2015) *Harmful societies: Understanding social harm*, Bristol: Policy Press.

Petrongolo, B. (2009) 'The long term effects of job search requirements: Evidence from the UK JSA reform', *Journal of Public Economics*, 93(11): 1234-53.

Petrongolo, B. and Van Reenan, J. (2011) 'Youth unemployment', London: CentrePiece, London School of Economics, Centre for Economic Performance, summer: 2-5, http://cep.lse.ac.uk/pubs/ download/cp338.pdf

Phillips, J. and Land, K. C. (2012) 'The link between unemployment and crime rate fluctuations: An analysis at the county, state, and national levels', *Social Science Research*, 41(3): 681-94.

Pitts, J. (2003) *The new politics of youth crime: Discipline or solidarity?*, Lyme Regis: Russell House.

Pleace, N., Fitzpatrick, S., Johnsen, S., Quilgars, D. and Sanderson, D. (2008) *Statutory homelessness in England: The experiences of families and 16–17 year olds*, London: London: Department for Communities and Local Government.

Ponticelli, J. and Voth, J. (2011). *Austerity and anarchy: Budget cuts and social unrest in Europe, 1919–2008*, Repositori, https://repositori.upf.edu/handle/10230/19893

Pople, L. and Smith, D. J. (2010) 'Time trends in youth crime and in justice system responses', in D. J. Smith (ed), *A new response to youth crime*, Cullompton: Willan.

Poverty and Social Exclusion (PSE) (2013) *Living Standards in the UK*, Bristol: PSE.

Presdee, M. (2000) *Cultural criminology and the carnival of crime*, London: Routledge.

Quilgars, D., Johnsen, S. and Pleace, M. (2008) *Youth homelessness in the UK. A decade of progress?*, York: Joseph Rowntree Foundation.

Raffe, D. (1984) 'The transition from school to work and the recession: evidence from the Scottish school leavers' survey', *British Journal of Sociology of Education*, 5(3): 247-265.

Raffe, D. (2003) 'Pathways linking education and work: A review of concepts, research, and policy debates', *Journal of Youth Studies*, 6(1): 3-19.

Raffe, D. and Willms, P. (1989) 'Schooling the discouraged worker: Local-labour-market effects on educational participation', *Sociology*, 23(4): 559-81.

Ramos-Díaz, J. and Varela, A. (2012) 'From opportunity to austerity: Crisis and social policy in Spain', in M. Kilkey, K. Farnsworth and Z. Irving (eds) *Social policy review 24: Analysis and debate in social policy, 2012*, Bristol: Policy Press

Rankin, N. and Roberts, G. (2011) 'Youth unemployment, firm size and reservation wages in South Africa', *South African Journal of Economics*, 79(2): 128-45.

Redhead, S. (ed) (1993) *Rave off: Politics and deviance in contemporary culture*, Aldershot: Avebury.

Rice, P. G. (1987) 'The demand for post-compulsory education in the UK and the effects of educational maintenance allowances', *Economica*, 48, 465-75.

Roberts, C., Burnett, R., Kirby, A. and Hamill, H. (1996) *A system for evaluating probation practice: Report of a method devised and piloted by the Oxford Probation Studies Unit and Warwickshire Probation Service*, Oxford: University of Oxford, Centre for Criminological Research.

Roberts, K. (1984) *School leavers and their prospects*, Milton Keynes: Open University Press.

Roberts, K. (1995) *Youth and employment in modern Britain*, Oxford: Oxford University Press.

Roberts, K. and Parsell, G. (1988) *Opportunity structures and career trajectories from age 16–19*, ESRC 16 to 19 Initiative, Occasional Paper Series, Swindon: Economic and Social Research Council.

Roberts, K. and Parsell, G. (1989) 'Recent changes in the pathways from school to work', in K. Hurrelmann and U. Engel (eds), *The social world of the adolescent: International perspectives*, New York: DeGruyter.

Roberts, K., Parsell, G. and Connolly, M. (1989) *Britain's economic recovery, the new demographic trend and young people's transition into the labour market*, ESRC 16–19 Initiative, Occasional paper no 8, London: City University.

Rodger, J. J. (2008) *Criminalising social policy: Antisocial behaviour and welfare in a de-civilised society*, Cullompton: Willan.

Rojek, C. (1985) *Capitalism and leisure theory*, London: Tavistock.

Rose, N. (1989/1999) *Governing the soul: Technologies of human subjectivity* (2nd edn), London: Routledge.

Rose, N. (1999) *Powers of freedom: Reframing political thought*, Cambridge: Cambridge University Press.

Rose, N. (2000) 'Government and control', *British Journal of Criminology*, 40: 321-39.

Rose, N. and Miller, P. (1992) 'Political power beyond the state: Problematics of government', *British Journal of Sociology*, 43(2): 173-205.

Rosenfeld, R. (2014) 'Crime and the Great Recession: introduction to the Special Issue', *Journal of Contemporary Criminal Justice*, 30(February): 4-6.

Rosenfeld, R. and Fornango, R. (2007) 'The impact of economic conditions on robbery and property crime: The role of consumer sentiment', *Criminology*, 45: 735-69.

Ross, A., Green, R., Brown, V., Pickering, K., Schoon, I., and Vignoles, A. (2011) *The impact of KS4 vocational courses on disengaged young people's engagement with education 15-18,* London: The Centre for Analysis of Youth Transitions / Depatment for Education

Rush, P. (1992) 'The government of a generation: the subject of juvenile delinquency', *Liverpool Law Review*, 14 (1) 3-43.

Saks, A. M. (2006) 'Antecedents and consequences of employee engagement', *Journal of Managerial Psychology*, 21(7): 600-619.

Savolainen, J. (2000) 'Inequality, welfare state, and homicide: Further support for the institutional anomie theory', *Criminology*, 38(4): 1021-42.

Schmidt, V. A. (2008) 'Discursive institutionalism: the explanatory power of ideas and discourse', *Annual Review of Political Science*, 11, 303-26.

Scottish Government (2005) *Mapping employability and support services for disengaged young people,* Edinburgh: Scottish Government. www.gov.scot/Publications/2005/10/2893835/38370

Scottish Government (2009) *Young offender learning and skills work stream report*, Edinburgh: The Scottish Government, www.scotland.gov.uk/Publications/2009/12/18103851/2

Scottish Government (2014), *JSA sanctions in Scotland: An analysis of the sanctions applied to claimants of Jobseeker's Allowance in Scotland*, www.scotland.gov.uk/Resource/0046/00462782.pdf

Seabrook, J. (2013) *Pauperland: Poverty and the poor in Britain*, London: Hurst.

Sheehy, K., Kumrai, R. and Woodhead, M. (2011) 'Young people's experiences of personal advisors and the Connexions service', *Equality, Diversity and Inclusion: An International Journal*, 30(3): 168-82.

Shildrick, T., McDonald, R., Webster, C. and Garthwaite, K. (2012) *Poverty and insecurity: Life in 'low-pay, no-pay' Britain*, Bristol: Policy Press.

Shore, H. (2002) 'Reforming the juvenile: gender, justice and the child criminal in nineteenth century England', in Muncie, J. Hughes, G. and McLaughlin, E. (eds). *Youth justice: critical readings*, London: Sage/Open University

Simester, A. and Von Hirsch, A. (2011) *Crimes, harms and wrongs: On the principles of criminalisation*, Oxford: Hart Publishing.

Silver, H. (1994) 'Social exclusion and social solidarity: three paradigms', *International Labour Review*, 133, 531-577.

Simmons, R. and Thompson, R. (2011) *NEET young people and training for work: Learning on the margin,* Stoke-on-Trent: Trentham Books.

Simmons, R. and Thompson, R. (2013) 'Reclaiming the disengaged: Critical perspectives on young people not in education, employment or training', *Research in Post-Compulsory Education*, 18(1-2): 1-11.

Simmons, R., Thompson, R. and Russell, L. (2014) *Education, work and social change: Young people and marginalisation in post-industrial Britain*, Basingstoke: Palgrave Macmillan.

Simon, B. (1974) *The politics of educational reform, 1920–1940*, London: Lawrence and Wishart.

Simon, J. (1996/2000) *Megan's Law: Governing through crime in a democratic society*, Unpublished manuscript, June 1996; later published in 2000, in *Law and Social Inquiry*, 25(4):1111-1150.

Simon, J. (2007) *Governing through crime: How the war on crime transformed American democracy and created a culture of fear*, New York: Oxford University Press.

Smith, C., Christoffersen, K. and Davidson, H. (2011) *Lost in transition: The dark side of emerging adulthood*, Oxford: Oxford University Press.

Smith, D. J. (2010) 'Key reforms: principles, costs, benefits, politics', in D. J. Smith (ed), *A new response to youth crime*, Cullompton: Willan.

Social Exclusion Unit (SEU) (1999) *Bridging the gap: New opportunities for 16-18 year olds not in education, employment or training*, London: HMSO.

Social Exclusion Unit (SEU) (2004) *Breaking the cycle*, London: HMSO.

Social Mobility and Child Poverty Commission (2014) *State of the nation 2014: Social mobility and child poverty in Great Britain*, London: HMSO.

Sodha, S. and Margo, J. (2010) *A generation of disengaged children is waiting in the wings*, London: DEMOS.

Solinger, D. J. (2007) 'Labor discontent in China in comparative perspective', *Eurasian Geography and Economics*, 48(4): 413-38.

Somavia, J. (2012) 'Giving youth a better start', *World of Work*, 74 (May): 4, 41, www.ilo.org/global/about-the-ilo/media-centre/statements-and-speeches/WCMS_182362/lang--en/index.htm.

Somavia, J./International Labour Organization (ILO) (2012a) Director-General's address to the plenary of the 101st International Labour Conference, Geneva, ILO, 6 June, www.ilo.org/global/about-the-ilo/media-centre/statements-and-speeches/WCMS_182362/lang--en/index.htm

Somavia, J./International Labour Organization (ILO) (2012b) Director-General's opening address to the 101st International Labour Conference, Geneva, ILO, 30 May, www.ilo.org/global/about-the-ilo/media-centre/statements-and-speeches/WCMS_181894/lang--en/index.htm.

Soothill, K., Francis, B. and Fligelstone, R. (2002) *Patterns of offending behaviour: A new approach, Findings, 171*, London, The Home Office, http://eprints.lancs.ac.uk/13452/1/r171.pdf (Full report).

Spitzer, S. (1975) 'Toward a Marxian theory of deviance', *Social Problems*, 22(5): 638-51.

Squires, P. (1990) *Anti-social policy: Welfare, ideology and the disciplinary state*, Hemel Hempstead: Harvester Wheatsheaf.

Standing, G. (2011) *The precariat: The new dangerous class*, London: Bloomsbury Publishing.

Stephenson, M. (2007) *Young people and offending: Education, youth justice and social inclusion*, Cullompton: Willan.

Stephens, M. and Blenkinsopp, J. (2015) *Young people and social security: an international review*, York: Joseph Rowntree Foundation.

Strandh, M., Winefield, A., Nilsson, K. and Hammarström, A. (2014) 'Unemployment and mental health scarring during the life course', *The European Journal of Public Health,* 24(3): 440-45.

Strathdee, R. (2013) 'Reclaiming the disengaged: Reform of New Zealand's vocational education and training and social welfare systems', *Research in Post-Compulsory Education*, 18(1-2): 29-45.

Stuckler, D., Basu, S., Suhrcke, M., Coutts, A. and McKee, M. (2009) 'The public health effect of economic crises and alternative policy responses in Europe: An empirical analysis', *The Lancet*, 374: 315-23.

Tadros, V. (2008) 'Crimes and security', *The Modern Law Review*, 71(6): 940-70.

Taylor, M. (1992) 'Post-16 options: Young people's awareness, attitudes, intentions and influences on their choice', *Research Papers in Education*, 7(3): 301-35.

Taylor-Gooby, P. (2013) *The double crisis of the welfare state and what we can do about it*, Basingstoke: Palgrave Macmillan.

Tedeschi, J. and Felson, R. (1994) *Violence, aggression and coercive action*, Washington, DC: American Psychological Association Books.

Thomas, R. J. and McFarland, D. A. (2010) *Joining young, voting young: The effects of youth voluntary associations on early adult voting*, CIRCLE Working Paper# 73, Center for Information and Research on Civic Learning and Engagement (CIRCLE).

Thomson, A and Stothard, M. (2015) 'Young Muslims lag behind white middle class in two-speed France', *Financial Times,* 19 January: 3.

Tombs, S. and Whyte, D. (2003) 'Unmasking the crimes of the powerful', *Critical Criminology*, 11(3): 217-36.

Tomlin, P. (2013) 'Extending the golden thread? Criminalisation and the presumption of innocence', *The Journal of Political Philosophy*, 21(1): 44-66.

Trades Union Congress (TUC)(2015)*Young Worker Issues*, Policy briefing, Organising and Services Department, 10 February, London: TUC, www.tuc.org.uk/sites/default/files/TUCYoungWorkerIssues.pdf

Treadwell, J., Briggs, D., Winlow, S. and Hall, S. (2012) 'Shopocalypse now: Consumer culture and the English riots of 2011', *British Journal of Criminology*, 53: 1-17.

Tussie, D. (2009) *The Politics of trade: The role of research in trade policy and negotiation*, Dordrecht: Brill.

Tyler, I. (2013) *Revolting subjects: Social abjection and resistance in neoliberal Britain*, London: Zed Books.

United Nations Department of Economic and Social Affairs (UNDESA) (2007) *Young People's Transitions into Adulthood: Progress and Change*, New York: United Nations

UNICEF (2013) *Child well-being in rich countries: A comparative overview*, Florence: Innocenti Research Centre/UNICEF.

United Nations Crime and Justice Information Network (2000) *Survey on crime trends and the operations of criminal justice systems*, New York: United Nations.

Upton, S. (ed) (2011) *Engaging Wales' disengaged youth*, Cardiff: Institute of Welsh Affairs.

US Department of Agriculture (2013) *Supplemental Nutrition Assistance Program participation and costs, data as of August*, www.fns.usda.gov/pd/SNAPsummary.htm

Vaughan, R. (2009) 'Top mandarin: 15% of NEETs die within 10 years', *The Times Educational Supplement*, 7 August, www.tes.co.uk/article.aspx?storycode=6019772

Verick, S. (2009) *Who is hit hardest during a financial crisis? The vulnerability of young men and women to unemployment in an economic downturn* (No 4359), IZA Discussion Papers, Geneva: International Labour Organization.

Vincent, D. (1991) *Poor citizens: The state and the poor in 20th-century Britain*, London: Longman.

Vincent, J. (1998) 'Jobseeker's allowance evaluation: Qualitative research on disallowed and sanctioned claimants: phase two after jobseeker's allowance', *Research Report RR86*, London: Department for Education and Employment.

Vincent-Jones, P. (2000) 'Contractual governance: Institutional and organizational analysis', *Oxford Journal of Legal Studies*, 20(3): 317-51.

Wacquant, L. (1999) 'Suitable enemies', *Punishment and Society*, 1(2): 215-22.

Wacquant, L. (2004/09) *Punishing the poor: The neo-liberal government of social insecurity*, Durham, NC: Duke University Press.

Wallace, C. (1987) *For richer, for poorer: Growing up in and out of work*, London: Tavistock.

Walters, W. (2000) *Unemployment and government: Genealogies of the social*, Cambridge: Cambridge University Press.

Walton, J. and Ragin, C. (1990) 'Global and national sources of political protest: Third world responses to the debt crisis', *American Sociological Review*, 55: 876-90.

Watts, B., Fitzpatrick, S., Bramley, G. and Watkins, D. (2014) *Welfare sanctions and conditionality in the UK*, York: Joseph Rowntree Foundation.

Weber, M. (1919/1965) *Politics as a vocation*, Philadelphia, PA: Fortress Press.

Webster, C. (2007) *Understanding race and crime,* Maidenhead: Open University Press.

Webster, D. (2014) *JSA Sanctions and Disallowances, House of Commons Work and Pensions Committee*, Second Report of Session 2013-14, Vol. II, London: House of Commons.

Wikstrom, P. O. H. and Loeber, R. (2000) 'Do disadvantaged neighbourhoods cause well-adjusted children to become adolescent delinquents?', *Criminology*, 38(4): 1109-42.

Wilkins, L. T. (1964) *Social deviance*, London: Tavistock.

Wilkinson, R. and Pickett, K. (2009) *The spirit level: Why more equal societies almost always do better*, London: Allen Lane.

Willis, P. E. (1977) *Learning to labour: How working class kids get working class jobs*, Farnborough: Saxon House.

Wilson, J. and Kelling, G. (1982) 'Broken windows', *Atlantic Monthly*, 249(3): 29-38.

Wolfbein, S. L. (1959) 'Transition from school to work: A study of the school leaver', *The Personnel and Guidance Journal*, 38(2): 98-105.

Woo, W. T. (2003) 'Confronting restructuring and stability', in S.J. Yao and X.M. Liu (eds), *Sustaining China's Economic Growth in the Twenty-First Century*, London: RoutledgeCurzon, pp. 13-40.

World Bank (2012) *World Development Report 2013: Jobs*, Washington, DC: World Bank, https://openknowledge.worldbank.org/handle/10986/11843 License: CC BY 3.0 IGO.

World Health Organization (WHO) (2011) *Impact of economic crises on mental health in Europe*, Copenhagen: WHO.

Worrall, J. (2005) 'Reconsidering the relationship between welfare spending and serious crime: A panel data analysis with implications for social support theory', *Justice Quarterly*, 22(3): 364-91.

Wright, G. (2011) *Governing marginalised populations: The role of coercion, support and agency*, Belfast: Department for Social Development.

Young, J. (1971) 'The role of the police as amplifiers of deviancy, negotiators of reality and translators or fantasy', in S. Cohen (ed), *Images of deviance*, Harmondsworth: Penguin.

Young Men's Christian Association (YMCA), England (2014) *Signed on and sanctioned*, London: YMCA.

Youth Justice Board / Ministry of Justice (2014), *Youth Justice Statistics, 2012/13, England and Wales*, London: Youth Justice Board / Ministry of Justice, www.gov.uk/government/uploads/system/uploads/attachment_data/file/278549/youth-justice-stats-2013.pdf

# Copyright material

The author and Policy Press gratefully acknowledge the permission granted to reproduce the following copyright materials in this book. All reasonable efforts have been made to identify the holders of copyright material and to obtain permission for their use. If we have unwittingly infringed any copyright, we apologise sincerely and would appreciate being corrected.

## Figures

The Local Government Association for Figure 1.1 Summary of the total hidden talent of young people (16 to 24-year-olds), England and Wales, Oct 2012-Sept 2013; and Figure 1.2 Total hidden talent, young people (16 to 24-year-olds), England and Wales. The Centre for Economic and Social Inclusion for Figure 3.1 Youth unemployment since 1969. Figure 3.3 Unemployment rate by age group, 1975-2010 is reproduced by kind permission of Barbara Petrongolo. The International Labour Organization for Figure 3.4 Global youth unemployment and unemployment rate, 1995-2015; and for Figure 3.5 Youth unemployment rates, European countries, 2008, 2013 and 2014. The Organisation for Economic Cooperation and Development for Figure 3.6 Youth vs adult unemployment, OECD/EU28 countries, 2013 (based on data from OECD (2015) DOI: http://dx.doi.org/10.1787/data-00046-en (Accessed on 29 September 2015)). The Low Pay Commission for Figure 3.7 Growth in the minimum wage and median earnings, by age, UK, 1999-2014; Figure 3.8 Nominal and real level of median earnings for 16 to 17-year-olds, by price index, UK, 1999-201; Figure 3.9 Nominal and real level of median earnings for 18 to 20-year-olds, by price index, UK, 1999-2014; and Figure 3.10 Percentage at or below minimum wage rates, by age, UK, 1999-2013. The Institute for Fiscal Studies for Figure 3.11 Change in real median weekly earnings since 2008 by age group. Figure 3.12 Monthly adverse decisions as percentage of all JSA claimants is reproduced by kind permission of the Joseph Rowntree Foundation, from *Welfare sanctions and conditionality in the UK* by Watts, B., Fitzpatrick, S., Bramley, G. and Watkins, D. published in 2014 by the Joseph Rowntree Foundation. Elsevier for permission to reproduce Figure 4.1 Unemployment, income inequality, welfare spending and incarceration in Britain, 1961-2006. Figure 6.1 Manifestations of crisis when reproduction processes are disturbed (pathologies) from Habermas, J. (1981/1987) *The theory of communicative action* (vol 2) *Lifeworld and system: A critique of functionalist reason*, Cambridge: Polity Press/Oxford: Basil Blackwell, is reproduced by kind permission of Polity.

# Index

Entries in **bold** indicate figures; those preceded by 'T' indicate a table. Page-numbers followed by 'n' (e.g. 116n) indicate an endnote. Entries in *italics* are book titles.

Lightning Source UK Ltd.
Milton Keynes UK
UKHW021327090519
342389UK00007B/243/P